SARDAR PATEL

SARDAR PATEL
Unifier of Modern India

RNP SINGH

Published by
Renu Kaul Verma
Vitasta Publishing Pvt Ltd
4348/4C, Ansari Road, Daryaganj
New Delhi-110 002
info@vitastapublishing.com

ISBN 978-81-19670-56-7
© Vivekananda International Foundation
First Edition 2025

MRP ₹595

All Rights Reserved.
No part of this publication may be reproduced, stored in a retrieval system, or transmitted in any form, or by any means—electronic, mechanical, photocopying, recording or otherwise—without the prior permission of the publisher. Opinions expressed in this book are the author's own. The publisher is in no way responsible for these.

Cover and layout by Vits Press
Printed by Vikas Computer and Printers

Contents

List of Illustrations	*vii*
Acknowledgements	*xiii*
Foreword	*xv*
Preface	*xix*
Integration of the Indian States	1
Eastern States	47
Greater Rajasthan	60
Travancore	69
Jodhpur	79
United State of Kathiawar	87
Bhopal	98
Junagadh	108
Hyderabad	123
Jammu and Kashmir	161

Patel's Historic Letter of 7 Nov 1950 to Nehru	205
Letter to Nehru, on China	212
Administrative Unifier and a Great Administrator	220
Patel: Greater than Bismarck	239
Appendices	247
Index	337

List of Illustrations

India before and after partition   xxiii
Source: https://priyamvadrai.files.wordpress.com/2016/07/integration-of-princely-states-3-638.jpg

Eastern States   46
Source: https://en.wikipedia.org/wiki/Chota_Nagpur_Tributary_States#/media/File:Chota_Nagpur_States-IGI_2.jpg

Greater Rajasthan   59
Source: http://www.rajras.in/wp-content/uploads/2016/07/Stage-4.jpeg

Travancore   68
Source: https://en.wikipedia.org/wiki/Madras_States_Agency#/media/File:Madras_map_1913.jpg

Jodhpur   78
Source: http://www.affordablehomesindia.com/admin/userfiles/images/mapp(7).PNG

United State of Kathiawar   86
Source: https://upload.wikimedia.org/wikipedia/commons/thumb/4/4e/Kathiawar_map.jpg/600px-Kathiawar_map.jpg

Bhopal   97
Source: https://discoverlakecity.files.wordpress.com/2012/07/bhopal-map.jpg?w=812

Junagadh   107
Source: http://www.thefridaytimes.com/tft/wp-content/uploads/2015/10/tft-37-p-20-e.jpg

Hyderabad 122
Source: https://upload.wikimedia.org/wikipedia/commons/6/6f/Hyderabad_state_from_the_Imperial_Gazetteer_of_India%2C_1909.jpg

Jammu and Kashmir 160
Source: https://s3.scoopwhoop.com/anj/KM/208342255.jpg

Sardar Patel in his teens. 318

In the late 1920s, Patel with his brother, Vithalbhai Patel. 318

Sardar Patel during the Nagpur Flag Satyagraha, 1923. 319

Sardar's Mother with her five sons in 1927 (Sardar-extreme right). 320

Maulana Azad, Sardar Patel, Abdul Ghaffar Khan and Kanayalal Munshi during a visit to Bardoli in 1928. The women here first addressed him as 'Sardar'. 320

Sardar, Bapu and Maniben during the Shimla Conference, 1945. 321

Maniben Patel with her father Vallabhbhai in 1946. 321

The Troika: Nehru-Gandhi-Patel, who led the last phase of India's freedom struggle from 1921 to 1947. 322

Gandhi's 'muscle man': Congress success lay in Patel lending his 'muscle' power as a great organiser to Gandhi's 'soul' force. The *Manchester Guardian* wrote: Without Patel, Gandhi's ideas would have had less practical influence, and Nehru's idealism less scope. 322

At a conference on the partition of India in June 1947 are (from left): President of the Indian National Congress Acharya JB Kripalani, Sardar Vallabhbhai Patel, Advisor to the Viceroy Sir Eric Melville, Pandit Jawaharlal Nehru and Lord Mountbatten. 323

A photograph taken during the Independence Day Session of the Constituent Assembly held on 15 August 1947. Standing in the first row can be seen Sardar Vallabhbhai Patel, KM Munshi, NV Gadgil and Amu Swaminathan. 323

Photograph taken on the occasion of Vallabhbhai Patel's visit to the Broadcasting House, New Delhi on 14 October 1947. 324

Sardar Patel was India's first Information and Broadcasting Minister. 324

C Rajagopalachari with Sardar Patel and Maniben Patel on arrival at aerodrome, New Delhi on 9 November 1947. Rajagopalachari was to act as Governor-General during the leave period of Lord Mountbatten. 325

Sardar Patel visited Calcutta in 8 January 1948. Photo shows Patel speaking at the Calcutta Club Lunch. 325

Photo taken on the occasion of Sardar Patel's visit to Calcutta in January 1948. 326

Sardar Vallabhbhai Patel's tour of Bombay and Ahmedabad (January 1948). Patel addressing a rally organised by the All-Mahajan Associations and Societies of Ahmedabad on 22 January 1948. 326

Nehru with Sardar Patel during Sardar's convalescence at Dehradun (1948). 327

Photo taken on the occasion of the Conference of Industrialists held under the agies of Sardar Patel in Mussoorie in May 1948, in connection with the Gandhi Memorial Fund. 327

Chandulal Trivedi, Governor of East Punjab and Chancellor of the East Punjab University presenting the degree of Doctor of Laws (Honoris Cause) to Sardar Patel at the first convocation of the University held at Ambala on 5 March 1949. 328

Lord Mountbatten greeting Sardar Vallabhbhai Patel at the Government House, New Delhi at reception held by Mountbatten in honour of the members of the Constituent Assembly, May 1949. At right is Lady Mountbatten. 328

Sardar Vallabhbhai Patel watching the Police tattoo at Phillaur Fort which he visited in March 1949. On his right appear Chandulal Trivedi, Governor of East Punjab, Maniben Patel is on the extreme right. 329

Sardar Patel, Deputy Prime Minister of India and the Minister-in-charge of States, administers an oath of office of the Rajpramukh to the Maharaja of Jaipur, at the inauguration ceremony of the Greater Rajasthan Union held at Jaipur on 31 March 1949. The new Union is the biggest union of Indian States comprising 15 ancient Rajput States with an area of 120,000 square miles, population of 13,000,000 and an approximate annual revenue of Rs 10 crore. 329

XIV Indian Athletic Championships, August 1949 in Delhi. A view of the distinguished visitors' gallery in the Irwin Stadium. Sardar Patel, the Deputy Prime Minister, Shankar Lal, President of the organising committee and the Maharaja of Patiala are seen in the picture. 330

Sardar Patel, RR Diwakar and Satyanarian Sinha photographed at the party held by Patel for the Members of the Constituent Assembly (MCAs) at New Delhi on 17 October 1949. Standing at extreme left is Maniben Patel. 330

Satyanarian Sinha, Rajendra Prasad, Sardar Patel and Acharya Kripalani photographed at the party which the Deputy Prime Minister held at New Delhi on 17 October 1949, to meet the MCAs. Maniben Patel stands behind. 331

Sardar Patel glances through a collection of telegrams that felicitate him on his 74th birthday on 31 October 1949. 331

Sardar Vallabhbhai Patel receives felicitations on 31 October 1949, his 74th birthday. 332

Air Chief Marshal Sir John Slessor, Chief of Air Staff-designate, RAF who was in Delhi on a three-day visit, called on Sardar Patel, Acting Prime Minister of India on 5 November 1949. He was accompanied by Air Marshal Sir Thomas Elmhirst, C-in-C, RIAF. 332

Sardar Patel in 1950, on the day the first President of Free India, Rajendra Prasad, took the oath of office at the Darbar Hall of the Government House. 333

The Cabinet of India on 31 January 1950, along with the newly appointed President Rajendra Prasad. (L to R sitting) BR Ambedkar,

Rafi Ahmed Kidwai, Sardar Baldev Singh, Maulana Abul Kalam Azad, Jawaharlal Nehru, Rajendra Prasad, Sardar Patel, John Mathai, Jagjivan Ram, Rajkumari Amrit Kaur and SP Mukherjee. (L to R standing) Khurshed Lal, RR Diwakar, Mohanlal Saksena, N Gopalaswami Ayyangar, NV Gadgil, KC Neogy, Jairamdas Daulatram, K Santhanam, Satya Narayan Sinha and BV Keskar. 333

JB Kripalani, Sardar Vallabhbhai Patel and Maniben Patel. 334

Rajendra Prasad, Sardar Patel, Maulana Azad and Khan Abdul Ghaffar Khan eating together. 334

Sardar Vallabhbhai Patel with TK Narayana Pillai, premier of the United State of Travancore-Cochin, V Shankar and others when he visited the Kanyakumari temple at Cape Comorin in May 1950. 335

Sardar Patel took his last breath on 15 December 1950. Seated beside is Maniben, the Sardar's daughter. 336

Acknowledgements

I gratefully acknowledge continuous support, encouragement and all care extended by Dr Arvind Gupta, former Deputy National Security Advisor and currently Director, Vivekananda International Foundation.

I am indebted for many kindnesses to General NC Vij, PVSM, UYSM, AVSM (Former Chief of the Army Staff & Founder Vice Chairman, National Disaster Management Authority), Former Director, Vivekananda International Foundation, who inspired, encouraged and provided all assistance to write this book.

I owe a special debt to Shri OP Sharma, former Governor of Nagaland, who besides being a source of inspiration, has been continuously supporting and extending invaluable suggestions.

I am deeply grateful to Lt General RK Sawhney, PVSM, AVSM (Former Deputy Chief of Army Staff & Former DGMI), Centre Head & Senior Fellow, Vivekananda International Foundation, who spared valuable time to peruse my manuscript and offer some precious suggestions. His continuous moral support provided strength to carry on my writing.

I express my deep regards and heartflet gratitude to Shri CD Sahay (Former Secretary Research & Analysis Wing, Cabinet Secretariat), Centre Head & Senior Fellow,

Neighbourhood Studies & Internal Security Studies, Vivekananda International Foundation for providing valuable inputs without which the book would not have been complete.

I owe a profound debt of gratitude to Shri Chetanya Kasyap, a philanthropist and currently Deputy Chairman of Planning Commission, Madhya Pradesh, for his continuous support in my academic persuit.

I wish to express my appreciation to my younger brother Shri SNP Singh, former Chief Manager, Punjab National Bank, for his unabated support to pursue my academic quest.

My grateful thanks to Smt Anuttama Ganguly, Joint Secretary (Administration & Finances), Vivekananda International Foundation, for taking all pains to enable me to complete this book.

I am thankful to Shri Ramanand Garge, Senior Research Associate, Vivekananda International Foundation for putting in hard labour in researching useful facts for the book.

My sincere thanks to Shri Sanjay Kumar, Librarian, Vivekananda International Foundation, who enabled me to get source material for the book.

I must express my thanks to Shri Kamal Singh, Executive Assistant, Vivekananda International Foundation, for extending helping hand and arranging the book in proper order.

I am thankful to all my friends, colleagues and well-wishers who extended helping hands in completion of this book.

Lastly, I doubt if I would have been able to complete the work I undertook for myself without the institutional facilities offered by Vivekananda International Foundation, New Delhi. More than the institutional facilities which are excellent, however, is the helpful attitude of every member of the VIF.

Foreword

India has had a galaxy of great men who were instrumental in winning independence from the British yoke. Standing tall amongst these luminaries was the 'Iron Man' of India, Sardar Vallabhbhai Patel. Sardar Patel bequeathed the idea of an integrated India after independence to the nation. His contribution in laying the foundation of the Union of India is unparalleled and chronicling his deeds for a historical profile is indeed a daunting challenge. I am glad that RNP Singh has taken up this gauntlet in this book on Sardar Patel. He has presented to the readers meticulously some original researched facts about the contribution of Sardar Patel, particularly towards building the free and integrated nation which India is today. Singh's work in presenting a true picture of Sardar Patel has been a commendable work.

Sardar Patel played a prominent role under Mahatma Gandhi in the national struggle, both during and after independence. He consolidated and unified the country and brought about stability in the Indian administration. Sardar Patel is thus aptly acclaimed as the 'Iron Man' and was a master strategist blessed with an uncanny foresight and a clear vision of where India's future lay. The greater part of his illustrious life was devoted to the struggle for freedom of the country and once independence was won, he dedicated himself to the monumental task of integrating the five hundred odd princely States into the Union of India. The integration of these princely States was a momentous challenge, not only in the history of modern India, but one which has not been witnessed or equalled in the history of any other nation.

Sardar Patel's singular commitment to the territorial integrity of the country was further underlined in the widely acclaimed accession of Junagadh and Hyderabad to the Indian Union. Sardar Patel was a visionary who was deeply rooted in the realism of the events of the day. As is well known, he was very unhappy that the Kashmir issue was referred to the United Nations. His mature and farsighted advice to deal with Chinese diplomacy analytically, was ignored by Nehru. The subsequent events proved that Sardar Patel's assessment was correct.

RNP Singh has presented a vivid account of the contribution of Patel in integrating India, replete with many well researched facts, which had hitherto escaped the notice of many earlier writers. Sardar Patel's total focus towards the integration of India, and saving it from Balkanisation, has been eloquently narrated by the author. He has not coloured the narrative with his own opinions and has treated the subject objectively which will enable the readers to exercise their own independent judgment. Sardar Patel's mature and decisive approach to the many debilitating issues that faced India at independence prevented any further division of India, which could well have become a mix of an India of the people and an India of the Princes. These sterling qualities which were the hallmark of his life and work are so much more required today as the country is faced anew with stresses appearing in our national rubric in many fields.

It is, therefore, an appropriate time to reflect on the contribution of this great unifier of modern India. The author has factually and comprehensively presented Patel's spirit and work with a view to guiding present and future generations of Indians, to meet the challenges of a growing India while retaining the spirit of its founding principles.

Finally, I will once again like to convey my compliments to RNP Singh, our Senior Fellow, for having produced such a masterly work.

General NC Vij
VSM, UYSM, AVSM (Retd) Former Director VIF
Former Chief of the Army Staff &
Founder Vice Chairman, NDMA
New Delhi 2018

Preface

Writing a book on the life and achievements of an outstanding personality like Sardar Vallabhbhai Patel would always be a huge challenge for anyone, but for me personally, it was especially so for multiple reasons—the primary one being the fact that I had only recently gone through the enormous task of examining this near contemporary history while writing a book, *Nehru: A Troubled Legacy*, that involved over three-four years' intensive research. On most of the issues and developments the two stalwarts, Nehru and Patel, were physically together but politically and intellectually wide apart. It was a stern intellectual test to analyse the events from two or more different perspectives and try to arrive at balanced and unbiased conclusions.

Vallabhbhai has been variously perceived by historians and contemporary analysts as a 'superman', and a leader with 'superlative brains'. He was none of that. What he was, was a statesman gifted with the rare quality of astuteness and pertinacity in his approach to problems. Despite his stern exterior, he possessed a generous heart, but in the pursuit of larger objectives, he never allowed emotions or sentiment to weaken his resolve.

Contrary to the general perception, Patel was totally committed to Mahatma Gandhi, yet at no time did he compromise with his deeply-felt convictions. For instance, despite his abiding faith in the Mahatma's leadership, he accepted non-violence, not as an ineluctable way of life, but in the circumstances then obtaining in India, as the only available weapon to compel British withdrawal from the country. And when the country achieved its objective, Patel was quick to advocate the creation of a strong defence force to guard its newly-acquired sovereignty.

Vallabhbhai's realism rested on the sound principle that the cause is always greater than the man. His perceived ruthlessness in enforcing organisational discipline in the Congress Party was derived from the conviction that only as a strong party could the Congress qualify to play the role of a competent 'receiver' after the end of foreign rule. His leadership of the peasants' revolt in Gujarat and of the flag *satyagraha* at Nagpur were designed to drill and discipline his countrymen to a life of suffering and sacrifice as a means of winning national freedom. In his scheme of things, there was indeed no place for vacillation, selfishness and cowardice, which he fought against, not with kid-gloves, but with the mailed fist. And because he was essentially a man of action, he lived, not in words, but in deeds.

Vallabhbhai has won for himself a glittering page in history as an annexationist and unifier far more resourceful and much bolder than Bismarck. Only a man of his resolute and persuasive abilities could have accomplished the unique feat of merging the five hundred odd mutually exclusive and fiercely self-regarding principalities into India's wider unity. The sacrifices demanded from the Princes were of staggering proportions and yet a majority of them willingly surrendered their most cherished possessions. It is not a small tribute to Patel's vision and sagacity that even after he had stripped the rulers of their powers, his relations with them, both individually and collectively, were most cordial. The bloodless revolution, representing the crowning achievement of his life, was accomplished at a time when the armed forces of the Government of India were dangerously inadequate.

To build up India of his dreams, Patel felt the need for an efficient and enthusiastic Civil Service. The ICS under the British Raj had earned renown for the ability and versatility of its members, but following the country's partition and independence in 1947, nearly 700 European and Muslim ICS officers out of a total of 1,150 had left. The burden of running the administration of a problem-ridden country fell upon a small number of officers.

Patel was indeed the only senior Congress leader who not only appreciated and admired their capabilities, but also won their confidence by fighting for their rights, privileges and immunities. He realised that the problems of the country, which were of such heart-breaking complexity, could be dealt with effectively only with their expert assistance.

After the exodus of a large number of the ICS and IP (Indian Police) men, Patel constituted the Indian Administrative Service and Indian Police Service in its place despite opposition from many State Chief Ministers to the creation of such an all-India cadre. Patel sternly discouraged divisive tendencies and impressed upon them the need for an interchange of officers in order to preserve the unity, integrity, independence, impartiality and the efficiency of the administration throughout the country. Never before in India's history since the Maurayan bureaucracy did India have a uniform system of administration, from which no part of the country was excluded. Nor was the country ever before unified as an unrestricted democracy.

Most of all, those who knew Sardar Vallabhbhai Patel, acclaimed him as a great man. An outstanding quality of his leadership was his capacity to dominate any situation, no matter how difficult it was. Alan Campbell-Johnson, who had rare opportunities of watching the Sardar in action, has referred to the Indian statesman in many places in his book, *Mission with Mountbatten*. Describing the Sardar as a man with Roman qualities, he recalls his conversation with Sir Archibald Nye whose knowledge of Indian affairs was also intimate and first-hand. Nye told him that, 'he was very impressed with Patel who was a real leader in the military sense'. 'Mountbatten', writes Campbell-Johnson, 'had been somewhat apprehensive about his first meeting with Patel, who had the reputation of being the strong man in the Congress High Command, but he very quickly detected a twinkle in the Sardar's eye. His approach to the whole problem was clear and decisive'.[1] In an extempore speech at the farewell banquet for him and Lady Mountbatten on 20 June 1948, Mountbatten referred to the Sardar thus: I was warned before I came to India that I should meet my match in a very 'tough guy', Sardar Vallabhbhai Patel; but when we met I came to the conclusion that he could not be quite as tough as the act that he put on. He is so very apparently hard and firm and unyielding, and I think he is like that because he does not want the world to know what a very warm heart beats behind the rugged exterior and I regard him as one of the greatest friends I have made here.[2]

'What was Vallabhbhai?', asked Rajagopalachari, and he himself answered: What inspiration, courage, confidence, and force incarnate Vallabhbhai was.... We will not see the likes of him again.[3] Nehru called him, 'the Builder and Consolidator of New India... a great captain of our forces in the struggle for freedom... a tower of strength which revived wavering hearts'.[4] Gandhi found in him a Colleague 'most trustworthy, staunch and brave'.[5] Vinoba Bhave called him, 'the accurate bowman of Gandhi's struggle, his disciple and his GOC. He knew no retreat'.[6]

Patel's international acclaim was equally eloquent. *The London Times* wrote of him on his demise, 'Little known outside his own country, "Sardarji" neither sought nor won the international reputation achieved by Gandhi or Mr Nehru. Yet, he made up with them the triumvirate that gave shape to the India of today'.[7] The *Manchester Guardian*'s tribute was more specific: Without Patel, Gandhi's ideas would have had less practical influence, and Nehru's idealism less scope. Patel was not only the organiser of the fight for freedom, but also the architect of the new state when the fight was over. The same man is seldom successful both as rebel and statesman. Patel was the exception.[8]

In spite of Patel being an unquestioned patriot, statesman, visionary and a unifier of modern India, dispassionate observers cannot help suspecting that there is almost a conspiracy of silence aimed at obliterating his memory. In certain circles he is painted as a reactionary, communalist and Hindu nationalist. His book of speeches, *Sardar Patel on Indian Problems,* has been out of print and no attempt has been made to reprint it. The original publisher was Government of India. A commemorative volume published on his 75th birthday, containing extracts from his speeches and life sketches by admirers, had a limited circulation.

In absence of the availability of material, it has been difficult to satisfy the curiosity of the student of history about what the Sardar was, and what he achieved as a fighter for freedom, as a powerful organiser and a great statesman. Some writers have thrown much mud at the Sardar's memory. This needs to be cleared by presenting hard facts. Patel's personality will then stand out clear and radiant for future generations to make their own estimate of his contribution towards building the free nation which India is today. In the present political flux, thinking men more than ever mourn the absence of Patel's leadership, his clarity of thought, his robust sense of realism, his firmness in decision and his iron will which none could bend; and they cannot help saying: Had Patel been alive for some more years, India would not have seen such dismal days.

Instead of a biographical narrative, I have in this book taken up only one aspect—that is his contribution to the integration of the Indian States in a factual and objective manner. I have tried to present the personality of Patel against the background of the political situation prevailing immediately after partition. My sole objective in writing this book is to present his personality to the reader in its proper colours—as one who left his mark not only on the map of India but also on the minds of the people.

References

1. Allen Campbell-Johnson, *Mission with Mountbatten*, Macmillan, 1985, p-101-282.
2. *Speeches by the Earl Mountbatten of Burma* (1947-48), Kaye, London, 1949, p-186.
3. *This was Sardar*, Commemorative volume-I, ed.GM Nandrukar, Sardar Vallabhbhai Smarak Bhavan, Ahmedabad, 1974, p-447-49.
4. Ibid.
5. Ibid.
6. *Harijan*, 26 January 1951, p-419.
7. *The London Times* (now *The Times*), 16 December 1950.
8. The *Manchester Guardian* (now *The Guardian*), 16 December 1950.

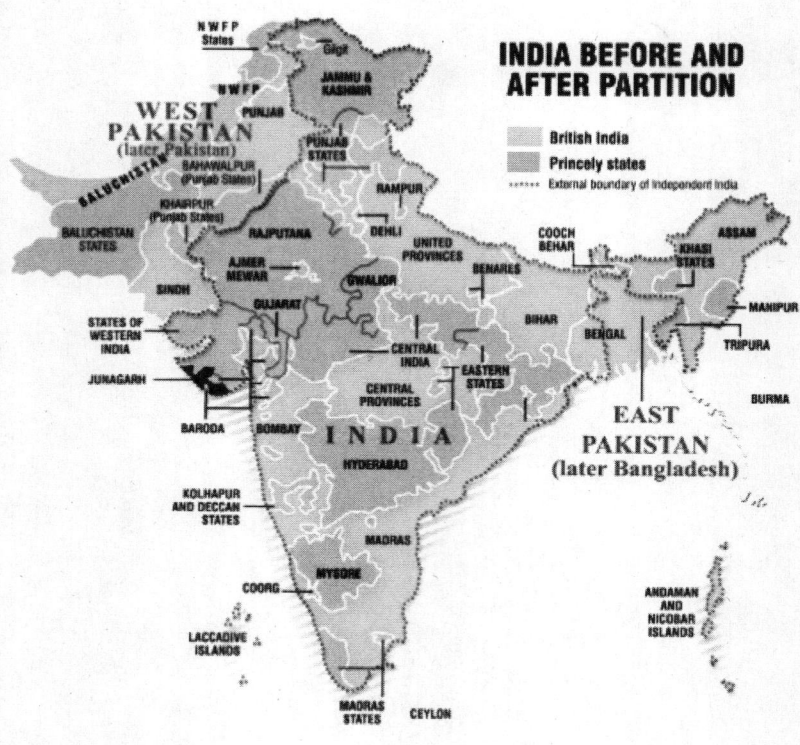

Integration of the Indian States

> *The masterly handling of the rulers (Princes) by Sardar was the foremost factor in the success of the accession policy. The rulers soon came to recognise him as a stable force in Indian politics and as one who would give them a fair deal. Added to this, his unfailing politeness to the rulers, viewed against his reputation as the 'Iron Man of India', endeared him to them and created such confidence that all accepted his advice without demur.*
>
> —VP Menon

AFTER SECURING the accession of States, Vallabhbhai Patel tightened his grip on the great movement which brought about their full integration with India. People were demanding the introduction of 'responsible government'. They were becoming restive due to violent outbreaks of discord. The safety of the rulers as well as of the people was in danger. Maintenance of law and order was becoming a problem and the Government of India was constrained to intervene wherever internal condition deteriorated. The States had no resources, no manpower and no stability. The rulers had become targets of the revolutionary impulses of those they had ruled. Their security depended on the goodwill of the people and the protection of the Central government. But the government could not support States which continued in their pre-independence form. Patel advised the rulers to surrender their power and authority to the Government of India, and in return accept the grant of privy purses and guarantees of their personal properties and privileges. The rulers saw the inevitable and wanted to salvage what they could. They negotiated for their privy purses.

Patel decided that the best course would be to secure their merger into a Union. He, therefore, explained to the rulers that the States could no longer continue their separate existence. Like little pools of water they had become stagnant. The transfer of power to the people had become inevitable. It was in the interests of the ruler that this should be effected in a peaceful manner. Most of States could not satisfy the demands of the people for minimum amenities of life, for they did not have the resources of money and manpower. By forming a Union of the States, the administration could be kept under control. The transfer of power might not be palatable to the Princes, but unless this was done, they would have to face more unpalatable prospects.

And then, from the realistic angle, he convinced them that the popular ministries (provincial governments) were sure to vote for merger into a Union of States. He asked them, would it not be safer for the Princes to agree to merger and thus safeguard their privy purses and their personal properties? The Princes agreed, and the United States of Kathiawad was formed on 15 February 1948. The movement for merger spread to other provinces. The Deccan and Gujarat States, scattered all over the province of Bombay, merged with it in June 1948. Kolhapur followed suit in March 1949. Vindhya Pradesh was established in January 1950. The Madhya Bharat Union was formed in May 1948.

The merger and integration of States gathered such momentum that the Punjab States formed the Patiala and East Punjab States Union in July 1948, the Rajasthan Union was formed in May 1949, by the merger of Matsya Union with Greater Rajasthan. Travancore and Cochin formed a Union in May 1949. Next month Mysore was integrated. In January 1949, Baroda had merged into the State of Bombay. On 7 November 1947, the Dewan of Junagadh found it impossible to carry on administration and requested the Government of India to take over the State.

Like a magician, Patel had picked up the fragments of States and from his basket produced compact and viable units. The map of India was changed completely. Out of 554 States, 216 had merged in the provinces, 310 had been consolidated into six Unions, five were put directly under the Centre as Chief Commissioner's Province, 21 Punjab Hill States formed the Himachal Pradesh and two States were made into separate Provinces. The 554 States were thus reduced to fourteen Unions and States.[1]

The administrative consolidation of these States and Unions, which varied much in their structure, was undertaken by loaning experienced officers to the Unions. The State forces were integrated in the Indian army. This process was completed by the Constitution of India which came into force on 26th January 1950.

Patel's policy of integration recognised the rights of the rulers, acquired by heredity and history which the people must honour. He said, 'Their dignities and privileges and their means of subsistence on a reasonable standard must be assured'.[2] He hoped that rulers would discard their former mentality, bred by autocracy, and devote themselves to the service of the people. He described the rulers as co-architects in the work of building the nation. He claimed that 'he had never used any coercion on the Princes. It was the compulsion of circumstances and events which forced the Princes to surrender. Some had intelligence to see the inevitable, others, who struggled against it, were ultimately forced in it'.[3]

Patel took all care to safeguard the genuine interests of the rulers. Some critics believed that Patel had been too generous to the Princes in respect of their privy purses and private properties. They ignored vital statistics. *The total amount of privy purses actually taken by rulers, before integration, was of the order of Rs 20 crore in values of the 1940s. In addition, customary taxes were collected from the people on such occasions as marriages and birth in the ruler's family, and even for purchase of a special car. On the other hand, the total cost of the privy purses after integration, as sanctioned by the Ministry of States, was Rs 5.8 crore.*

The amount in the case of each ruler was fixed in consultation with the Ministry or the leaders of the Union. They were granted for life and the successors' privy purses were to be fixed at the discretion of the government. Only eleven rulers got more than Rs 10 lakh. They were Gwalior (Rs 25 lakh), Indore (Rs 15 lakh), Patiala (Rs 17 lakh), Baroda (Rs 26.5 lakh), Jaipur (Rs 8 lakh), Jodhpur (Rs 17.5 lakh), Bikaner (Rs 17 lakh), Travancore (Rs 18 lakh), Bhopal (Rs 11 lakh), Mysore (Rs 26 lakh), and Hyderabad (Rs 50 lakh in Hyderabad currency). Ninety-one rulers were given privy purses of more than one lakh rupees. Fifty-six rulers had less than one lakh and the remaining 396 rulers were given privy purses less than Rs 50,000 per annum.[4]

As against this cost, the gain to India was considerable when the States were taken over. *The new State governments inherited cash balances and investments exceeding Rs 77 crore.* The rulers surrendered over 500 villages, thousands of acres of land and their palaces, museums and buildings. For instance, the Nizam surrendered his personal estate with a net revenue of Rs 1.24 crore in return for a compensation of Rs 25 lakh per annum during his life time. He invested over Rs 40 crore in government securities and shares and, in addition, gave an annual loan of Rs 50 lakh for the Tungbhadra Project. *Besides, the government acquired about 12,000 miles of railways without payment of compensation.*

The country has reason to be grateful to Sardar Patel who laid the foundations of an integrated India, wherein regional loyalties were overshadowed by the desire to build a strong and united nation. *By partition, India had lost 3.6 lakh square miles of territory with a population of 81.5 million. By the integration of States, she acquired 5 lakh square miles of territory with a population of 86.5 million.* Artificial barriers between the States and the rest of India were demolished. Almost overnight, the superstructure of the modern system of government was introduced in these States.

The Sardar performed a miracle. In his own words: The great idea of geographical, political and economic unification of India, an ideal which for centuries remained a distant dream and which appeared as remote and as difficult of attainment even after the advent of Indian independence, was consummated by the policy of integration.

However, he was too much of a realist to ignore that real integration had still to take place in the minds of the people. He said: We have to weave new fabrics into old materials; we have to make sure that simultaneously the old and the new are integrated into a harmonious whole—a design that would fit well into the pattern of all India.[5]

Historical background of the idea of integration

The Indian States, with their total subservience, formed the main arch of the British power in India. After the great National Revolt of 1857, when Victoria, the Queen of England, assumed the role of the Empress of India, the British government clearly drew its lessons from the rebellion and felt that the native governments had acted and could act as breakwaters for any nationalist storm, which would otherwise have swept away the Empire in one great move. For over ninety years, these States, petrified under British control, continued to play an important part in maintaining foreign rule in India. With ever-changing doctrines and devices regarding their subservience and sovereignty, they provided the strongest bulwark against the rising tide of nationalism.

Successive British statesmen continued to prize the loyalty of the Princes who ruled over the backward populations under the 'control' of British Residents or Agents. During the twentieth century, when British India was astir with national aspirations, new constitutional doctrines were evolved by the British in India. All the States, with full powers of jurisdiction, were now equal in sovereignty; the treaties made by them with East India Company were sacrosanct. But, where the British interests were affected, the undefined word 'Paramountcy' overrode all obligations. This doctrine was avidly accepted by the rulers as their charter of independence.

The British Empire started annexing Indian States and provinces, as subsidiaries of the Empire, after 1858. 'The Indian Princes were seen as feudal subsidiaries of the British crown, especially after the Royal Titles Act of 1876.'[6] The crucial thing at this time for the imperial state was the question of heir or successor of the kingdom. It was not only an idea of conquest but also an idea of hegemonic administrative control under the mark of governability and accountability that the colonial state emphasised, which it carried forward in everyday formal-legal bureaucratic-governmentalised spheres of life.

The division of colonial India into British and Princely India was structured along various hierarchies and divisions overlapping social, cultural, economic, political and ideological differences between these two parts of the population. Princely States formed about two-fifths of the territory and a quarter of the population of colonial India. In order to better manage and control the Princely States, the colonial state deputed residents, political agents and Crown representative in those States. The Montague-Chelmsford Reforms of 1919 were the first in this regard to initiate the process of sharing powers between the empire and its constituents. The most important recommendation of the Montague-Chelmsford report related to the codification of political practice. The next twenty-five years saw the genesis and emergence of the constitutional history of India, providing measures addressing issues of political representation, autonomy and division of power between the Centre and States. The Government of India Act 1935, the Cripps Proposal of 1942 and the Cabinet Mission Plan of 1946, among others, were significant exercises in this regard.

Under the Government of India Act 1935, States were to accede to the Indian federation. It provided for a constitutional relationship between the Indian States and British India on a federal basis. A special feature of the scheme was that, whereas in the case of the provinces, accession to the federation was to be automatic, in the case of the States it was voluntary. A State was considered to have acceded when its ruler executed an 'Instrument of Accession' and after it was accepted by His Majesty. This instrument would empower the federal government, the federal legislature, the federal court and any other federal authority to exercise in relation to the State such functions as might be vested in them by or under the Act, but the authority to perform such functions was to be exercised only in respect of those matters accepted by the ruler as 'federal' in his Instrument of Accession and subject to such limitations as might be specified in it. An instrument of accession would become operative only when His Majesty had signed his acceptance of it.

The relationship of the Indian Princes with the paramount power was safeguarded by creating a Crown Representative in addition to the Governor-General. In the conduct of their affairs as members of the federation, the States were to deal with the Governor-General as head of the federal government, whereas in their relation with the paramount power, they were to deal with the Crown Representative.

The Government of India Act of 1935, other than the part relating to federation, came into force on 1 April 1937. From that date, the functions of the Crown in its relations with the States were entrusted to the Crown Representative; those functions included negotiations with the rulers for their accession to the federation. The Viceroy who succeeded Lord Willington in 1936 was the Marquess of Linlithgow who came to India with the ambition to inaugurate the federation during his tenure of office. He thought that a direct personal approach to the rulers would persuade many of them to accept it. He, therefore, planned to send his own personal emissaries to various States to clear the rulers' doubts so that they could make a final decision without delay. The emissaries were provided with draft copies of the Instrument of Accession, which had already been sent to the rulers, as well as with the written instructions from the Viceroy.

The three emissaries chosen were Sir Courtenay Latimer, Sir Francis Wylie and Sir Arthur Lothian, all of whom belonged to the Political Service. The three emissaries toured the various States in the Winter of 1936-37 and met the rulers and their advisors. The rulers made it clear that they did not urge unity. The question which agitated them was not whether the federation would benefit India, but whether their own position would be better and safer inside the federation than outside it.

They conveyed their concern with these words: We are being given the opportunity of entering a federation from which, when once we are in, there is no escape. Nor, since the ultimate interpreter of the federal constitution is the Federal Court, can the Government of India or anyone else predict the course of future events or anticipate the use which federation will make of its powers. We owe it, therefore, to ourselves and to our successors to safeguard to the utmost our own position inside the federation. That is the light in which you must regard the limitations which we have proposed, and if they seem unduly numerous and too widely drawn, remember that we have good reasons for making them so.[7] Limitations proposed by the rulers were mainly their desire to safeguard—their sovereignty and their financial position.

The emissaries submitted their reports to the Viceroy in early 1937. The reports indicated that the rulers were in bargaining mood and suggested many far-reaching concessions to induce them to join the federation. The Princes also sent their replies to the Viceroy, stating the terms on which alone they were prepared to come in.

Meanwhile, several rounds of talks between the Indian government and the rulers were held, with no result. No assurances they wanted was forthcoming. The federation was still as distant as ever. Such was the position towards the beginning of August 1939. In the meantime, the provincial part of the Government of India Act of 1935 had been put into operation and elections to the provincial legislatures had been held in 1937. The Congress had swept the polls in six provinces and in July of that year, it had formed ministries. A little later, with the support of a few independent members, Congress ministries were also formed in two other provinces, viz. Assam and North-West Frontier Province.

The overwhelming success of the Congress encouraged the States' subjects to agitate for civil liberties and responsible government. There were unrests in Mysore, Travancore, Kashmir, Hyderabad, Jaipur, Rajkot and the Orissa States. The Congress reiterated its objective of standing for the same political, social and economic freedom in the States as in the case of the rest of India, and of considering the States as integral part of India.

Lord Linlithgow realised that unless some radical reforms were brought about in the States, it would only be a question of time before they succumbed to the Congress agitation. The bigger States were capable of looking after themselves, it was the future of the middle-sized and small States about which he was anxious. He felt that, with regard to the latter, the policy of abstention from interference, which the British government had for some years pursued, could no longer be defended and should be abandoned; that active pressure should be brought to bear on these States to effect administrative reforms. Lord Linlithgow wanted to bring stronger pressure to bear on the rulers than had hitherto been the case in the matter of sponsoring representative institutions and establishing some form of constitutional government within the States. However, these proposals were not to the taste of the Political Department back home.

The Secretary of State was in agreement with Lord Linlithgow's proposal on administrative reforms. But, as regards the constitutional advance, he considered that, on both political and practical grounds, the initiative and onus of responsibility must continue to rest with the rulers themselves. He felt that constitutional development in the States, once begun, could not be regulated and limited in the same way as administrative advance and that no policy conceived by the British government could by itself maintain the rulers or ensure against their eventual capitulation to the Congress agitation. In the meantime, the Second World War broke out. The position then was that owing to the unyielding attitude of the rulers, as well as of the major political parties in British India, the federal scheme was in its last gasp.

Due to breaking out of the Second World War, the Empire needed the help of the Princes in men, money and material. It was not the time to rub them the wrong way. On 11 September 1939, Lord Linlithgow announced in his address to both Houses of the Central Legislature that, 'while the federation remained, as before, the objective of His Majesty's Government, the compulsion of the present international situation and the fact that, given the necessity for concentrating on the emergency that confront us, we have no choice but to hold in suspense the work in connection with preparation for federation'.[8] This marked the close of a crucial chapter in modern India's political history.

Cabinet Mission and Constituent Assembly

When the war entered its acute phase with the fall of France, Neville Chamberlain resigned and Winston Churchill formed a National Coalition Government in which LS Amery became the Secretary of State for India. On 8 August 1940, Linlithgow put forward some new proposals on behalf of His Majesty's Government. He offered a certain number of seats in the Governor-General's Executive Council to Indian representatives. He also proposed a War Advisory Council with members from the representatives of the States and of British India. Lastly, he promised that after the conclusion of the war, a body of representatives of the principal elements in India's national life would be called upon to devise the framework of a new Constitution. The Congress rejected the offer, the Muslim League followed suit.

The British government made no further overtures to the political parties. But, towards the close of 1941, the war situation had changed for the worse. On March 1942, Churchill declared in the House of Commons that 'the crisis in the affairs of India arising out of the Japanese advance has made Britain wish to rally all the forces of Indian life to guard their land from the menace of this invader'.[9] He announced that the War Cabinet was sending out Sir Stafford Cripps to India, with a set of proposals approved by the Cabinet, in order to remove the doubts and apprehensions in the minds of the Indian parties and to convince their leaders how those proposals constituted a far-reaching advance towards satisfying Indian aspirations.

Sir Stafford Cripps, who arrived in India on 22 March 1942, revealed his two offers at a press conference on 29 March. His offer consisted of a proposal that a constitution-making body would be set up to frame the Constitution of a new Indian Union which would have the full status of a 'Dominion' with the power to secede, if it chose, from the British Commonwealth. This body would be elected by an electoral college consisting of the members of lower houses of the provincial legislatures, for which fresh elections would be held. The British government undertook to accept and implement forthwith the Constitution framed by this body on two conditions. Firstly, any province or provinces which were not prepared to accept the new constitution would be entitled to frame, by a similar process, a *constitution of their own* giving them the same full status as the Indian Union. The second condition was that a treaty should be negotiated between the British government and the constitution-making body to cover all matters arising out of the transfer of responsibility, particularly the protection of racial and religious minorities.

The Princes were not associated with Cripps in any discussions. The rulers felt that the scheme for making a new constitution after the war applied to all-India and hence they were deeply concerned. They met Sir Stafford Cripps and raised several questions of their interest. While replying to their questions, Cripps said that in any case, it was definite that the British government did not contemplate transferring the Paramountcy of the Crown to any other party Paramountcy would continue to be in force in the case of States which join the union; intention was to revise the treaties only so far as might be required in the new situation; and the British government could not be expected to coerce any party into such arrangements, although their good offices would be available to resolve differences. The Cripps offer was rejected by both the Congress Working Committee and the Muslim League. Cripps left for London, his mission a failure.

By the end of 1944, events had overtaken Britain's colonial plans. The defence of Stalingrad had halted Hitler, and his armies were thrown on the defensive. Japan had been effectively checked, leading to the victory of the Allies. The Labour Party withdrew from the coalition government in Britain after the victory, thus, forcing an early general election, in which the Conservatives were defeated. On 26 July 1945, the Labour Party was invited to form a new government. Clement Attlee became Prime Minister and Lord Pethic-Lawrence assumed the duties of Secretary of State for India.

In September of the same year, Lord Wavell went to England and on his return announced his second plan. The announcement reaffirmed the King's government's determination to do their utmost, in conjunction with the leaders of Indian opinion, to promote the early realisation of 'full self-government' for India and expressed the hope that India's political leaders would assume ministerial responsibilities in all the provinces after the elections, which had already been announced.

The announcement made it clear that His Majesty's Government intended to convene, as soon as possible, a constitution-making body to draft a future Constitution of India but, as a preliminary step, the Viceroy had been authorised to consult representatives of the provincial assemblies as to whether the concrete proposals in the Cripps declaration required any modification. It was against this background that the annual session of the Chamber of Princes was held on 17 January 1946. (The Chamber of Princes was brought into being by a Royal Proclamation on 8 February 1921.) In his address, the Viceroy assured them that no changes in their relationship with the Crown or the rights guaranteed to them by treaties and engagements would be initiated without their consent. At the same time, he expressed his confidence that the States would take their full part in the constitutional discussions which were to be held later in the year, as well as, in the proposed constitution-making body.

On 19 February 1946, Attlee announced the decision of the British Cabinet to send three cabinet ministers to India to settle with the Indian leaders, in association with the Viceroy, the procedure of framing a new Constitution for the country.

It was decided that the Mission should interview (1) Chancellor of the Chamber of Princes (2) the rulers of Patiala, Bikaner and Nawanagar jointly as representing the middle States (3) rulers of Dungarpur and Bilaspur jointly representing the smaller States (4) the Anwar of Chhatari (Hyderabad), Sir CP Ramaswami Iyer (Travancore) and Sir Mirza Ismail (Jaipur) individually. A suggestion that the Mission should interview the representatives of the States' subjects was not acceptable either to the Political Department or to the Chancellor.

As per this decision, the Cabinet Mission met the representatives of the Princes. Broadly, the position taken up by the State representatives was that the Paramountcy should not be transferred to a successor government, but that it should lapse; that the States should not be forced to join any Union or Unions; that there should be *prima facie* no objection to the formation of a Confederation of States, if the rulers so desired and that there should be no interference in their internal affairs by British India.

Imperial Strategy of Pakistan-Hindustan-Princestan

On 16 May 1946, the Cabinet Mission and the Viceroy, in consultation with His Majesty's Government, issued a statement embodying their own suggestions and recommendations towards a solution of the Indian problem. This was subsequently known as the 'Cabinet Mission Plan'.

Referring to the States, 'the Mission said that it was quite clear that with the attainment of independence by British India, whether within or without the British Commonwealth, the relationship which had hitherto existed between the States and the British Crown would no longer be possible. Paramountcy could neither be retained by the British nor transferred to the new government'. The statement went on to say that: the rulers had assured the Mission that they were ready and willing to cooperate in the new development of India. However, the precise form which that cooperation would take must be a matter for negotiation during the building up of the new constitutional structure and it by no means followed that it would be identical for all the States.[10]

Under the proposed plan, the States were to retain all subjects and powers other than those ceded to the Union, namely foreign affairs, defence and communication. In the preliminary stage, they were to be represented in the Constituent Assembly by a Negotiating Committee. In the final Constituent Assembly, they were to have appropriate representation not exceeding 93 seats.

The method of selection was to be determined by consultation between the parties concerned.

The Cabinet Mission Plan of 16 May 1946, though expressed in the form of a recommendation, was really in the nature of an award, as the Mission had been unable to bring about a general agreement between the Congress and the Muslim League. The Congress agreed to participate in the Constituent Assembly to be convened under the plan for framing a new constitution. The Muslim League at first accepted the full plan while reiterating that attainment of a sovereign Pakistan still remained its unalterable objective, but after a somewhat acrimonious controversy between the Congress and the League over interpretation of the plan, the Council of Muslim League revoked its acceptance.

On invitation from the Viceroy, Jawaharlal Nehru formed an Interim Government. The League representative also joined the government. In the meantime, elections to the Constituent Assembly were held in accordance with the procedure laid down in the plan. The Muslim Leaguers who were elected to that body refused to join it. The Constituent Assembly, for the first time, met on 9 December 1946. It elected Rajendra Prasad as the President and appointed various committees to draft the different sections of the Constitution.

Patel, as Home Member in the Interim Government, realised that with the promise of separate constitutions for the princely States, His Majesty's Political Department harboured designs to Balkanise the Indian subcontinent. The Princes were under the exclusive charge of the Viceroy as Crown Representative, but were directly responsible to the Secretary of the Political Department. He, in turn, could directly report to the Secretary of State in London. The British were to terminate Paramountcy simultaneously with the transfer of power to India, so that they could make the Princes independent, and thus, enable them to negotiate, individually or jointly, with the new government in British India on equal terms. This was an attempt to implement

Churchill's 'Imperial Strategy' of which Wavell records in his Journal on 29 March 1949: He seems to favour partition into Pakistan, Hindustan, Princestan etc.[11] This was the tip of the iceberg. What was being maneuvered underneath hardly anyone could see or know. Patel was no exception.

Such maneuvering followed the two pronouncements of the Cabinet Mission: the Memorandum of 12th, and the Plan of May 16th. The former stated: When a new fully self-government or independent government or governments came into being in British India... HMG will cease to exercise the powers of Paramountcy... the rights of the States which flow from their relationship to the Crown will no longer exist and that all the rights surrendered by the States to the Paramount Power will return to States. Political arrangements between the States, on the one side, and the British Crown and British India, on the other, will, thus, be brought to an end. The void will have to be filled either by the States entering into a federal relationship with the successor government or governments in British India, or, failing this, entering into particular political arrangements with it or them.[12]

Though Patel was then a helpless witness, he commented later: Nobody could have been so innocent or ignorant as to presume that overnight small rulers could be converted into 'Their Majesties'. That position would have been full of dangerous possibilities and potentialities.[13] In its 16 May 1946 statement, the Mission virtually put a seal on the Princely States' sovereign status by declaring, 'Paramountcy can neither be retained by the British Crown nor transferred to the new government'.[14]

The Cabinet Mission made another dangerous move in the suggestion that, for the seats allotted to the Princes in the Constituent Assembly, the Chamber of Princes should nominate a 'Negotiating Committee' for parleys with its counterpart from British India. Two dangers lurked in that. Since, practically every matter which concerned the State had been committed to the care of the States' Negotiating Committee, Patel wondered whether their Negotiating Committee had to settle the question of determining the method of election of the States' representatives to the Constituent Assembly, or whether the Negotiating Committee had even a wider field of discussing other subjects concerning the States. Further, Patel wrote to KM Munshi: Another important question for us to decide is whether the Constituent Assembly will have any say in the matter of grouping of States, which the Chamber of Princes might decide on, or which any group of States independently might agree upon. He also told Munshi in his letter of 7 December 1946: You know efforts are being made to form groups of States, either independently or under the inspiration of the Chamber of Princes.[15]

Not much later, such fears came out in the open when Bhopal and Conrad Corfield, Secretary of the Political Department, began organising the Princes into blocs.

An accident of history changed the course of events and determined the fate of the country. An official file, casually falling into Patel's hands after taking charge of Home in the Interim Government, in September 1946, opened his eyes to the dangers India faced. Bastar, whose 'Raja was a minor and a weakling and the Prime Minister a foreigner' and a land which had rich mineral and other resources, was being 'mortgaged to Hyderabad State by means of long lease' and was to be 'exploited to the prejudice of India'.

His Majesty's Political Department evaded Home Member Patel's enquiries on the matter. He was told that those in charge of the Department were 'guardians of the minor' and that they 'could enter into the contract in the interests of the minor'. Patel told them that 'they (the British) were now going away and they should not bother about their wards. Their guardianship would now devolve on us (free India), and they should do nothing without our agreement, or which was contrary to the interests of the people' of India.

Not satisfied with the Political Department's response, Patel also called for the Prince. 'When I saw the ruler', he records, 'how young and inexperienced he was, I felt that it was a sin to make him sign such an agreement. It was then that I was made fully conscious of the extent to which our interests were being prejudiced in every way by the machinations of the Political Department, and came to the conclusion that the sooner we were rid of these people, the better. Their main aim was to further their own interests and to cause as much damage to India as possible. I came to the conclusion that the best course was to drive out foreigners even at the cost of partition of the country. It was also then that I felt that there was only one way to make the country safe and strong—and that was the unification of the rest of India'.[16]

Meanwhile, on 20 February 1947, Prime Minister Attlee made a declaration in the House of Commons in course of which he set a date not later than June 1948 by which time Britain would transfer power to responsible Indian hands. It was also announced that Mountbatten would replace Lord Wavell as Viceroy. With regard to the States, the declaration stated: As was explicitly stated by the Cabinet Mission, His Majesty's Government do not intend to hand over their powers and obligations under Paramountcy to any government of British India. It is not intended to bring Paramountcy, as a system, to a conclusion earlier than the date of the final transfer of power, but it is contemplated that for the intervening period the relations of the Crown with the individual States may be adjusted by agreements.[17] This announcement had a considerable influence on the two Negotiating Committees at their joint meeting on 1 March 1947. Nehru contended that the British government's declaration had introduced an additional element of urgency and it would be greatly to the advantage of the States.

The imminence of Partition and the British government's clear indication, that the treaties and Paramountcy relationships between them and the princely States would cease and that all arrangements, usage etc. that bound them in fiscal and other matters would terminate immediately lent great importance and urgency to the problem of future relationship between the future Indian Dominion and the States.

Patel, who always had before him the picture of a united India embracing both British India and the States, was deeply concerned over this issue. He had no illusions about the future of India without this unity and integration. In fact, he was one of the few in the Congress party who had a clear idea of what this implied both in theory and practice and how much depended on the solution of this problem, not only from the point of view of peace and prosperity of the Indian Dominion but also from the point of view of the future relationship between India and Pakistan-to-be and its economic progress.

He had also complete information as to the designs and intentions of the League leaders, who were straining their ingenuity to see that the Princes remain a perpetual problem for the future Indian Dominion and that as many of them as possible out of those who might associate themselves with the future Indian Dominion keep themselves aloof from such an association. To top it all there was the Political Department led by Sir Conrad Corfield. It comprised a coterie of officials, practically all of them British, who had dominated the Princes, so far. It was chary of giving up that domination, was hostile to Indian aspirations and was believed to be inspiring moves among the Princes to form unions of their own even at the cost of the unity and integrity of the future India.[18]

Sardar Patel's views were further explained in his letter of 2 February 1947 wherein he said, 'Sovereignty in England vests in the people of England and not in his Majesty the King.... No man in his senses in the world believes that sovereignty vests in any single individual, whether he be a prince or a monarch, a czar or a Hitler'.[19] On 26 February 1947, after Attlee's policy statement of 20th February, Patel wrote to a friend: From June 1948, there will be no Sovereign in India, and Paramountcy will evaporate in the air.[20] By such utterances, he was forewarning the British and checkmating their designs in India. No other Indian leader had Patel's boldness and courage. Later, after the transfer of power, he grew still bolder and declared: Paramountcy can never be annihilated. It must ever reside in the central authority, for, it belongs to the people. Whoever will challenge it will perish.[21] That was the warning to the Princes playing into the hands of Bhopal and Corfield.

The fear of Churchill's strategy of 'Princestan' always haunted Patel. His fears were later confirmed by some of the Dewans of the States. No less a person than Corfield himself admitted at Mountbatten's Staff meeting on 26 March 1947 that he was supporting Bhopal's conspiracy with some Princes against their joining the Indian Union, and that he was making efforts to set up the 'Princes as a potential third force',[22] which was another name for Churchill's Princestan. At a conference of Residents and Political Officers, held in the second week of April 1948, Corfield asked them 'to enable the States to stand on their feet, to encourage them to hold together and, at the same time, to cooperate fully with British India'.[23] There was also a sinister motive in the Political Department's proposal to hand over to the States the Crown Representative's police force. Ingeniously, Patel killed the proposal by immediately changing the name to the Central Reserve Police Force. In the hands of the States, the force could have been a source of potential mischief.

All through, while dealing with the rulers and British negotiators, Patel maintained his characteristic coolness, an attitude of conciliation and compromise rather than confrontation, and yet he was firm in his resolve, and when an occasion demanded, he was blunt in expressing his views. In an effort to woo the Princes, he told them that the policy of the Congress was to befriend the Princes.

In contrast, Nehru's occasional outbursts scared the Princes. On 18 April 1947, addressing the annual session of the All-India States' People's Conference, Nehru declared 'that any State which did not come into the Constituent Assembly would be treated by the country as a hostile State'. Such a State, he added, 'would have to bear the consequences of being treated'.[24]

This speech provoked a prompt rejoinder from Liaquat Ali Khan, the leader of the Muslim League in the Central Legislature and the Cabinet, who in a press statement declared that the Congress had no right to coerce the States; and that, according to the Cabinet Mission Plan and the clarifications issued by His Majesty's Government from time to time, the States were perfectly within their rights in refusing to have anything to do with the Constituent Assembly. Liaquat Ali Khan appealed to the States to disregard the idle threat.[25]

Meanwhile, Lord Mountbatten, the new Viceroy, arrived in India on 22 March 1947, and took charge two days later. In the course of his first speech he said that his was not a normal viceroyalty. The British government was resolved to transfer power by June 1948, and solutions had to be found in a few months' time. His earnest determination to carry out the decision of His Majesty's Government to transfer power to Indian hands smoothly and speedily created a deep impression.

Mountbatten did not like Nehru's inflexible attitude. He privately rebuked Nehru for two reasons: first, it would scare the Princes from joining the Indian Union, and second, 'for his demagogy', especially as a Member of the Interim Government, who ought not to speak in such terms without Cabinet approval. Pandit Nehru took this castigation meekly, explaining that he was speaking in a personal capacity as President of the States' People's Conference.[26]

The Standing Committee of the Chamber of Princes held many meetings and even sought the Political Department's advice on several issues. At their Bombay conference, on 29 January 1947, the Princes resolved that the Constitution of each State, its territorial integrity and the succession of its reigning dynasty shall not be interfered with by the Indian Union, nor should the existing boundaries of a State be altered except by its free consent. Far more alarming was their decision that the Constituent Assembly was not to deal with questions affecting the internal administration or Constitutions of States. The resolution 'provoked a good deal of controversy'; in particular, 'Public opinion was considerably agitated over the statement made by some rulers that, if the fundamental prepositions were not accepted by the Congress, they would boycott the Constituent Assembly'.[27]

This was all because of Bhopal who was playing into Jinnah's hands. Cochin and Baroda were the only States who were not a party to the Bombay resolution. The Maharaja of Cochin had announced earlier, on 30 July 1947, his decision to participate in the proceedings of the proposed Constituent Assembly through popular representatives, elected by the State's Legislative Assembly. After that, Baroda, guided by its Dewan, BL Mitter, announced its decision to join the Constituent Assembly. However, the majority of Princes were still with the Chamber of Princes under Bhopal's influence. Bhopal seemed to have received a shot in the arm with Travancore and Hyderabad joining his battle.

CP Ramaswami Iyer, the Dewan of Travancore, said on 17 March 1947 that his State 'will be an independent State and will revert to the 1750 status'.[28] Earlier, on behalf of the Nizam, Syed Abdul Latif had declared on 27 February 1947 that Hyderabad would automatically become a kingdom on transfer of power and that the Nizam would proclaim himself, 'His Majesty the King of Hyderabad'.[29] This was just after Attlee's statement of 20th February.

Beginning of the End of Chamber of Princes

While addressing the joint meeting of two Negotiating Committees on 8 February 1947, Patel and Nehru suggested to the Princes to decide to enter and participate in the work of the Constituent Assembly, in the larger interest of the country. The suggestion did not find favour with the rulers. Bhopal, as the Chancellor of the Chamber of Princes, had laid down certain fundamental prepositions on which they wanted satisfactory assurances before they could enter the Constituent Assembly. When things were heading towards a deadlock, the Maharaja of Patiala intervened and checkmated Bhopal's move for a deadlock through postponement by seeking a clarification of the position as it had emerged from the previous days' meeting. Because of Nehru's persuasive approach and conciliatory statement, the atmosphere became friendly.

The meeting was adjourned till 1 March. The two committees asked the Secretaries of the Constituent Assembly and the Chamber of Princes to jointly work out a scheme for distribution of the seats allotted to the States. At such a time when the two committees should have been sorting out the problem, Attlee's original statement of 20th February 1947 was watered down and another adopted instead.

By this resolution, 'the conference reiterated the willingness of the States to render fullest possible cooperation in framing an agreed Constitution and towards facilitating the transfer of power on an agreed basis. It redefined the general understanding reached between the two Negotiating Committees and demanded that ratification of that understanding by the Constituent Assembly should precede the participation in the work of the Constituent Assembly of the representatives of such States as might desire to do so at the appropriate stage'.

The resolution noted that Attlee's statement of 20th February 1947 further confirmed that the 'States would be in position as independent units to negotiate freely in regard to their future relationship with others concerned'.[30]

Attlee's statement of February 20th threw overboard whatever limited progress the talk seemed to have made. The statement served as an encouragement to Bhopal and his group of princes to sit on the fence by declaring Britain's intentions not to hand over their powers and obligations under Paramountcy to any government of British India, as also not to bring Paramountcy, as a system to a conclusion earlier than the date of the final transfer of power.

Sensing trouble ahead, Patel, at the meeting of 1st March 1947, spoke to the Princes in a mixed tone of frankness and deliberate pessimism. He is reported to have said, 'freedom is coming. But I am afraid it may not last long. Before that happens, nothing may be left of the Princes as well'.[31] It was a stern warning, which turned the tide in his favour. Such pessimism on the part of India's 'iron man' surprised many Princes, especially Bikaner and Patiala, on whom, because of the closeness of their States to Pakistan and because of the happenings in Punjab, a new realisation dawned: how vulnerable their States could be to new dangers. They, therefore, refused to follow Bhopal's policy in their negotiations with the Congress. Impressed by the realism of Patel, the Bikaner-Patiala group assured him of its cooperation in achieving a united, strong India. Prime Minister of Bikaner, KM Panikkar, informed Patel on 10 March 1947, of Bikaner's decision to participate in the Constituent Assembly. Patel replied, 'I am glad that so many Princes are getting out of the cordon (of Bhopal). Let us hope that they will come in now... you have seen what is happening in Punjab. I hope there will be no sympathy from any quarter for the Muslim League any more, not even amongst any of the Princes'.[32]

The differences between Bikaner and Bhopal were now in the open. Their interviews revealed the full scale of split among the Princes. According to Campbell-Johson, 'There is great grief to Bhopal, who feels that Bikaner and the other "dissidents", by allowing themselves to take part in the Constituent Assembly, are becoming tools of the Congress and undermining the whole bargaining position of the States... Bhopal thought the time-limit was quite impossible, and, if enforced, must involve bloodshed and chaos'. That sounded Jinnah-like to some of the Princes. Bikaner, on the other hand, held Bhopal responsible for the split, 'who, by his attitude to the Interim Government, had caused the communal issue to be raised against them (the

Princes)'. The real danger, however, lurked in the support Bhopal had of Corfield, who at his meeting with Mountbatten, on 26 March 1947, 'argued with some bitterness that Bikaner, by taking his place in the Constituent Assembly, had seriously weakened the bargaining power of the Princes'.[33]

Bhopal, however, was contained in his efforts to influence the Princes. Bikaner now openly questioned the advisability and wisdom of such a policy. Bikaner countered Bhopal's move by arguing that it was in the interest of the Princes to have a strong Central government. The only safe policy for the States was to work fully with the stabilising elements in British India to create a Centre which would safeguard both the States and British India in the vacuum that would be created by the withdrawal of the British government. The interests of the people of the States obviously lay in joining hands with British India in establishing a strong Centre. Bikaner was followed by Patiala who, in a public statement, deprecated the policy of sitting on the fence.

A new group formed by the Maharaja of Bikaner, though in minority, had a salutary influence on the Princes. As a result, the original draft was watered down, and another was adopted instead, which reiterated the willingness of the States to render fullest possible cooperation in framing an agreed Constitution and towards facilitating the transfer of power on an agreed basis. Seeing the situation going out of hand, Bhopal played a trump card suggesting to Patiala, who was pro-chancellor, 'that rulers who held offices in the Chamber should adhere to its recommendations on such vital matters not withstanding any personal differences of opinion'.

The Maharaja of Patiala promptly replied that the fact that 'he happened to hold the office of pro-chancellor imposed no special obligations on his government, nor did it detract from his decision to adopt such policy about vital matters as he considered necessary in the interests of his State'. He told Bhopal that 'he was sending his representatives to the Constituent Assembly, because he felt that the stage for the States' participation in the constitution-making process had definitely come, and that any delay in doing so would be prejudicial not only to his own interests but also to the wider interests of the country'. VP Menon characterised the wind of change as 'the beginning of the end of the united front put up by the Chancellor of Princes (Nawab of Bhopal)'.[34]

Mountbatten's 3rd June Plan

Meanwhile, Lord Mountbatten announced the plan of 3rd June 1947, according to which, His Majesty's Government would be prepared to relinquish power to two governments, India and Pakistan, on the basis of Dominion status, and this relinquishment of power would take place much earlier than June 1948. In regard to the States, the plan laid down that the policy of His Majesty's Government towards the Indian States, contained in the Cabinet Mission memorandum of 12 May 1946, remained unchanged. This announcement introduced a maximum degree of urgency into the situation.

Lord Mountbatten elucidated the plan next day at a press conference. No fresh ground was covered so far as the States were concerned. But to a question whether it was the intention of His Majesty's Government to confer dominion status on any State which declared itself independent, he replied emphatically in the negative. It was at this conference that he gave the first public indication that the date of transfer of power would be on 15 August 1947.

The general tendency among the Princes was to make the most of the bargaining position in which the lapse of Paramountcy placed them. The fact that during Second World War many of the major States had strengthened their armed forces could not be ignored. The decision therefore, that with the withdrawal of the British, Indian States, comprising two-fifths of the land, must return to a state of complete political isolation was fraught with the gravest danger to the integrity of the country.

Patel saw this danger in the big chunk of supporters for the Chamber of Princes Bhopal had built as a bastion to give the Congress a strong fight. His statesmanship lay in turning the disunity among the Princes to his advantage. Now he rode among them like a rancher, gently shepherding his scattered flock back home. The operations had to be completed before the return of Paramountcy to the Princes on 15 August. Patel told the Princes on 15 April, 'In a short time India will be free.... I congratulate those Princes who have wisely sided with the Congress. Only those Princes will be able to rule who carry their people with them; those who fail to do so will find their thrones disappear.... Many of the Princes are yet sitting on the fence, waiting to see what shape coming events will take.... I appeal to such Princes to join us now. It would not behove them to do so in the hour of their defeat'.

Patel further told them, 'Many Princes seem to believe that they should collect arms to establish their authority. But India is not the same today as she was when the British came here.... In the end, every State will have to come in. But those who come in the last will deny themselves the honour they will enjoy now. It will be said of those who come in now that they helped bring about unity and establish peace in India. The rest will be classed as mere spectators'. He, however, assured the Princes, 'we want to uphold the Princes' prestige, their honour.... Those amongst them who have ability, intelligence and bravery can take up leadership of the Army. They can also enjoy the glory of serving India abroad as our Ambassadors. What for are you rotting in your small pits? Come out into the open ocean of national life'.[35]

Due to the salutary effect of Patel's speech many important Princes including Baroda, Bikaner, Cochin, Jaipur, Patiala and Rewa took their seats in the Constituent Assembly. This set the ball rolling and as a result, other States began coming in one after another. Some of the States still kept aloof. An official document says: Bhopal... was acting as an agent of Pakistan..., he was circulating to other rulers false statement to the effect that, as a result of his group of rulers, the Instrument of Accession was being revised, and that, if all of them stood firm, they would be able to obtain or extract more favourable terms.[36] Bhopal tried to convince the Princes by telling them that lapse of Paramountcy would take place prior to the actual transfer of power, so that they could be in a better position to bargain with the successor government. Bhopal succeeded in misleading many States, especially those strategically placed which included Jodhpur, Jamnagar and Travancore.

'After announcement of the participation, the rulers on our side of the border realised that they should strengthen the Indian Union and so were gradually coming into the Constituent Assembly. They were, however, very jealous about their Sovereignty and I felt strongly that they should not be rubbed the wrong way. At the same time, the attitude of some of the rulers of big States was disconcerting and Pakistan was playing with the idea of getting some of the border States to cast in their lot with her. Sardar told me (VP Menon) that the situation held dangerous potentialities and if we did not handle it promptly and effectively, our hard-earned freedom might disappear through the States' door.'[37]

The concept of the lapse of Paramountcy was, according to Menon, 'the greatest disservice the British had done us as well as the rulers'.[38] Patel held the same opinion. *The disservice lay in the 3rd June Plan, which was to sow seeds of disruption by making Paramountcy lapse simultaneously with the transfer of power: on August 15th; whereas under the Cabinet Mission Plan, Paramountcy would have lapsed only after the Constitution had been set up and power transferred to the successor governments.*

Even as late as 3rd June, when the Pakistan demand had been conceded, Corfield and Jinnah endeavoured to aggravate the situation for India by trying to establish the States' sovereign status under the Plan. Jinnah stated on 18 June 1947 that every Indian State was a sovereign State and that the States were 'fully entitled to say they would join neither Constituent

Assembly nor....' Liaquat Ali was more explicit in stating, 'The Indian States will be free to negotiate agreements with Pakistan or Hindustan as considerations of contiguity or their own self-interest may dictate....'[39] This was fishing in Indian waters, not without purpose. If he could force acceptance of his interpretation, Jinnah expected accession to Pakistan not only of Kashmir, Hyderabad and Bhopal, but also Indore, Jodhpur, Junagadha, Jamnagar and even Baroda.

The situation was taking dangerous shape. Patel was very much alive to the situation. Patel outmaneuvered Jinnah and Corfield and thwarted their design. Bhopal faced the futility of his efforts in Patel's success in Jodhpur, Kathiawar and even Travancore. Patel's assumption of charge of the newly-created States Department (not a ministry yet) on 5 July 1947 was significant in the prevailing confused, complex and dangerous situation. The new department was to replace His Majesty's Political Department without the latter's functions, powers and records. With Patel these things mattered little. He was capable of creating his own functions and powers that suited the nascent nation's interests. And he did create them.

Princes were drawn towards Patel because of his powerful personality, which gave them firm assurance of a hopeful future in an atmosphere of trust, and the benign friendship of one who exuded humanity, humility and broad-mindedness. Ample evidence of this was seen in Patel's policy statement on taking charge as Minister of States. 'The statement was acclaimed as a masterpiece of diplomatic finesse, reflecting Patel's transparent sincerity. He stirred up the nobler sentiments of the Princes by recalling the Princes' proud, glorious past when ancestors of some had played highly patriotic roles in the defence of their family honour and the freedom of their land.'[40]

Patel proudly told the Princes that among them, 'I am happy to count many as my personal friends'. He reminded them, 'It is the lesson of history that it was owing to her politically fragmented condition and our inability to make a united stand that India succumbed to successive waves of invaders. Our mutual conflicts and internecine quarrels and jealousies have, in the past, been the cause of our downfall and our falling victims to foreign domination a number of times. We cannot afford to fall into those errors or traps again'. He told them, 'we are on the threshold of independence…. The safety and preservation of the States, as well as of India, demand unity and mutual cooperation between its different parts'.

Patel urged the Princes to consider that in the exercise of Paramountcy, 'there has undoubtedly been more of subordination than cooperation', and that 'now that British rule is ending, the demand has been made that the States should regain their independence. In so far as Paramountcy embodied the submission of States to foreign will, I have every sympathy with this demand, but I do not think it can be their desire to utilise this freedom from domination in a manner which is injurious to the common interests of India, or which militates against the ultimate Paramountcy of popular interests and welfare, or which might result in the abandonment of that mutually useful relationship that has developed between British India and Indian States the last century'.

He told them, 'we are all knit together by bonds of blood and feeling, no less than of self-interest. None can segregate us into segments; no impossible barriers can be set up between us…. I invite my friends, the Rulers of States and their people, to the councils of the Constituent Assembly in this spirit of friendliness and cooperation in a joint endeavour, inspired by common allegiance to our motherland, for the common good of us all'. Patel gave them assurance that, 'it is not the desire of the Congress to interfere in any manner whatsoever with the domestic affairs of the States'.

He further assured them, 'They (the Congress) are no enemies of the Princely Order, on the other hand, they wish them and the people under their aegis all prosperity, contentment and happiness. Nor would it be my policy to conduct the relations of the new department with the States in any manner which savours of the domination of one over the other; if there would be any domination, it would be that of our mutual interests and welfare'.

While concluding his masterly speech, Patel declared, 'we are all at a momentous stage in the history of India. By common endeavour, we can raise the country to a new greatness, while lack of unity will expose us to fresh calamities. I hope the Indian States will bear in mind that the alternative to cooperation in the general interest is anarchy and chaos, which will overwhelm great and small in a common ruin if we are unable to act together in the minimum of common tasks. Let not the future generations curse us for having had the opportunity but failed to turn it to our mutual advantage. Instead, let it be our proud privilege to leave a legacy of a mutually beneficial relationship which would raise this sacred land to its proper place amongst the nations of the World and turn it into an abode of peace and prosperity'.[41]

Patel's speech moved many a prince, big and small. In a rich compliment, Bikaner said, 'May I take this opportunity of sending you my best wishes in the onerous duties which have fallen upon you.... The fact that one of the most respected and mature statesmen and leader of your experience and judgment has been chosen is, I feel, a happy augury. It is most gratifying to recall that you have always shown a realistic and cordial attitude towards the States. The friendly hand that you have so spontaneously extended to the Princes and States, as evidenced by your statement is, I need hardly assure you, greatly appreciated by us. We are confident that we may look forward to an association of full cooperation with you and a sympathetic understanding at your hands of the very important problems vitally affecting the States at the present transitional stage, thus enabling the States to take their due and honoured place in the future Union of India, in the making of which we are all proud to give our wholehearted support. I know that the interests of the Princes and States are safe in your hands'.[42]

In view of Patel's statesmanship quality and mature leadership even Mountbatten preferred Patel to Nehru. He wrote, 'I am glad to say that Nehru has not been put in charge of the new State Department, which would have wrecked everything. Patel, who is essentially a realist and very sensible, is going to take it over'.[43] He told the Princes at his last conference with them, on 25 July 1947, 'In India the States Department is under the admirable guidance of Sardar Vallabhbhai Patel… you can imagine how relieved I was, and I am sure you will yourselves have been equally relieved, when Sardar Vallabhbhai Patel, on taking over the States department, made, if I may say so, a most statesman-like statement of what he considered were the essentials towards agreement between the States and the Dominion of India'.[44] Mountbatten thought that Patel, being the 'strongest pillar of the Cabinet', alone could help him fulfil his assurance to the King on two matters, India's membership of the Commonwealth, and fair treatment for the Princes.

Patel and Mountbatten worked together in dealing with the Princes. Mountbatten was happy to get Patel's strong support for the Commonwealth membership. On the other hand, Patel was satisfied with Britain's decision that the Indian States could not enter the Commonwealth as independent Dominions. Patel secured another point. While giving his consent to India's membership of the Commonwealth, he stipulated a condition: 'Let Paramountcy be dead, you do not directly or indirectly try to revive it in any manner…. The Princes are ours, and we shall deal with them.'[45]

As recorded by HV Hodson about a meaningful dialogue between Patel and Mountbatten, prior to the former's acceptance of the charge of the States Ministry, Patel said, 'I am prepared to accept your offer provided you give me a full basket of apples'. 'What do you mean?' asked Mountbatten. 'I will buy a basket with 565 apples, but if there are even two or three missing, the deal is off', Patel said. 'This', said the Viceroy, 'I cannot completely accept, but I will do my best. If I give you a basket with, say 560 apples, will you buy it?' 'Well, I might' replied Patel.[46]

Patel on his part showed tact and diplomacy in his handling of the Princes. They feared his firmness, even his wrath; but they could enjoy his genuine friendship if they did not override the country's interest. Presiding over a press conference addressed by Menon, on 5 July 1947, Patel gave a blunt warning. 'Whoever denounces such agreements takes the responsibility for the consequences.'[47]

The States entitled to separate representation on the Constituent Assembly were now reassured that there was no threat to their separate existence. This development aroused among them consciousness of a community of interests, and joint consultations by this group, with the exception of States like Hyderabad and Bhopal. The smaller States, on the other hand, became apprehensive regarding the attitude of the major States. On 11 June 1947, Sir CP Ramaswami Iyer, Dewan of Travancore, announced that Travancore had decided to set itself up as an independent sovereign state. A similar announcement was made the next day on behalf of the Nizam of Hyderabad. The same Dewan of Travancore had earlier gone to the extent of announcing his intention to appoint a Trade Agent in Pakistan. These events had earlier given rise to apprehension that if other States adopted a similar attitude, then India will be split into fragments.

On 5 July 1947, Patel, through a statement, appealed to the Princes to accede on three subjects. It pointed out, 'The States have already accepted the basic principle that for defence, foreign affairs and communications they would come into the Indian Union. We ask no more of them than accession on these three subjects in which the common interests of the country are involved'. The statement went on: 'This country with its institutions is the proud heritage of the people who inhabit it. It is an accident that some live in the States and some in British India, but all alike partake in its culture and character.

We all are knit together by bonds of blood and feeling no less than of self-interest. None can segregate us into segments; no impossible barriers can be set up between us. I suggest that it is therefore, better for us to make laws sitting together as friends than to make treaties as aliens. I invite my friends, the rulers of States and their people, to the councils of the Constituent Assembly in this spirit of friendliness and cooperation in a joint endeavour, inspired by common allegiance to our motherland for the common good of us all'.[48]

A number of Princes and States' ministers met at Patel's residence. Patel urged that the States, which had joined the Constituent Assembly, should forthwith accede to India on three subjects, and pointed out that such a course would enable them to have a direct voice in shaping the policies of free India's Central government. The States' delegation appreciated the logic of the suggestion, but emphasised that the matter required careful consideration and a cautious approach. It was decided to hold a series of informal discussions with the Princes and their advisors. It was this conference which at last broke the ice, clearing away a mass of vague suspicions which the Princes had entertained about the new States Department.

Patel continued to canvass individually with many of the Indian Princes who mattered. Much feverish activity to persuade the rulers to accept accession on three subjects and enter into Standstill Arrangements, by the time the British regime ended, were going on behind the scenes. The problem of dealing with the Princes collectively, however, appeared to be a formidable one, the delicacy of the task being heightened by the presence of disruptive elements among the Princes who were inspired either by the League leaders themselves or some of their own brother Princes who were out and out League sympathisers. Jinnah went to the extent of making a public announcement that he would guarantee the independence of the States in Pakistan.

At the meeting of the Princes which Patel had convened it was agreed that a conference of the rulers would be held on 25

July 1947, at which matters of accession, Standstill Agreement and other issues concerning the functioning of the State Department would be discussed. However, the question as to how this should be done in the face of doubts and uncertainties harboured by the Princes and the manoeuvres and machinations of those who were out to sabotage this development caused deep mental anguish to Patel. Finally, he decided that if he himself took a leading part in the meeting, it might lead to open agreements, notwithstanding the contrary or hostile acts by the League leaders. He also felt reassured that Mountbatten would be able to lend his help effectively in bringing about the aspired to results. Patel, therefore, secured Cabinet approval for Lord Mountbatten to deal with this question in his capacity as the Crown Representative. In the meantime, a draft Instrument of Accession and revised draft of the Standstill Agreement had been prepared by the Political Department of the British Government in India.

On 25 July, amid scenes of pomp and pageantry, the conference of Princes and representatives of States was held in the Chamber of Princes and Lord Mountbatten in a very persuasive and appealing speech advised the Rulers to accede to their appropriate dominion on the subjects of Defence, External Affairs and Communications. He made it plain that under compulsion of geography, a vast majority of the States were linked with the Dominion of India and if they were prepared to come, it was much better their coming in before 15 August than afterwards. He announced the personnel of the Negotiating Committee, who would consider the items on the agenda in detail, and then clarified a number of points raised by the Princes and their ministers.

The atmosphere was a combination of majesty and splendour, informality and cordiality. To this was added a compelling sense of urgency. In the midst of the divided counsels that prevailed, it seemed quite clear that most of the princes would play for safety and consequently follow the path of least resistance.

After the conference was over, the matter was remitted to the closed door discussions of the Negotiating Committee which, during the following week, sorted out the different problems the various States had and succeeded in enlisting the support of most of the Princes. Behind the scene, there was no doubt that Lord Mountbatten was exercising his influence in a remarkable manner in favour of accession for he was convinced that the Princes had no choice in their own interests but to accede.

Knots untied for unification of India

By 31 July 1947, all the hurdles had been crossed and all the knots unraveled and the Instrument of Accession and the Standstill Agreement were approved by the full Negotiating Committee. During the subsequent week, most of the Princes signified their willingness to sign the two precious documents but some stood out, the prominent among them being Hyderabad, Jammu and Kashmir, Travancore, Bhopal, Indore, Dholpur, Nabha, Junagadh and Jodhpur. All of them had mixed motives for their aloofness. Hyderabad held on to a dream of independence and separate existence. 'In view of the special position and peculiar problems of Hyderabad both Nehru and Patel felt that Lord Mountbatten should continue to negotiate with Nizam even after 15 August. Accordingly, on 12 August, Lord Mountbatten informed the Nizam that offer of accession would remain open in the case of Hyderabad for a further period of two months.'[49]

Jammu and Kashmir had its difficulties, 'which Sardar fully appreciated and for which he was prepared to wait'.[50] Travancore asserted its independence on transfer of power. Bhopal believed in the evolution of a third force and was more in line with the ideas of Sir Conrad Corefield on this subject. Jodhpur got himself involved in unfortunate intrigues with Jinnah 'who gave him a blank cheque if he acceded to Pakistan'.[51] Indore, Dholpur, and Nabha were prepared to follow the lead of Bhopal.

Lord Mountbatten actively engaged himself in trying to persuade CP Ramaswami Iyer, the Dewan of Travancore, to accede to India. He finally persuaded him to agree to accession. In fact, CP Ramaswami Iyer was the first to declare a revolt against his State joining the Indian Union, accused the British of duplicity and of 'inconsistent and dissimilar approaches to the Princes and the Congress'.[52] Travancore's accession was followed by Patel's instructions to the Travancore Congress Committee to suspend their campaign of direct action.

The Maharaja of Jodhpur had literally to be enticed away during the course of one of his visits to Jinnah and tackled by Patel, who was a friend of his father and towards whom the Maharaja displayed an attitude of veneration and respect. Thereafter, the Maharaja was taken to Lord Mountbatten and after he had successfully persuaded him into doing so, he signed the Instrument of Accession.

The Nawab of Bhopal, who was a personal friend of Lord Mountbatten, had not attended the meeting on 25 July, but later was persuaded to sign the Instrument of Accession. Characteristically, the Nawab made it a condition that his signature should not be announced for some days after the transfer of power. This was because he was deeply committed to the Maharaja of Indore, Dholpur and Nabha to oppose accession and felt that a premature disclosure would compromise his position. Finally, however, all of them, Dholpur, Bharatpur, Bilaspur and Nabha, signed the Instrument of Accession before 15 August 1947, since they realised that if they did not do so, they might be treated in a different category altogether after Independence.

Hyderabad, Junagadh remained. Patel had met the Prime Minister of Kashmir, Ram Chandra Kak, late in June 1947, when question of accession of Kashmir had been discussed, but he did not force the issue and was content to leave Kashmir, in view of the complications involved, out of the accession list. Through some of the emissaries of the Maharaja, who had sought Patel's advice, Patel had counselled caution and patience and was against any hurried commitment.

After expressing his intention to accede to India, the Nawab of Junagadh became the victim of Pakistani intrigue in which the leading participants were Sir Shah Nawaz Bhutto, who was Dewan, and Sir Mohammad Zafrullah Khan, Nawab's advisor on constitutional matters. Under these influences, the Nawab changed his mind and signed an accession to Pakistan contrary to every compelling factor that was relevant to the issue. This upset Patel considerably and he felt that the problem of Junagadh should be tackled with determination and speed.

Junagadh, situated as it was in the midst of Kathiawar State, and with a sea-front of its own posed a substantial security risk to India, if Pakistan secured a foothold there. Apart from this, Junagadh constituted the solitary defeat of Patel's policy regarding the States, on which he had set his heart and for which he had laboured hard and skillfully. Henceforth, Junagadh became an issue of patriotism and prestige for him and he began to organise in his own quiet and efficient way, resistance to accession to Pakistan from within the State itself. In this task, he roped in the services of the Kathiawar Princes, led by the Jam Saheb of Nawanagar and the leading subjects of Junagadh outside the State led by Samaldas Gandhi, a nephew of Gandhiji.

So determined was Patel to bring about a change in the shortest possible time that these matters became the continuous preoccupation of VP Menon and the States Department. The accession of States like Mangrol, Manavadar and other small principalities which were taken to be the feudatories of the State of Junagadh was secured. The organisation of the Provisional Government or *Arzi Hukumat* led by Samaldas Gandhi was finally accepted in order to secure quick results. 'In the process, it is interesting to recall that Patel turned down Lord Mountbatten's idea that the question of Junagadh might be referred to the United Nations Organisation.'[53]

Energetic action was taken on the military front to preserve the peace and security of Saurashtra that was threatened by this development and one by one, the feudatory States of

Junagadh were taken over by the Government of India whilst *Arzi Hukumat* secured control over the Junagadh Islands in Saurashtra. A battle of words, in the meantime, was going on between India and Pakistan. 'It resulted in an angry exchange of telegraphic correspondence and also heated discussions at the joint meetings of leaders of India and Pakistan. Sardar displayed firmness and determination in dealing with the issue and resisted any attempt on the part of Lord Mountbatten to find a via media and even to soften the measures in the hope of avoiding an open conflict.'[54]

As regards Hyderabad, on 21 June 1948, three days after the breakdown of negotiations with Hyderabad, Lord Mountbatten left India and was succeeded as Governor-General by C Rajagopalachari. Lord Mountbatten was extremely disappointed at the breakdown of the negotiations.

Hyderabad, politically under the control of Razakars,[1] neither agreed to accession nor to responsible government. The minority community which was holding a virtual monopoly of all offices under the State government, could not view with equanimity the grant of responsible government for that would spell the end of their privileged position. The Nizam and his advisors were possessed by the notion that India would be unable to take any action against Hyderabad because her hands were full with Kashmir and other problems. The anti-Indian attitude of a section of the British press, and the plea for Hyderabad's independence voiced by some British political leaders, bolstered the Nizam's uncompromising attitude.

After the failure of the negotiation in June 1948, it was only a question of time when a major operation would be initiated. The entire staff for the purpose had been alerted

---

1   The Razakars were a private militia organised by Qasim Razvi to support the rule of Nizam Osman Ali Khan and resist the integration of Hyderabad State into the Dominion of India in 1947-48. It's parent organisation was Majlis-e-Ittehadul Muslimeen

and the timing depended on how long it would take for Patel to overcome a foreseen resistance to this course by Governor-General Rajagopalachari and by Pandit Nehru, who found in Rajagopalachari an intellectual support for his non-violent policy towards Hyderabad. Patel had already made up his mind. For instance, speaking at a meeting with Indian and foreign journalists in Delhi on 29 January 1948, after unification of Kathiawar States, he said: One State remains which is still causing us some anxiety. It is the State of Hyderabad.... Accession in the case of Hyderabad is inevitable and will.... The people there must get their due and I would only appeal to H E H the Nizam to appreciate this situation and to do the right thing in time.[55]

Even earlier, at Junagadh, on 13 November 1947, before negotiations for a Standstill Agreement had been finalised, Patel had said, 'If Hyderabad is to be saved, it must effect a radical change in its methods and policy. In the world of today, only those who have guts can make their voice felt. If Hyderabad wishes to be heard, it must follow bravely and courageously the popular will. Otherwise, Hyderabad's fate will sooner or later be the same as those of other rulers and dynasties who had attempted to thwart the popular will only at the cost of their existence'.[56]

He was even more forthright in his speech at Patiala, at the time of the inauguration of PEPSU (Punjab and East Punjab States Union), on 15 July 1948, when he said: 'Many have asked me the question, what is going to happen to Hyderabad? They forget that when I spoke at Junagadh, I said openly that if Hyderabad did not behave properly, it would have to go the way Jungadh did. The words still stand and I stand by these words... up to the last Lord Mountbatten was hopeful of a settlement, that hope never materialised owing to the intransigence of the Nizam and fanaticism of the forces at his back. But I should like to make one thing clear. The terms and the talks which Lord Mountbatten had, have gone with him. Now the settlement with the Nizam will have to be on the lines of other settlements with the States.'[57] Thus, Patel's views, which were already quite strong in 1947, had begun to stiffen in January 1948, but after the failure of Lord Mountbatten's mission, they had crystalised into a need for action. In fact, by that time, the word had gone out to the Armed Forces and the provinces to be ready for a confrontation and take-over of the Hyderabad administration, if need be.

On 9 September 1948, after a careful evaluation of all considerations and only when it was clear that no other alternative remained open, the Government of India took the decision to send Indian troops into Hyderabad to restore peace and tranquility inside the State and a sense of security in the adjoining Indian territory. This decision was communicated to the Southern Command, who ordered that the Indian forces should march into Hyderabad in the early hours of 13 September 1948. The Indian forces were commanded by Major-General JN Chaudhuri under the direction of Lt General Maharaj Shri Rajendrasingji, who was then the General Officer Commanding-in-Chief, Southern Command. This operation was given the name 'Operation Polo' by the Army Headquarters.

On the evening of 17 September 1948, the Hyderabad army surrendered. On the 18th, the Indian troops, under Major-General Chaudhuri, entered Hyderabad city. The operation had lasted barely 108 hours. Major-General Chaudhuri took charge as Military Governor on 18 September 1948. Immediately after the installation of the Military Governor's administration, the Nizam issued a proclamation which brought the Hyderabad State into line with the other States on accession and other matters.

'The masterly handling of the rulers by Patel was the foremost factor in the success of the accession policy. The rulers soon came to recognise him as a stable force in Indian politics and as one who could give them a fair deal. Added to this, his unfailing politeness to the rulers, viewed against his reputation as the 'Iron Man of India', endeared him to them and created such confidence that all accepted his advice without demur.'[58] Patel had come to a decision about which Reginald Coupland had speculated in 1945: 'An India deprived of the States would have lost all coherence. They stand between all four quarters of the country... India could live if its Moslem limbs in the north-west and north-east were amputated, but could it live without its heart?'[59] And that is what Patel instinctively meant when he stated, 'Hyderabad is, as it were, situated in India's belly. How can belly breathe, if it is cut off from the main body?'[60] The States formed India's heart and Patel's genius lay in preserving, integrating and strengthening that heart at all costs and thereby saving India from the frightening prospects of Balkanisation. Patel prevented a situation which was fraught with the gravest danger to the integrity of the country.

Jinnah could not forgive India, in particular, Patel, for forcing him to accept in the end a Pakistan that was 'truncated and moth-eaten' when the British left India. It was the end of the dream, which the British from Churchill to Attlee had purposefully built to serve Britain's own interests. They had nearly succeeded in handing Jinnah his dream empire but for the 'Man of Iron' in Patel, who blocked their way like a rock. Jinnah had made all efforts to secure accession or association of Jodhpur, Junagadh, Kathiawar, and even Hyderabad, not forgetting the invasion of Kashmir through frontier tribesmen.

References

1. KL Punjabi, *The Indomitable Sardar*, Bhartiya Vidya Bhavan, Bombay, 1990, p-207.
2. Ibid, p-222.
3. Ibid.
4. Ibid, p-224.
5. Ibid, p-222.

6. Dick Kooiman, Invention of Tradition in Travancore: A Maharaja's Quest for Political Security, *Journal of the Royal Asiatic Society* 15(2): 15-64, 2005.
7. VP Menon, *Integration of the Indian States*, Orient Black Swan, New Delhi, 2014, p-34.
8. Ibid, p-42.
9. Ibid, p-44.
10. Ibid, p-59-60.
11. *Wavell: The Viceroy's Journal*, ed:Pauderal Moon, Oxford University Press, 1973, p-120.
12. Sardar Patel, *In Tune with Millions*, Vol II, Appendix-I, Sardar Patel Smarak Bhavan, 1975, p-330.
13. Ibid, p-37.
14. KM Munshi, *Pilgrimage to Freedom*, Bhartiya Vidya Bhavan, Bombay, 1967, p-150.
15. Ibid, p-151-52.
16. Harekrushna Mahatab, *The Beginning of the End*, published in Cuttuck by the Book Co, 1972, Patel's Preface, p-8-9.
17. VP Menon, *Integration of the Indian States*, Orient Black Swan, New Delhi, 2014, p-68.
18. V Shankar, *My Reminiscences of Sardar Patel*, vol-I, Macmillan Co of India, 1974, p-66.
19. *Sardar Patel's Correspondence*, vol V, ed. Durga Das, Navjivan Publishing House, Ahmedabad, 1971, p-401.
20. Ibid, p-407.
21. Sardar Patel, *In Tune with Millions*, vol III, Sardar Vallabhabhai Patel Smarak Bhavan, 1975, p-57.
22. Alan Campbell-Johnson, *Mission with Mountbatten*, Macmillan Publishing Company, 1985, p-46.
23. VP Menon, *Integration of the Indian States*. Orient Black Swan, New Delhi, 2014, p-73.
24. Ibid, p-72.
25. Ibid.
26. HV Hodson, *The Great Divide: Britain-India-Pakistan*, OUP, 1977, p-358-59.

27. VP Menon, *Integration of the Indian States*, Orient Black Swan, New Delhi, 2014, p-66.
28. *The Indian Express*, 18 March 1947.
29. *The Indian Express*, 28 February 1947.
30. VP Menon, *Integration of the Indian States*, Orient Black Swan, New Delhi, 2014, p-70-71.
31. Major-General Himatsinhji Maharaj, Recorded interview given to Balraj Krishna on 6 September 1970.
32. *Sardar Patel's Correspondence*, vol V, p-384.
33. Alan Campbell-Johnson, *Mission with Mountbatten*, Macmillan Publishing Company, 1985, p-43-46.
34. VP Menon, *Integration of the Indian States*, Orient Black Swan, New Delhi, 2014, p-71-72.
35. *Sardar Patel's Speeches,* in Hindi, Publication Division, Government of India, p-592-95.
36. *Sardar Patel's Correspondence*, vol-V, ed. Durga Das, Navjivan Publishing House, Ahmedabad, 1971, (Note by AS Pai of the States Department) p-342-43.
37. VP Menon, *Integration of the Indian States*, Orient Black Swan, New Delhi, 2014, p-86.
38. Ibid, p-87.
39. HV Hodson, *The Great Divide: Britain-India-Pakistan*, OUP, 1997, p-361.
40. Balraj Krishna, *Sardar Vallabhbhai Patel*, Rupa, New Delhi, 2005, p-307.
41. *For a United India: Speeches by Sardar Patel*, Compiled by Publication Division, Ministry of Information & Broadcasting, Govt of India, 1967, p-3-5.
42. *Sardar Patel's Correspondence*, vol-V, p-392.
43. HV Hodson, *The Great Divide: Britain-India-Pakistan*, OUP, 1997, p-364.
44. *KM Munshi Papers: Indian Constitutional Documents*, vol-II, Bhartiya Vidya Bhavan, Bombay, 1967, p-415-16.
45. Sardar Patel, *In Tune with Millions*, vol. III, Sardar Vallabhbhai Smarak Bhavan, 1975, p-175.
46. HV Hodson, *The Great Divide: Britain-India-Pakistan*, OUP, 1977, p-367-368.

47. VP Menon, *Integration of the Indian States*, Orient Black Swan, New Delhi, 2014, p-92.
48. Ibid, p-91.
49. Ibid, p-109.
50. V Shankar, *My Reminiscences of Sardar Patel*, vol-I, Macmillan Company of India, 1974, p-87.
51. Ibid.
52. *The Hindu*, CP Ramaswami Iyer's review of EWR Lambay's book, *The Transfer of Power in India*, March 21, 1958.
53. V Shankar, *My Reminiscences of Sardar Patel*, vol-I, Macmillan Company of India, 1974, p-89.
54. Ibid.
55. Ibid, p-122-23.
56. Ibid, p-123.
57. Ibid, p-123.
58. VP Menon, *Integration of the Indian States*, Orient Black Swan, New Delhi, 2014, p-110-111.
59. Sir Reginald Coupland, *India: A Re-statement*, Oxford University Press, 1945, p-278.
60. *For a United India*, Sardar Patel's speeches, compiled by Publication Division, Ministry of Information & Broadcasting, Government of India.

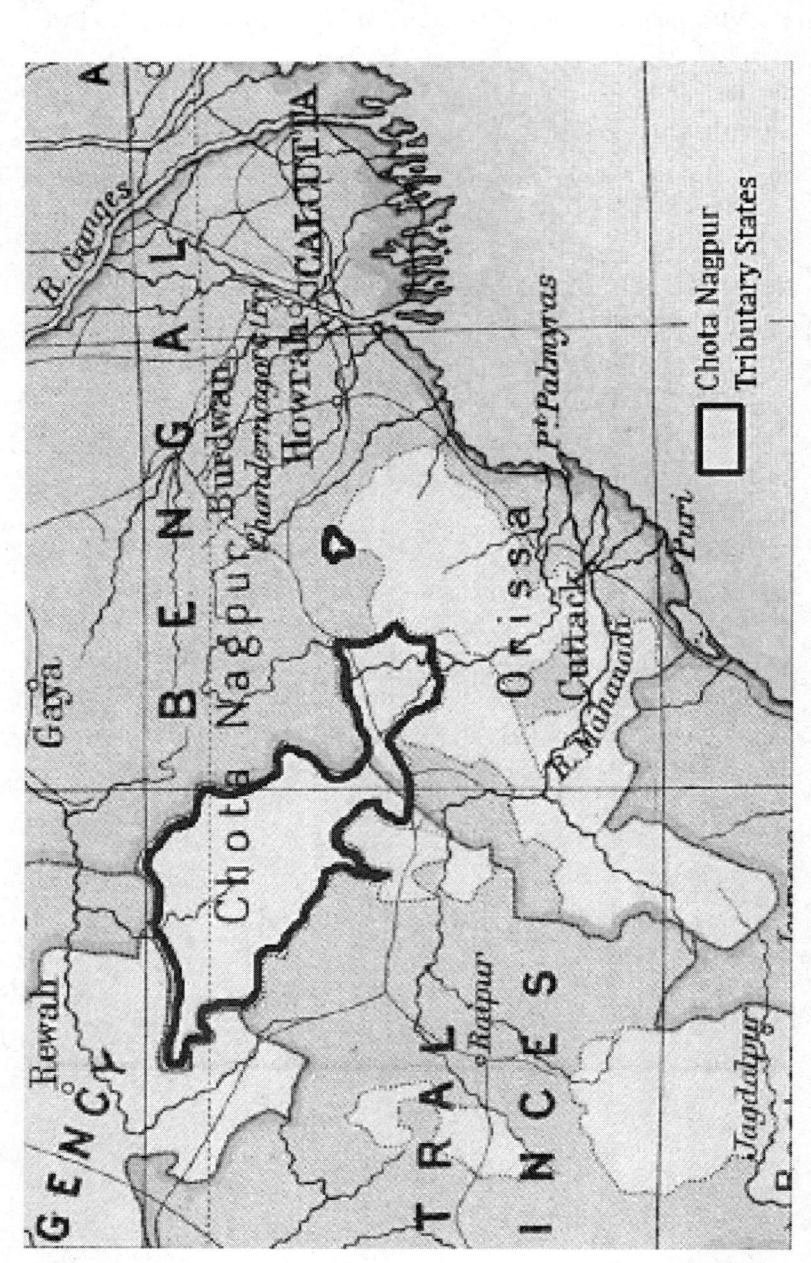

Eastern States

The merger of Eastern States, 'electrified the whole atmosphere... the Indian States could not long remain citadels of autocracy.' The bastions gradually began to give way.
—Sardar Patel

15 AUGUST 1947 was epoch-making. India saw the dawn of freedom after more than 150 years of British rule. Equally significant was simultaneous accession of the Princely States to the Indian Union. It was Patel's personal achievement, for which he was acclaimed as the Bismarck of India. On this day Patel began his historic march towards the creation of One India through the unification and consolidation of princely States as an integral part of India. An India-wide process of integration was triggered in December 1947 by the merger of Orissa and Chhattisgarh, actually of forty-one States. Patel claimed in January 1948 that postponement of the merger would have

been a serious risk and that it would have been foolish to 'let slip an opportunity'.[1]

The Orissa States were 26 in number—eleven 'A' class, twelve 'B' class and three 'C' class—exercising varying degrees of jurisdiction. The biggest, Mayurbhanj, had an area of 4,000 square miles and a population of about 10 lakh. The smallest was Tigira, with an area of 46 square miles and a population of a little more than 20,000.

The Chhattisgarh States numbered 15. The largest was Bastar with an area of 13,000 square miles and a population of well over half a million, whilst the smallest was Sakti with an area of 138 square miles and a population of about one lakh.

These States in 1948, particularly in Orissa, constituted one of the greatest forest areas in the country, forest revenue being for some of them the largest source of their income. Excellent iron ore was available in Myurbhanj as well as in Bastar; a vast coalfield underlined much of Sarguja and Korea; Talchar was also an outlying coalfield. Quantities of manganese, copper, iron ore, coal, limestone, mica etc abounded all over this region.

The origin of these States is obscure. Some of the rulers had descended from Rajput pilgrims who, having come on pilgrimage to Puri, stopped on their way back and carved out principalities for themselves; while others had descended from petty aboriginal chiefs. Most of them were under the suzerainty of the Mughals and later under the Maratha Bhonsles of Nagpur. When they came under the suzerainty of the British government, doubts cropped up as to their rightful status. Their recognition as rulers was conceded to them, in the case of the Chhattisgarh States in 1863, and in the case of the Orissa States in 1888. The provincial governments were nevertheless inclined to treat them as mere Zamindars and none of them exercised the same measure of internal sovereignty as the rulers of the older and more firm States.

In most of these States, there had been prolonged periods of minority administration, when an officer responsible to the

Political Agent was in charge. Even otherwise, there were Agency officials in charge of important departments. If external control were to have been removed, there was always the danger that many of these States would have relapsed into their previous backward condition.

After announcement of the Cabinet Mission proposals, some of the rulers of the Orissa and Chhattisgarh States formed the Eastern States Union, which started functioning from 1 August 1947. The biggest States, Mayurbhanj and Bastar, as well as some of the smaller States had kept out of the Union. The Union had an elaborate constitution. The head of the Union was Raja of Korea. The Union had a premier. It also had a chief secretary, a joint police organisation under an Inspector-General of Police and an appellate court. The Union had no legislature. It was financed by contributions from constituent States. The joint police organisation was headed by an Englishman and the police force contained a large number of Pathans and Punjabi Muslims.

It had been the small State of Nilagiri (now Balasore district) that first issued a valedictory proclamation on 14 November 1947, for merger. The princely fragment of territory embedded in then Orissa province lacked size, money and competent men. Its ruler was locked in a struggle with a Prajamandal (people's representatives' group) that was pressing for popular rule. Its Adivasis (tribes) were in strife with non-Adivasis. Communists appeared to be involved. Patel's anxiety on this score was enhanced by his knowledge that in the State of Hyderabad, Communists had links with the Razakars. With Nilagiri's administration collapsing, the Centre asked the provincial government of Orissa, in November 1947, to run the State. The takeover was swift and smooth; the Raja of Nilagiri admitted in his proclamation that he had been unable to look after his State, and Patel, who thought that some of Nilagiri's sister States were likely to experience a similar unrest and breakdown, had an instant vision of all the Orissa and Chhattisgarh States, as they were called, merging with Orissa or the Central Province (CP).

Merger with Orissa or CP was not necessarily the only solution for these States. Recognising and widening the Eastern States Union was another. Alternatively, the States and the Province or provinces surrounding them could be asked to coordinate their affairs. In the third week of November, Patel discussed these options with VP Menon and Harekrushna Mahatab, the Premier of Orissa. The Eastern States Union found no support in this discussion. It lacked the men to govern a large and complex area and Patel saw a gulf between the rulers and their subjects.

The coordination idea was also readily dismissed. In July 1947, Patel had assured the States that the Government of India 'would scrupulously respect their autonomous existence' in all matters other than defence, external affairs and communications. Could he now, in November and December 1947, contemplate the extinction of some forty of them? Though admitting that merger meant 'setting aside' the 'guarantee', Patel said that he felt 'quite sure' that the rulers of these States lacked 'the capacity to secure the wellbeing of their subjects. Moreover, merger seemed the only way of saving the rulers from the fury of their subjects'. Coordination might be tried for the bigger States.[2]

Since merging rulers would surrender their States once and for all time, it was, as VP Menon put it, 'Since they were surrendering their States for all time, it was elementary justice that some form of *quid pro quo* should be conceded to them'. Recalling that the British government had given liberal pensions to rulers whose territories it took over, Patel and Menon concluded that merging rulers should receive privy purses for their maintenance 'and that such allowances should not be terminated with the present rulers but should be continued to their successors'.[3]

As regards the basis on which the privy purses were to be fixed, there had been two precedents to guide. The first was the formula evolved by the Political Department in 1945 in consultation with a sub-committee of the Chamber of Princes. This formula gave the rulers a privy purse on the basis of a percentage of the average revenues of the State for the previous five years. The percentages suggested were 25 per cent for all revenues (in the 1940s values) up to Rs 5 lakh; 20 per cent for Rs 5 lakh to Rs 10 lakh; 15 per cent for Rs 10 lakh to 25 lakh; 10 per cent for Rs 25 lakh to rupees one crore; 7 per cent for the second crore, 5 per cent for the third crore; 3 per cent for the fourth crore and an overall maximum of Rs 25 lakh for revenues above Rs 4 crore.[4]

The second precedent before Menon and Patel was the award of a Congress sub-committee consisting of Rajendra Prasad, D Pattabhi Sitarammayya and Shankarrao Deo in connection with the formation of the Deccan States Union. This was known as the 'Deccan States formula'. Under this formula, the rulers were to get privy purses at the rate of 15 per cent on the first Rs 5 lakh of the average annual revenue; 10 per cent on the next five lakh and 7.5 per cent on the revenue above Rs 10 lakh. The Deccan States formula did not fix a ceiling but it provided a minimum of Rs 50,000 per annum in reimbursement.[5]

It was thought that the Political Department's formula was on too generous a scale, while the Deccan States formula was not sufficient. Therefore, Patel felt that there should be a maximum privy purse but he was against fixing any minimum. In the formula that was devised (subsequently known as the Eastern States formula), the rulers were to get 15 per cent on the first lakh of the annual revenue; 10 per cent on the next Rs 4 lakh, and 7.5 per cent on all revenues above Rs 5 lakh, subject to maximum of Rs 10 lakh. The financial year 1945-46 was taken as the basic year for the calculation of the privy purse.[6]

Patel also felt that the privy purses should be tax-free (the rulers were immune from taxes in their own territories); private properties, including palaces, should stay with the rulers; succession to the *gaddi*[II] should be assured; and the personal

---

[II] Seat of power, a colloquial usage in Hindi

privileges of the ruler, his wife, his mother, the heir-apparent and the latter's wife should be guaranteed. He decided, finally, that the Centre rather than a Province should take over a State, though the Centre would thereafter ask the province to run it.

On 21 November 1947, Patel asked Menon to fix two meetings in the middle of December, one in Cuttack with the rulers of the smaller Orissa States, and another in Nagpur with the rulers of the smaller Chhattisgarh States. He had not intended to take part in these meetings; Menon and the provincial premiers were to do the needful. However, a few days before Menon was to leave for Cuttack, Patel announced that he would go too. Behind the decision lay Patel's feeling that the bigger States too might have to merge. The co-ordination plan was not standing up to scrutiny. A half-way house between the *status quo* and merger would be far too cumbrous. But it was not until Patel and Menon had arrived in Cuttack and conferred with Mahatab and his colleagues in the Orissa cabinet and with Chandulal Trivedi, the Governor, that it was decided to ask the bigger States too to merge. According to Mahatab, Patel spent the evening and night of 13 December 'examining (the Premier's) grip over the administration' and his capacity to cope if the rulers proved recalcitrant. Evidently Vallabhbhai also probed 'the capacity of the people to agitate' if the rulers rejected his advice to merge. 'If necessary', Mahatab told the Sardar, 'all the States will be taken over the day you leave'.[7]

Next morning (14 December), Patel met the rulers of the smaller Orissa States. Patel told them, in a most persuasive speech, that their safety as well as safety of their subjects was in danger. He had come only to tender friendly advice. They, the rulers, were in no position either to suppress the cry for responsible government or to provide it. Why should they continue to expose themselves as target in troublsome times? If they divested themselves of all power and authority, the Government of India would guarantee their privileges, honour and dignity. But, if his advice was not heeded, and the rulers, after being ousted by the people, came to Delhi for his help, he might be unable to offer it.

The young Raja of Ranpur wanted to know whether he would be allowed to stand for election to the Orissa Assembly. Vallabhbhai replied at once in the affirmative and added, in characteristic fashion, that 'instead of diving in a narrow well, the ruler would be entitled to swim in an ocean'.[8] The main part of the discussions turned to the privy purses. Menon explained how these amounts were fixed.

There was a strong demand that the privy purses should be increased. Patel was firm and said that 'if the privy purses were to be settled in perpetuity, he did not wish them to be fixed so high as to become target of attack'.[9] The Princes asked for some time to consider the agreement. But it was only a formal request. They realised that their continued existence depended on the goodwill of their people and the support of the Government of India, both of which they lacked and that if, owing to agitation, the administration of their States were ultimately taken over by the Government of India, they might not even get the privy purses which was being guaranteed to the them at this point in time.

The same evening Menon met the rulers again. Patel was not present at this discussion. 'Ultimately, twelve rulers agreed to the merger and signed the Agreement. It was decided to ask the rulers of the remaining three States who had been prevented from attending by illness, or for other reasons, to sign later'.[10]

By this time Patel had had discussions with the rulers of the bigger Orissa States. The Maharaja of Mayurbhanj, the largest, was told that in view of the size, population and the revenue of his State he could be left out of the discussions to consult his ministers. The others, led by Maharaja of Patna, fought hard for coordination with Orissa rather than merger. When the Maharaja of Patna asked for further consideration of merger, Patel 'almost lost his patience at this and said that if the friendly advice which he tendered was not acceptable and the problem remained as before, he could not answer for the consequences'.[11]

Menon then suggested that the Princes consider the proposal for a few hours and, after that, meet him at ten in the night.

Patel was very much disappointed with the Princes' attitude. Patel and Menon were to proceed to Nagpur the next day for talks with the Chhattisgarh rulers. Would they have to take the news of a failure with them? Or of a forcible take over? Menon's resourcefulness and admirable patience ensured that they took word of success. After midnight, he contacted the Raja of Dhenkanal, one of the bigger Orissa States. This Raja was in difficulty with the Prajamandal in his State and sought the Government of India's favours. Menon told him that 'all his reasonable demands would be conceded' if he agreed to merge his State with Orissa. The Raja 'readily agreed'. He agreed again when Menon requested him to tell the other rulers at once of his decision and to pass on another message: if the Princes did not sign, Menon would issue orders then and there confining the rulers to Cuttack, and the State Ministry would occupy their States as soon as sufficient policemen could be assembled.[12]

The Dhenkanal ruler went post haste to the Maharaja of Patna, who knocked on Menon's door in the very early hours of the morning of 15 December. To him Menon repeated the threats of confinement and a takeover. When the Maharaja asked why the extreme step was being considered, Menon, who knew that Patna State was free from trouble, could only reply that agitation was bound to hit Patna, the ruler asked if Menon was prepared to convey the threat in writing. Menon said yes, whereupon the Maharaja brought in the other rulers. A clause by clause consideration of the agreement then began. Menon made some minor alterations in the rulers' favour. They all signed, but the rulers of Patna, Kalahandi and Baudh asked for and obtained the letter that Menon had agreed to provide. It said, 'I am glad that you have signed the agreement. I mentioned to you the peculiar position which your State occupies among the Orissa States. The Government of India are most anxious to maintain law and order. We cannot allow your State to create problems for the Government of Orissa and if you had not signed the agreement, we would have been compelled to take over the administration of your State'.[13]

Menon had been with the Princes all of the night on 14 December 1947, and until nine on the morning of 15 December. Later, he would recall: 'Sardar was very pleased when I handed him the merger agreement signed by the rulers of the "A" class States... I told Sardar about the letter I had given to some of the rulers which I felt might occasion some criticism, but Sardar assured me that there was no need to worry'.[14]

It may never be known whether or not Menon obtained Vallabhbhai's consent before issuing his threats. But what is established is that Patel had received Mahatab's assurance that the States could be taken over on the day of his departure, and also that Vallabhbhai defended Menon. Even if unauthorised, Menon's ingenuity served Patel's plan and was not disowned by him. The Maharaja of Kalahandi afterwards made the charge that he had been coerced, however, there was no truth in the stories of rulers being locked in a room in Cuttack.

Menon's letter to three rulers found its way into print, and Patel sent Menon with his version of the Cuttack events to Gandhi and Nehru. Jawaharlal merely listened, but the Mahatma, so claims Menon, 'Gandhiji listened patiently and professed himself entirely satisfied. In his characteristic way, he told me that the merger of the States was like giving castor oil to children. It was for the ultimate good of the rulers. He also told me that I was at liberty to quote his approval'.[15] Neither Nehru nor the Cabinet had been consulted before this merger was decided upon and executed. In due course, the Cabinet approved the agreements relating to the merger of the Orissa and Chhattisgarh States. Jawaharlal, though, could not criticise the merger without damaging his own anti-feudal image, but raised procedural objections, complaining to the Mahatma that, 'many decisions have been taken by the States Ministry without any reference to the Cabinet. For my part, I agree with those decisions; but it seems to me a wrong procedure for these decisions to be taken without reference to the Cabinet or the PM'.[16]

On this Vallabhbhai's comment was that he had only 'anticipated a Cabinet decision. Postponement of the decisive act', he added, 'would have been fraught with serious consequences and would have let slip an opportunity which would have perhaps recurred only after considerable patience, toil and trouble to all concerned'.[17]

After the Cuttack capitulation, there was no chance of Chhattisgarh States holding out. Patel met 14 rulers or representatives of these States in Nagpur in the afternoon of 15 December 1947. Big and small, all signed. The ruler of Korea had asked whether the privy purse would be included in the Constitution and whether a new Government of India would be able to renege on it. 'Sardar assured him that the agreement which the rulers were signing embodied a guarantee given by the Government of India and that intention was to incorporate it in the new Constitution.'[18] The promise was implemented; the guarantee was written into the Constitution. However, the ingenuity of a later decade altered the Constitution and swallowed the privy purse.

The Maharaja of Mayurbhanj, who had kept aloof from the merger on the ground that he would not move without consulting his ministers, came to Menon after one year, on his own, and confessed to Menon that it was a mistake on his part not to have merged his State, alongwith the other Orissa States, with the province. He pleaded that the State should be taken over by the Government of India at once. On 17 October 1948 the Maharaja signed an Instrument of Merger. The State was taken over by the Government of India on 9 November 1948. On 1 January 1949, Mayurbhanj was merged with Orissa.

Patel had won his first unique victory—so quick and so non-violent was the surrender that his mind went back to the glorious past of the region. Filled with justifiable pride, Patel reminded his countrymen: 'Centuries ago, it was the proud privilege of Kalinga to arouse awakening in a great monarch... few had dreamt, and none had imagined, that it would be the same land that will usher in a revolutionary change which would achieve for India the same measure of unity, strength and security which India had once attained under the distinguished ruler, Ashoka.'[19]

The merger of the Eastern States, as Patel correctly claimed, 'electrified the whole atmosphere... the Indian States could not long remain citadels of autocracy. The bastions gradually began to give way'.[20]

Unification of over 560 princely States took around 18 months. It moved fast, with the speed of a soft whirlwind, gently drawing the Princes into its warm embrace, hurting none. Patel was watched with wonder and admiration for redrawing the map of India: first with Accession, followed by merger of neighbouring States, and, finally, with formation of large, viable unions on par with the provinces.

Reference

1. Narhari D Parikh, *Sardar Vallabhbhai Patel*, Navjivan Publishing House, Ahmedabad, 1953, p-42.
2. Prajabandhu, Quoted in *Sardar Vallabhbhai: From Civic to National Leadership*, DN Pathak and PN Sheth, Navjivan Publishing. House, Ahmedabad, 1980, p-47.
3. VP Menon, *Integration of the Indian States*, Orient Black Swan, New Delhi, 2014, p-145-46.
4. Ibid, p-146.
5. Ibid.
6. Ibid.
7. Rajmohan Gandhi, *Patel: A Life*, Navjivan Publishing House, Ahmedabad, 1991, p-452.
8. VP Menon, *Integration of the Indian States*, Orient Black Swan, New Delhi, 2014, p-149
9. Ibid.

10. Ibid.
11. Ibid, p-150.
12. Narhari D Parikh, *Sardar Vallabhbhai Patel*, Navjivan Publishing House, Ahmedabad, 1953, p-36.
13. VP Menon, *Integration of the Indian States*, Orient Black Swan, New Delhi, 2014, p-153.
14. Ibid.
15. Ibid, p-155.
16. Note dictated by Gandhi to Jagdish Munshi, August 1944, reproduced in KM Munshi's *Pilgrimage to Freedom*, p-439.
17. Narhari D Parikh, *Sardar Vallabhbhai Patel*, Navjivan Publishing House, Ahmedabad, 1953, p-92.
18. VP Menon, *Integration of the Indian States*, Orient Black Swan, New Delhi, 2014, p-154.
19. *Sardar Patel, In Tune with Millions*, vol-II, Sardar Vallabhbhai Patel Smarak Bhavan, Ahmedabad, 1975, p-106.
20. Ibid, vol-III, page 92.

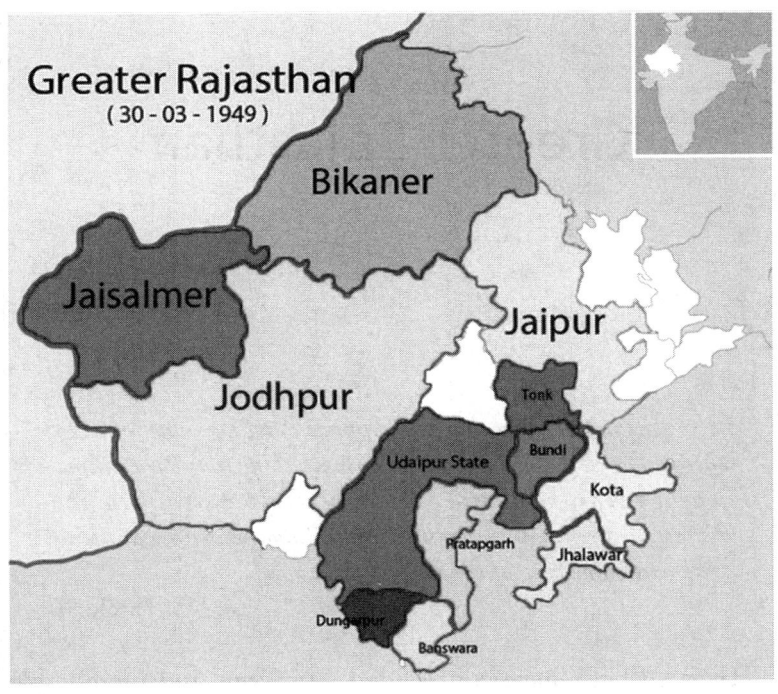

Greater Rajasthan

... Many are amazed that Vallabhbhai Patel was able to sweep them away in so short a time. The Puranas say that Parasurama fought twenty-one battles before he could exterminate the Kshatriya princes, but the new Parasurama needed no battle to make a clean sweep of kingship in India ...

—KM Panikkar

THE RAJPUTS have contributed a glorious and memorable chapter to the early history of India. Before the Muslim invasion, the whole of northern and Central India was parcelled among various Rajput clans. Against the Muslim invaders the Rajputs put up a heroic resistance. Their race has become synonymous in the Indian mind with chivalry.

Akbar led series of campaigns against the Rajput rulers. Ultimately, he was able to subdue most of them, Udaipur (or Mewar) being the only kingdom which resisted Mughal domination. Akbar realised, however, that without cooperation of the Hindus, especially the Rajputs, he could not build up an enduring empire in India. By policy of religious toleration and respect for their pride and sentiment he won over the Rajputs. During his time and that of his two successors the Rajputs, in fact, played a big part in the consolidation of the Mughal Empire. Akbar's wise policy was not followed by Aurangzeb—which was one of the reasons for the final disintegration of the Mughal Empire.

In the wake of the decline of the Mughal Empire, the Marathas appeared on the scene. The Rajput rulers were compelled to become tributary either to Scindia or to Holkar. By the end of the eighteenth century, ravaged by the Marathas, the Pindaris and the Pathans, the Rajput States were reduced to abject helplessness. Yet, the Marathas failed to utilise the Rajputs in the consolidation of *their* empire.

Lord Hastings realised the immense strategic and political advantages which would accrue from British alliances with the Rajputs. After the defeat of the Marathas in the Third Maratha War (1817–1818, during George III's rule), the British freed the Rajput States from the suzerainty of the Scindia and the Holkar and took them under their protection. Colonel James Tod was appointed to settle the problems of Rajasthan.

The formation of the Union of Greater Rajasthan on 30 March 1949 was momentous and historic. Not only did it integrate a divided Rajasthani people, but it was no less strategic from the viewpoint of national security. Rajputana States (the present Rajasthan) comprised 19 salute States and 3 non-salute States. Except for the tiny island of British Indian territory, Ajmer Merwara, the States formed one solid block of territory. The integration of these States was done in five stages. The first was formation of the Matsya Union, which embraced the four States of Alwar, Bharatpur, Dholpur and Karauli. The second was the formation of the first Rajasthan Union with Banswara, Bundi, Dungarpur, Jhalawar, Kisengarh, Kota, Partapgarh,

Shahpura and Tonk. The third was the inclusion of Udaipur in the first Rajasthan Union. The fourth was the creation of Greater Rajasthan by the inclusion of the remaining Rajput States of Jaipur, Jodhpur, Bikaner and Jaisalmer; and the fifth stage was the incorporation of the Matsya Union with Greater Rajasthan.

The whole of Rajasthan brimmed with centuries-old ancestral Pride. On 30 March 1949, Patel inaugurated at Jaipur the Union of Greater Rajasthan, almost as large as Italy, comprising 14 States with a combined population of nearly 153 lakh, an area of 128,424 square miles and an annual revenue of over Rs 18 crore. Patel evoked such pride among the Rajput Princes and nobles assembled to hear him—resplendent in their rich brocades, conspicuous in their manly beards and multi-coloured turbans and Jodhpuris. Patel stated, 'what we have achieved today is merely the fulfillment of the desires and aspirations of Maharana Pratap'.[1] Patel's tribute to Pratap took in one sweep the proud Rajputs back three and half centuries and reminded them not only of the nationalist fervour that coursed through the veins of Pratap, who fought the Mughals till death for the freedom of his motherland, but also of the circumstances under which some quislings from among the brave Rajputs had surrendered to Akbar.

The Princes were reminder of how Akbar's Empire was 'the outcome of the coordination of Mughal prowess and diplomacy and Rajput valour and service'.[2] Prior to fighting Pratap, Akbar had secured the submission of Jaipur, Bikaner and Jaisalmer and the services of able Rajput generals like Man Singh. And it was diplomatic of him to have cemented his relationship with the Rajputs through marriage. History seemed to be repeating itself, though somewhat differently, in 1947. Akbar's realism that his empire could not be built without subjugation of Rajputs appeared to have been the motive for Jinnah's design on Rajasthan and Kathiawar through his manoeuvres to secure the accession of Jodhpur and Jaisalmer in Rajasthan and Junagadh in Kathiawar. Patel defeated all such moves, and even put to an end the fissiparous tendencies and internal feuding among the Rajput princes and Kathiawar rulers. In Greater Rajasthan he was proud to have 'achieved a unity most unknown in the past recorded history'. Patel was equally proud to say in his speech at Jaipur that with the union of Rajput States, Indian unity 'can now be said to be complete'.[3]

Patel knew that there were formidable forces against him. To deal with Rajput States was not merely a jigsaw puzzle, but it was also like facing steel armour, not so easily penetrable. Glorifying in their ivory-tower aloofness, the highly-sensitive Princes were too proud of their status, privileges, ancestry, territories and, no less, the number of guns salute the British had conferred upon them to be fired in their honour on ceremonial occasions. They did not concern themselves with the reality that all that they had so long enjoyed was in name only—under the watchful eyes of the British Resident and at his pleasure; and all the splendour was only permitted by the British to feed their ego.

Rajasthan, therefore, required careful handling; and Patel believed that any word or action there would affect the entire region. The ruling class, the Rajputs and the Muslims, were considerably agitated. A procession in Jaipur openly indulged in anti-Congress and anti-Indian slogans. Jodhpur was no better. Patel, therefore, moved very cautiously, playing cool and showing imperturbable and almost inexhaustible patience in his handling of the Rajasthan Princes. He was wise enough at promoting friendliness rather then arousing opposition and enmity with them. Patel's policy in this strategically-important region lay in his belief: 'It would be best to avoid upsetting the feudatory element. The element can be tackled as soon as possible when the proper time comes and things are ripe.'[4]

Patel waited for nineteen months, between 15 August 1947 and March 1949, for implementing Rana Pratap's dream. The task was complex, delicate, difficult and could prove explosive. Patel could penetrate the Rajput rulers' steel armour only through political maneuvering. It required two prerequisites:

first, integration of the neighbouring small Rajput States so as to break the back of the bigger ones and second, since the Rajput States were like a hornet's nest, Patel wanted to put his finger into it only when the wasps had lost their sting, and their aggressiveness was diluted. He expected opposition mostly from Bikaner, Jaipur and Jodhpur, and not from Udaipur whose ancestor was Maharana Pratap. Patel, therefore, proceeded diplomatically to cut through the complex and delicate tangle without a violent shake-up which would have harmed India as much as the Princes.

Patel was looking for the earliest opportunity to achieve his objective. Such an opportunity came to him on its own with Gandhi's assassination, when rumours of Alwar's and Scindia's complicity in the crime were in the air. It was alleged that Alwar had been an important training and propaganda centre for the RSS (the Rashtriya Swayamsevak Sangh), and that some of the conspirators responsible for the murder had been sheltered in the State. In view of NB Khare's (Premier of Alwar) pronounced pro-Hindu bias, the allegations gained some credence.

Patel did not hesitate to strike. Both the rulers had been badly shaken by the prevailing hostile opinion among their subjects, even when they had no direct involvement. Both rushed to Delhi to clear their position with Patel. While Scindia complied with whatever the Sardar wanted, Alwar was ordered to stay on in the capital till the police enquiry into his kingdom's involvement in Gandhi's murder was completed. It was this surrender that made Patel's task easier—the formation of the United States of Matsya on 17 March 1948, comprising Alwar, Bharatpur, Dholpur and Karauli. With this, Patel killed the nefarious designs that the Jats and Rajputs from these States, particularly Alwar and Bharatpur, seemed to be hatching. Thereafter, Patel proceeded with the integration of the Maratha States of Gwalior, Indore and Malwa in Madhya Bharat, to be followed by the Rajasthan Union comprising smaller States of Kota, Banswara, Bundi, Dungarpur, Jhalwar, Pratapgarh, Shahpura, Tonk and Kishengarh.

Patel felt much distressed over the news that Gandhi's assassination had been celebrated in Alwar with the distribution of sweets. He wanted 'to proceed against both the Maharaja of Alwar and premier, NB Khare'. Alwar 'being the hotbed of dissident elements, a threat to the Central government so close to Delhi could not be tolerated'. Patel decided to act against the advice of Mountbatten and the others. He placed the Maharaja of Alwar and his Prime Minister, Khare, under house arrest in Delhi. Patel's anger was, perhaps, fuelled by Mountbatten's advice that, 'in terms of the Indian Independence Act transferring power to the Princes, the States, even though they had signed the Standstill Agreement, were foreign territories where the Indian Government did not exercise any extradition rights'.[5]

Patel could not accept this. To him, in a free India, it sounded illogical.

The British had themselves never accepted such a position; for them Paramountcy of the crown was always supreme. Patel was, therefore, determined to prove that on behalf of independent India, he alone exercised such rights. Before the house arrest of the Maharaja and Khare, Patel had seen to it that he segregated Bharatpur from Alwar and thereby killed any designs Alwar and Bharatpur were reportedly hatching among Jat rulers of the region. Patel's second bold step was to send Indian troops to Alwar to take control of the State. However, the result of the enquiry into the allegations against the Maharaja of Alwar and Khare was that both were exonerated. An enquiry into similar allegations against the Maharaja of Bharatpur produced the same result; the Maharaja was completely exonerated.

Having thus created the right climate, Patel visited Alwar to talk to the people face-to-face at a public meeting on 25 February 1948, where he bluntly said, 'Small States cannot subsist as independent entities any longer without endangering Indian unity... Many rulers have realised their duty by merging themselves in bigger entities. Rajasthan has to march with the times'. In the same breath he tickled their Rajput pride and roused their dormant nationalist patriotism with the observation, 'It is your privilege and duty to bear the sword. It is equally your responsibility to ensure that the sword is not used to harass the weak, but to protect them. You should use it in a manner that the world will say, you are the inheritors of an ancient civilisation and are true to the real traditions of the chivalry of Rajasthan'.[6]

Patel had, thus, prepared ground for his next step—the formation of the Matsya Union. The formation of the Matsya Union opened the way to the formation of similar other unions in quick succession in the neighbouring States: On 25 March 1948, the Union of Rajasthan; in early April, the Union of Vindhya Pradesh (Rewa and the States of Bundelkhand); on 15 July, the PEPSU (Patiala, Kapurthala, Nabha, Jind, Faridkot, Malerkotla, Nalagarh and Khalsia); on 29 May, the Union of Malwa comprising 25 big and small States. Patel's message on each occasion had a historic significance—as lesson for the Princes to take seriously.

He told the Rajputs of the smaller Union of Rajasthan, 'placed as they are today, small units, unable to support themselves according to modern requirements, cannot afford to remain in precarious isolation. The history of the world in the last two centuries amply demonstrates that it is only by coming together that smaller States can retain their distinctive culture, safeguard their economic interests and take their due share in the political life of the country'.[7] He reminded the rulers of Vindhya Pradesh: 'For several centuries in the past, Central India had been the cockpit on this great subcontinent. Under a strong imperial regime, it was generally either a transit route for armies on the march or a stepping-stone for expeditions to the South. Under a weak Central Kingdom, it was divided up into small principalities under a feudal rule, which made any progress or prosperity impossible.' Patel told them, 'the consequence has been that this tract of land, intended by a bounteous nature to flourish in wealth and plenty, has been one of the most backward tracts of India'. He was, therefore, happy 'to find that both the rulers and the people of Rewa and Bundelkhand States have decided to pool their resources in order to bring out to the full glory of this ancient territory...'[8]

KM Panikkar, who had witnessed the whole drama of States integration unfolding from close quarters as Dewan of Bikaner, paid a most handsome tribute to Patel when he said: How all those grand and grandiose title-holders were swept under the carpet of history in the twinkling of an eye. Many are amazed that Vallabhbhai Patel was able to sweep them away in so short time. The *Puranas* say that Parasurama fought twenty-one battles before he could exterminate the Kshatriya princes, but the new Parasurama needed no battle to make a clean sweep of kingship in India. One by one they queued up to sign their Instrument of Accession, collected their pensions and left with good grace.[9]

References

1. Sardar Patel, *In Tune with Millions*, vol-III, Sardar Vallabhbhai Patel Smarak Bhavan, Ahmedabad, 1975, p-69.
2. RC Majumdar, *An Advanced History of India*, Macmillan, London, 1953, p-449.
3. Sardar Patel, *In Tune with Millions*, vol-III, p-70.
4. *Sardar's Letters-Mostly Unknown*, ed: GM Nandrukar, Sardar Vallabhbhai Patel Smarak Bhavan, Ahmedabad, 1975, vol-V, p-61.
5. Balraj Krishna, *Sardar Vallabhbhai Patel*, Rupa, New Delhi, 2013, p-409.
6. *For A United India: Speeches of Sardar Patel*, compiled by Publication Division, Ministry of Information & Broadcasting, Government of India, p-34.
7. Sardar Patel, *In Tune with Millions*, Sardar Vallabhbhai Smarak Bhavan, Ahmedabad, 1975, vol-II, p-92.
8. Ibid, p-94-95.
9. *KM Panikkar: An Autobiography*, Oxford University Press, 1977, p-190-91.

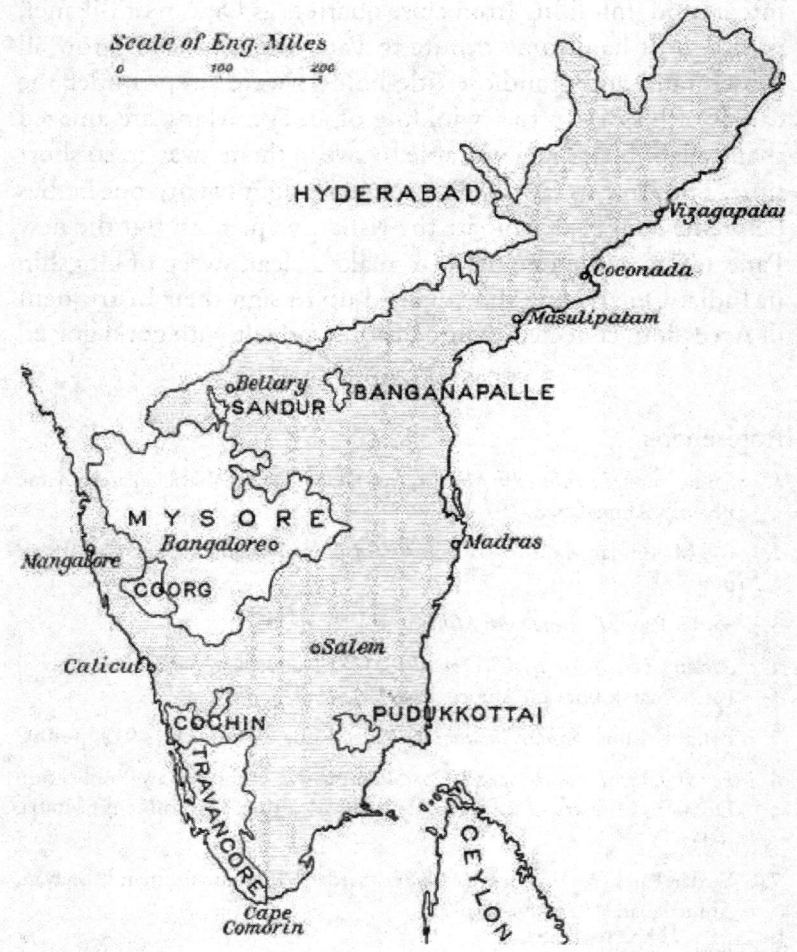

Travancore

... The Rulers of Travancore and Cochin, the two Premiers and their colleagues, and the local Congress organisations have given by this act of union an unmistakable proof of these virtues and the complete unity of purpose and devotion to duty thus symbolised by them are a happy augury for the success of this unique enterprise.
—Sardar Patel

TRAVANCORE, THE southernmost Indian State, occupies the south-west portion of the Indian peninsula. The natural beauty of Travancore induced Lord Curzon, during his visit to this place, to declare: I have for many years heard so much of its exuberant natural beauties, its old-world simplicity and its arcadian charm. Who would not be fascinated by such a spectacle? Here nature has spent upon the land her richest bounties; the sun fails not by day, the rain falls in due season, draught is practically unknown, and eternal summer gilds the scene....[1]

Travancore has evolved a distinctive custom and culture of its own. The area is divided from the rest of India by the Western Ghats; and if a visitor was to cross the Ghats and enter Malabar, he could not fail to be struck by the change in scenery as well as in the life and customs of the people.

The ruling family traced its descent from the ancient Chera Kings of South India. In later historic times, Travancore was split into a number of petty principalities. The consolidation of these into a single State was the achievement of Raja Marthanda Varma, who ruled in the first half of the eighteenth century. He brought the whole of Travancore under his sway, established order and settled the country. In January 1750, he formally and solemnly dedicated the State to Shri Padamnabha, the tutelary deity of his family and he and his successors had ever since ruled as *Dasas*, or servants of that deity. The ruler in 1948, Sir Rama Varma, succeeded to the *simhasana*[III] at the age of twelve and was invested with full ruling powers in November 1931.

Sir CP Ramaswami Iyer, who was the first non-Travancorean Dewan of the State, was the first person to have raised the banner of revolt against the Accession of Travancore in the Indian Union. Sir CP, who was interviewed on 9 April 1947, did not regard the treaties as of any particular value to the States and was not disposed to lay too much emphasis on them. However, on the issue of Paramountcy, he was of the unequivocal opinion that it could not be transferred to a successor government. During the interim period, Paramountcy would have to be preserved, but the machinery of the Political Department would have to be revised if there was to be no undue friction.

CP suggested the appointment of an Adviser to the Viceroy, chosen by the States and working in conjunction with a committee or Advisory Council selected in consultation with the States. He felt that it was impossible to conceive of 601

[III] Throne in Indian languages

States being effective factors in the future unless they grouped themselves. He thought that the smaller States should be told that, if they did not group themselves, they would be left to their fate, in which case they would acquiesce.

CP Ramaswami Iyer was an acknowledged intellectual, Dewan of a premier State, and a stalwart who had occupied the centre of the political stage during the Home Rule Movement. He was Secretary to its founder, Annie Besant. This was in 1916-17, prior to Gandhi's emergence on the political horizon. KM Munshi writes, 'I had known Sir CP Ramaswami Iyer since 1915-16 when we were working together in the Home Rule League; he was not only a patriot, but one of the most far-seeing statesmen. His attitude came to me as a rude shock'.[2]

The seriousness of his revolt lay in Travancore's strategic position: a premier Hindu State at the southernmost tip of India, with a sizeable seaboard and ancient maritime tradition. And it was trotted out that, with the discovery of uranium deposits, for Travancore 'the lapse of Paramountcy now assumes new strategic significance'.[3]

Patel was among the first to have sensed that CP Ramaswami Iyer was spearheading a dangerous move among the Indian States. According to KM Munshi, his 'intransigence gave a new ray of hope to those Princes who had been dreaming of evolving a "Third Force" out of the States'.[4] In the words of Ali Yavar Jung, an ex-official of the Hyderabad State, 'they were looking to the wizard of Travancore who at least had seaboard for the export of coconuts and uranium'.[5]

On 3 June 1947, Lord Mountbatten met the members of the States' Negotiating Committee and explained the plan to them. CP Ramaswami Iyer, at the meeting, appealed to the Viceroy for loosening or lapse of Paramountcy before the transfer of power. He pleaded that such a course would enable the States to negotiate on equal terms with the prospective governments of the two Dominions. He felt that there might be States which were not likely to join up with either Dominion and it was even more essential for the bargaining powers of these to be improved.⁶ Mountbatten, did not commit to appease any such appeal but said that, 'He would, however, consider the premature lapse of Paramountcy in special cases, if it would be proved to him that its continuation constituted a handicap to negotiation.'⁷

Brimming with hope and confidence, CP Ramaswami Iyer, 'on 11 June 1947 announced that Travancore had decided to set itself up as an independent sovereign State. A similar announcement was made the next day on behalf of the Nizam of Hyderabad. These events gave rise to apprehension lest other States should adopt a similar attitude and India be split into fragments'.⁸ Going a step further, CP roused people's emotions by raising the slogan: 'Travancore for the Travancoreans', and he went on to say, 'the future for the next hundred years at least of Travancore is in the making... The Maharaja does not act, has not acted, will not act as an autocrat. He conceives himself as the trustee and the seapoint of Travancore's activities and of Travancore's will, and I am making this appeal on behalf of the Maharaja and with his special permission, and on his behalf of the dynasty he represents'. He asserted, 'There is no question that Travancore is ever going to enter the Constituent Assembly and there is no question that Travancore is now going to join the Indian Union. Travancore will be an independent State, and will function as an independent State from August 15. I have told the Viceroy—and this is no secret—that from the next day, next to the 2nd of this month on which I met him, namely the 3rd instant I propose to prepare Travancore to fulfil its role and play its part as an independent State.'⁹

The Dewan of Travancore went to the extent of announcing his intention to appoint a Trade Agent in Pakistan. The general tendency among the rulers was to make the best of the bargaining position in which the lapse of Paramountcy placed them. Many of the major States had also strengthened their armed forces in the last two decades. The decision therefore, that with the withdrawal of the British, the Indian States comprising two fifths of the land must return to a state of complete political isolation 'was fraught with the gravest danger to the integrity of the country. And so the prophets of gloom predicted that the ship of Indian freedom would founder on the rock of the States'.[10]

On the heels of CP's declaration had come that of the Nizam of Hyderabad, on 12 June 1947. Jinnah was quick to add fuel to fire by stating on 17 June that 'Constitutionally and legally, the Indian States will be independent Sovereign States on the termination of Paramountcy and they will be free to decide for themselves to adopt any course they like, it is open to them to join the Hindustan Constituent Assembly or Pakistan Constituent Assembly, or decide to remain independent.... Neither the British government, nor the British Parliament, nor any other power or body can compel them to do anything contrary to their free will and accord'.[11]

CP Ramaswami Iyer's stand was vehemently criticised by the former Dewan of Cochin, RK Shanmukham Chetty. He stated, 'the most disquieting feature of the Indian political situation is not so much the fact of division or the potentialities of communal troubles, but the declaration of some of the Indian States they intend to remain as independent Sovereign States on the termination of British Paramountcy... the creation of the separate state of Pakistan may not be a damaging blow to India's prestige or influence.... The real danger to the unity and prestige of India is the attitude of certain Indian States. If a considerable number of Indian States choose to follow the example of Travancore and Hyderabad, it would mean the Balkanisation of India'. Chetty, therefore, regretted, 'It is one of the ironies of fate that the Dewan of Travancore, who has been the champion of pure Indian nationalism and a strong Central government, should now make an alliance with Jinnah'.[12]

CP Ramaswami Iyer's attitude perturbed Gandhi who could not withhold his deep concern. He stated, on 25 June 1947, that, 'If the Travancore Dewan was allowed to have his way and his example was followed by others, India would be split into several States—a disaster too dreadful to contemplate. Those many States would need an Emperor, and the Emperor who was leaving might even return with redoubled force'.[13] However, in spite of these disturbing developments, Patel was firm on his stand. He had earlier unequivocally stated at the AICC meeting, on 16 June 1947, that, 'Probably the statesmen who made declaration of independence and sovereignty did not understand the implications of those terms. So long as the Congress continues to have a foothold in Travancore, there is no question of independence and sovereignty'.[14]

Meanwhile, the Travancore State Congress had threatened a campaign of 'direct action' to begin from 1 August 1947. The Congress press in India had been extremely caustic in its comments on Sir CP Ramaswami Iyer. In fact, there had been sharp exchange of words between the Congress leaders and Sir CP in the newspapers. The situation was hotting up every day. Lord Mountbatten, therefore, invited Sir CP to New Delhi. 'On 20 July 1947, I (Menon) had an exploratory talk with him (CP). I explained to him the advantages which would accrue to Travancore as a result of Accession…. Sir CP referred to the proposal of the Union Consultative Committee to divert to the Centre the revenues from customs, import and export duties. He pointed out that Travancore was a maritime State deriving half of its total revenue from these heads and if it were to accede on these conditions, it would be reduced to a fifth-rate State.' VP Menon assured him that the present Accession Plan 'had nothing to do with the new Constitution and that what we were asking for was Accession on three subjects under the Government of India Act of 1935, without any financial or other commitments. Sir CP admitted that he had not been aware of this approach'.[15]

VP Menon further tried to convince Iyer on the emerging dangerous situation if Travancore did not accede to the Indian Union. 'I (Menon) begged him (CP) not to take any precipitate action. Whatever might be his grievances against the Congress, the utterances of its leaders ought not to deflect him from what he considered to be in the best interests, not only of Travancore but of India as a whole. Sir CP replied that he could not give an answer immediately but he assured me that, "coming from a sincere will-wisher of the States and of myself in particular, your comments will have my closest attention".[16]

'Sir CP met Lord Mountbatten on 21 July 1947, when the latter tried to pin him down on the question of Accession. Lord Mountbatten said that all other questions could be adjusted by negotiation and agreement later on. He added that here was a golden opportunity for Travancore to play its part. The Accession of Travancore would be hailed throughout India as a great act of statesmanship. He said that it would not entail any financial loss to the State. On the other hand, in shaping of the future destinies of India, Travancore could play a very important part since its representatives would be sitting in the Dominion Legislature. Sir CP stated that 'he would not agree to Accession but to some agreement on three subjects'.[17]

Sir CP remained adamant in further talks too with Lord Mountbatten and VP Menon but after a lot of persuasion by the former, he agreed that Accession was inevitable. As he had to be back in Trivandrum on 25 July 1947, in connection with the death ceremony of the former ruler of Travancore, he took with him the draft Instrument of Accession and personal letter to the incumbent Maharaja from Lord Mountbatten, promising to return on 27 July. Before he could do so, a personal attack was made on Sir CP by the State communists when he was attending a cultural function at Trivandrum and he was wounded. Immediately after the incident, the Maharaja telegraphed to Lord Mountbatten his acceptance of the Instrument of Accession and Standstill Agreement. This announcement had a distinct effect on other rulers who were still wavering. In the meantime, the Travancore State Congress suspended their campaign of direct action.

The inauguration of the United State of Travancore and Cochin on 1 July 1949, was one of the happiest and momentous events for Patel. He could not attend the inaugural function in

Trivandrum owing to ill-health. However, his message described the union as 'the culminating point of the policy of consolidation of States, which was inaugurated not more than eighteen months ago; and which, with the cooperation and assistance of the rulers and the support and consent of the people of the States, has been my proud privilege to implement'.

Not taking all the credit for himself, Patel paid handsome tributes to all those concerned with its success: 'It has also been my unique pleasure to find among the Princes and the people, a willingness to make sacrifices in the cause of the country—that sense of public duty which only true patriots can exhibit, and that realisation of the urgency and pre-eminence of the country's interests, which calls forth the best and the truest in human beings. The Rulers of Travancore and Cochin, the two Premiers and their colleagues, and the local Congress organisations have given by this act of union an unmistakable proof of these virtues, and the complete unity of purpose and devotion to duty thus symbolised by them are a happy augury for the success of this unique enterprise.'[18] The historic significance of Patel's success was underlined by Mountbatten: 'The adherence of Travancore, after all CP's declaration of independence, has had a profound effect on all other States and is sure to shake the Nizam.'[19]

References

1. VP Menon, *Integration of Indian States*, Orient Black Swan, New Delhi, 2014, p-248.
2. KM Munshi, *Pilgrimage to Freedom*, vol-I, Bhartiya Vidya Bhavan, Bombay, 1967, p-165.
3. Allen Campbell-Johnson, *Mission with Mountbatten*, Macmillan, 1985, p-54.
4. KM Munshi, *Pilgrimage to Freedom*, Bhartiya Vidya Bhavan, Bombay, 1967vol-I, p-165.
5. Ali Yavar Jung, *Hyderabad in Retrospect*, Bennet Colemen (Times of India Publication), p-18.

6. VP Menon, *Integration of Indian States*, Orient Black Swan, New Delhi, 2014, p-74.
7. Ibid.
8. Ibid, p-83.
9. MJ Koshy, *Last Days of Monarchy in Kerala*, Kerala Historical Society, Karala, 1973, p-271-72.
10. VP Menon, *Integration of the Indian States*, Orient Black Swan, New Delhi, 2014, p-84.
11. *The Bombay Chronicle*, 23 June 1947.
12. Ibid.
13. Ibid, 25 June 1947.
14. Ibid, 16 June 1947.
15. VP Menon, *Integration of the Indian States*, Orient Black Swan, New Delhi, 2014, p-105.
16. Ibid.
17. Ibid.
18. Sardar Patel, *In Tune with Millions*, vol-III, Sardar Vallabhbhai Smarak Bhavan, Ahmedabad, 1975, p-74-75.
19. HV Hodson, *The Great Divide: Britain-India-Pakistan,* Viceroy's Personal Report No 15, August I, 1947, OUP, 1945, p-378.

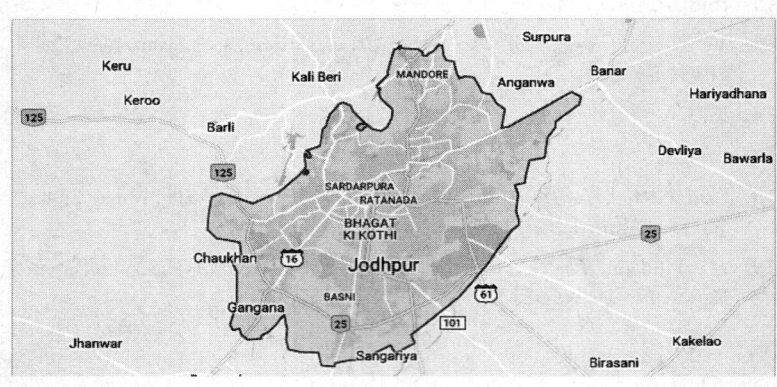

Jodhpur

Jinnah signed a blank sheet of paper and gave it to Maharaja Hanwant Singh of Jodhpur along with his fountain pen, saying you can fill in your conditions.

—VP Menon

JODHPUR (OR MARWAR) was one of the three principal States of Rajputana. The Maharaja was head of the Rathor clan of Rajputs. Offshoots of Jodhpur were the States of Bikaner and Kishangarh in Rajputana, Idar (later merged with Bombay), Ratlam, Jhabua, Sitamau and Sailana, then forming part of Madhya Bharat. Jodhpur State had been founded in 1459 when the seat of the government was transferred to the present capital. But a foothold was acquired in the thirteenth century when Mallani and the neighbouring tract was conquered by Siahji, a grandson of Jaichand, the last king of Kannauj. Like other Rajput States, Jodhpur entered into subsidiary alliance with the

British in 1818. At the time of merger with the Government of India, the Maharaja was Sir Hanwant Singhji. He died in a plane accident in 1952.

The Maharaja of Jodhpur continued to be intractable in 1947. Jinnah and Muslim League leaders had a series of meetings with him. Jinnah's fishing in distant waters of Travancore and Hyderabad was to achieve his objective of weakening the government in New Delhi. Kathiawar, including Junagadh, was on Jinnah's priority list, but that did not provide so favourable a situation to Pakistan as Jodhpur. The State lay across Pakistan's border and was most strategic from the point of view of making inroads into the heart of India. 'The case of Jodhpur', admits Hodson, 'illustrates the lengths to which Jinnah was prepared to go in order to wean States from India'.[1]

Events in Jodhpur took a dramatic turn in June 1947 with the sudden demise of Maharaja Umed Singh and the succession to the throne by his son, Hanwant Singh, who was young, rash, headstrong and given to irresponsible, emotional outbursts. Hanwant Singh's father had cast his lot with India and was among the first few princes whose representatives took their seats in the Constituent Assembly on 28 April 1947.

On the occasion of the crowning ceremony on 21 June 1947, the new Maharaja announced that Jodhpur would continue to be associated with the Constituent Assembly of India. He even expressed the desire that Jodhpur, in close association with the participating States in the Assembly, would work wholeheartedly for the formation of a Union of India. But the manoeuvring of Bhopal in Jodhpur was a most disturbing factor in an otherwise quiet situation. The Nawab of Bhopal, in a secret mission, went to Jodhpur under cover of felicitating the young Maharaja and played the role of an emissary from Jinnah. On Jinnah's behalf he was to arrange a few meetings in New Delhi, at which Bhopal, alongwith his Legal Advisor, Mohammad Zafrullah, were to be present to assist Jinnah in winning over Jodhpur, and thus weaning the Maharaja away from India. Jinnah harboured a grand plan—a Karachi-Jodhpur-Bhopal axis, which Patel considered to be a dagger into the very heart of India. 'This way, Jinnah wanted to avenge Patel's forcing on him a truncated Pakistan. Jodhpur's defection would have given a fatal blow to Patel's dream of unification of the Rajput States, which stretched along Pakistan's eastern border and [it was the] Rajput's disunity, distrust and friction in the past which had helped Mughals to build their Empire in India. Jinnah seemed to be angling for a similar role for Pakistan, with Jodhpur repeating history by playing a quisling.'[2]

CS Venkatachar, the Prime Minister of Jodhpur, came to know about Bhopal's secret mission. Deeply concerned at what was ominously taking shape, he sent HVR Iyengar, Home Secretary to the Government of India, a handwritten note, through a special messenger, giving news of the utmost gravity for the very stability of India. The note stated that 'the ruler had been approached by Jinnah and had been persuaded to stay out of the Indian Dominion'.[3] Iyengar took the note to Patel and apprised him of the gravity of the situation. A great danger lurked in Bhopal, Indore and a few other Central Indian States forming an independent federation under Bhopal's leadership with ultimate Accession to Pakistan. Bhopal expected Baroda to join his group on Jinnah's promise that he would be allowed to exercise control over his port of Bedi Bandar on the Saurashtra coast. Jinnah was hopeful of roping in the Jamsaheb of Nawanagar as well in his plan.

Jodhpur, along with the Maharajkumar of Jaisalmer, met Jinnah. The ambitious Maharaja of Jodhpur was tempted by four offers: a sea-outlet through the use of Karachi as a free port; free import of arms and continuance of manufacture of firearms in his State; jurisdiction over the Jodhpur-Hyderabad (Sind) railway; and a large supply of grains for famine relief. This was Jinnah's basket of apples, which Bhopal had already successfully sold to Jodhpur. The Maharaja of Jodhpur seemed to be so happy that he approached Udaipur to join him in acceding to Pakistan. With

Jinnah's blessings, he attempted to project Pakistan right across India through the States of Jodhpur, Udaipur, Indore, Bhopal and Baroda. The territories would extend from the borders of Pakistan to Bhopal in the east and Navsari in the Surat district of Gujarat in the south.[4]

When the Maharaja of Jodhpur took the Bhopal plan to the Maharana of Udaipur, the reply was to shock Jodhpur: My choice was made by my ancestors. If they had faltered they would have left us a kingdom as large as Hyderabad. They did not. Neither shall I. I am with India.[5] Bikaner also refused to accompany Jodhpur to Jinnah.

Anxious not to let the fish escape from his net, 'Jinnah signed a blank sheet of paper and gave it to Maharaja Hanwant Singh of Jodhpur along with his own fountain pen, saying "you can fill in your conditions"'. A discussion followed. The Maharaja was prepared to line up with Pakistan. He then turned to the Maharajakumar of Jaisalmer and asked him whether he would follow suit. The Maharajakumar said he would do so on one condition:'If there was any trouble between Hindus and Muslims, he would not side with the Muslims against the Hindus.'[6] This was a bombshell that took Maharaja Hanwant Singh by surprise. Zafrullah (Legal Adviser of Bhopal) tried to make light of the whole affair and pressed Jodhpur to sign the Instrument. Taking advantage of his vacillation, the Maharaja's ADC, Col Thakur Kesri Singh, whispered into his ear, 'your Highness, before you sign, you must ask your mother'. The Maharaja greatly respected her. Known as Rajdidi,[IV] she was 'a woman of great character, power and influence'.[7]

The Maharaja now felt unable to take a decision. He suggested to Jinnah that he would go to Jodhpur and return the next day. The Maharaja remained at Jodhpur for three days. The atmosphere in the State was hostile to the idea that Jodhpur

---

[IV] Maharani Badan Kunwar Sahiba

should cast its lot with Pakistan; the *Jagirdar*s and nobles were decidedly opposed to it. The Maharaja began to waver.

Patel, thus, faced three extremely intrepid, intractable and unpredictable men in Jinnah, Bhopal and Jodhpur. The first was astute and clever, proudly basking in the glory of his victory in getting away with Pakistan and hunting for opportunities to stir up trouble for India by other ways. The second was a peerless Machiavelli who carried influence with some of the Princes as chancellor of the Chamber of Princes. And the third, the Maharaja of Jodhpur, was headstrong, emotional and impulsive, capable of committing any rash act irrespective of the consequences.

The Maharaja returned to New Delhi after a three-day stay at Jodhpur for a final round of talks with Jinnah and Bhopal. He didn't seem to be the same as earlier—apparently subdued by his mother's pep talk as also by what his *guru*, a *swami* told him: how could a Hindu State like Jodhpur agree to accede to Pakistan which would be a Muslim State? Yet, Venkatachar did not leave matters to chance. He followed him to New Delhi to keep a watch on his moves. VP Menon too moved into the arena of manoeuvring.

'When he (Hanwant) returned to Delhi after three days, I (Menon) was informed that unless I handled the Maharaja quickly, the chances were that he might accede to Pakistan. I went to the Hotel Imperial and told the Maharaja that Lord Mountbatten wanted to see him.'[8] It was decided, as part of strategy, that before Patel stepped into the scene, Mountbatten might handle the Maharaja first. The latter agreed to do so, rather hopefully. Without losing time, Menon drove the Maharaja to the Viceroy's House.

Lord Mountbatten made it clear that from a purely legal stand point, that there was no objection to the ruler of Jodhpur acceding to Pakistan; but the Maharaja should, he stressed, 'consider seriously the consequences of his doing so, having regard to the fact that he himself was a Hindu, that his State was populated predominantly by Hindus and that the same applied to the States surrounding Jodhpur'. Mountbatten argued that, 'In the light of these considerations, if Maharaja were to accede to Pakistan, his action would surely be in conflict with the principle underlying the partition of India on the basis of Muslim and non-Muslim majority areas; and serious communal trouble inside the State would be the inevitable consequence of such affiliation'.[9]

The Maharaja started at once to ask concessions. 'I (VP Menon) told him plainly, if you want to sign on false hopes, I will agree to your demands, adding that most of the demands could not be conceded. He then told us that Jinnah had given him blank paper in which he could put down all the concessions he wanted. I (Menon) urged him not to be swayed by false promises. After a great deal of discussion, I gave him a letter conceding some of his demands.'[10] Thereafter, Jodhpur signed the Instrument of Accession.

One drama was over. Another began soon after, at the Viceroy's House. Immediately after the Instrument of Accession had been signed, Mountbatten went out of the room. During his short absence, in a fit of emotional outburst, narrates Menon, 'the Maharaja whipped out a revolver, levelled it at me and said, I refuse to accept your dictation. I told him that he was making a very serious mistake, if he thought that by killing me or threatening to kill me, he could get the Accession abrogated. Don't indulge in juvenile theatricals, I admonished him. Shortly after, Lord Mountbatten returned and I told him what had happened. He made light of the episode and turned it to jest. The Maharaja returned to normal and we departed in company. After leaving him at his residence, I returned to office. The whole episode became a standing joke between us later on'.

In the settlement of Jodhpur affairs, a great calamity was averted. Both Patel and Mountbatten played their respective but complementary roles. The ultimate success was, nevertheless, due to Patel. He made Jinnah suffer a humiliating defeat. It was for Bhopal too. Patel's greatest gain, however, was winning the abiding loyalty of the Maharaja. While the Maharaja struck a deep, warm, lifelong friendship with Menon, his relations with Patel grew deeper and warmer from then onwards. Hanwant Singh gave Patel the reverence he would have offered to his late father. His devotion to Patel led the Maharaja to serve him as an errand boy, who happily flew in his aircraft from Prince to Prince and from State to State, carrying Patel's messages. He always felt proud to accompany Patel to various places.

References

1. HV Hodson, *The Great Divide: Britain-India-Pakistan*, OUP, 1997, p-379.
2. Balraj Krishna, *Sardar Vallabhbhai Patel*, Rupa, New Delhi, 2013, p-313.
3. HVR Iyengar (ICS), Sardar's Ways: Focus on Main Tasks, *The Indian Express*, 31 May 1965.
4. KM Munshi, *Pilgrimage to Freedom*, Bhartiya Vidya Bhavan, Bombay, 1967, p-162.
5. KM Munshi, *Pilgrimage to Freedom*, vol-I, Bhartiya Vidya Bhavan, Bombay, 1967, p-163.
6. VP Menon, *Integration of Indian States*, Orient Black Swan, New Delhi, 2014, p-106.
7. HVR Iyengar (ICS), recorded interview, May 17, 1969.
8. VP Menon, *Integration of Indian States*, Orient Black Swan, New Delhi, 2014, p-106.
9. Ibid, p-106-107.
10. Ibid, p-107.

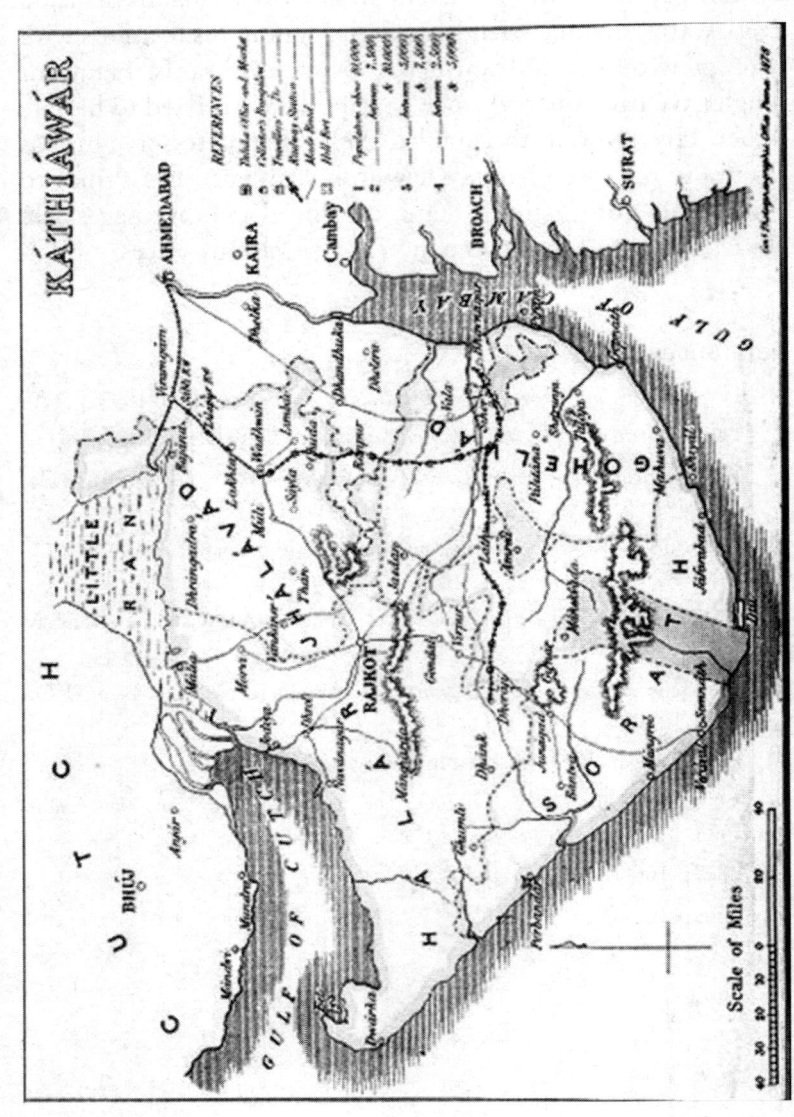

United State of Kathiawar

Little pools of water tend to become stagnant and useless, but that if they are joined together to form a big lake, the atmosphere is cooled and there is universal benefit.

—Patel, addressing a public meeting at Bhavnagar on 15 January 1948

KATHIAWAR WAS governed by the lieutenants of the Maurya kings, about 300 BCE. It also formed part of the Gupta Empire, whose viceroys governed from Wanthali. Later on, the *senapati*s[V] became kings of Kathiawar and established themselves at Vallabhinagar (modern Vala). When the Guptas were ousted, the Vallabhi dynasty extended its sway over Kutch and

---

[V] The generals

Lat Desha (between Gujarat and Rajputana). In the eleventh century Kathiawar came under Muslim authority. The sack of Somnath by Mahmud Ghazni in 1024 CE and the capture of Anhilwad by Muslims in 1194 were the prelude to the conquest of Kathiawar by the Khiljis and Tughlaks. In 1573, Gujarat was conquered by Akbar, and his viceroys at Ahmedabad exacted periodical tribute from Kathiawar through troops sent there from time to time. In the latter half of the eighteenth century, the Marathas supplanted the Mughals and every year Kathiawar was visited by Maratha forces for the collection of tribute. In 1803, some of the *talukdar*s of Kathiawar applied to the British Resident at Baroda for protection.

In 1807, the forces of the East India Company and of the Gaekwar, under Colonel Alexander Walker, advanced into Kathiawar 'with an object of relieving the province of the double scourage of periodical invasions and internecine conflicts'.[1] The rulers and talukdars[VI] of Kathiawar were guaranteed security from the visitation of Maratha forces, in return for which they agreed to pay volountarily a fixed and settled tribute to the East India Company, to keep the peace and to maintain order within their own limits. The framework of Colonel Walker's settlement remained practically undisturbed till the transfer of power in 1947.

The States in Kathiawar comprised the fourteen salute States of Junagadh, Nawanagar, Bhavnagar, Dharangadhra, Porbandar, Morvi, Gondal , Jafrabad, Wankaner, Palitana, Dhrol, Limbdi, Rajkot and Wadhwan; Seventeen non-salute States; and 191 other small States exercising varying degree of jurisdiction. The area was a little over 22,000 square miles with a population of nearly four million.

The administration of Kathiawar States was complicated by the fact that many of them had scattered islands of territory

---

[VI] Officials of Department of Land Records

outside their individual State boundaries. Nawanagar, Gondal and Junagadh, for instance, had respectively nine, eighteen and twenty-four separate areas of territory. Thus, the map of Kathiawar was divided into about 860 different jurisdictions. Communications were in primitive conditions. Internal trade was rendered difficult by the export and import duties which the various units levied at different rates, and this encouraged extensive smuggling and black market operations. Since an offender in one State could escape easily to another State, administration of justice and maintenance of law and order were greatly handicapped. In fact, all the worst effects of political fragmentation were to be seen in Kathiawar.

Four years before the transfer of power, the Political Department had, under their Attachment Scheme, joined some of the smaller units to the neighbouring big States. The Scheme covered an area of 7,000 square miles with a population of 800,000. It provoked bitter opposition from the rulers of the smaller States. After the transfer of power, the position of these attached units became a problem by itself. Their rulers asserted that since Paramountcy had lapsed, they were no longer bound by the Attachment Scheme and this had deleterious results in many parts of Kathiawar.

The Jamsaheb of Nawanagar's position in Kathiawar was strategically no less important than that of the Maharaja of Jodhpur in Rajasthan. If the unification of Rajasthan States largely depended on Jodhpur, equally so was that of Kathiawar on the attitude of the Jamsaheb, who, unlike the Maharaja of Jodhpur, commanded a position of respect and influence among the Princes of Kathiawar. A sinister situation, similar to that in Jodhpur, was developing in Jamnagar around May-June 1947. On 1 July 1948, BL Mitter, Dewan of Baroda, wrote to Nehru, 'the Jamsaheb is reported to be negotiating with Jinnah regarding his port of Bedi Bander. If this port and Veraval, the Junagadh port, come into the orbit of Karachi, Bombay will be seriously affected'.[2] And with the Accession of Veraval and

Junagadh to Pakistan, the whole of Kathiawar would have come under Jinnah's domination.

Earlier, on 22 November 1946, Mitter had informed Patel: The Chamber of Princes is playing Jinnah's game... the Jamsaheb has bought his immunity by selling his soul to the Political Department. His confederation plan is sponsored by the Department.[3] Again Mitter wrote to Patel on 26 March 1947, that the Chief of Wadia (in Kathiawar) had told him, 'the Jamsaheb was strengthening his armed forces... was aspiring to be the overlord of Kathiawar'.[4] About mid-June in 1947, a gathering of Kathiawar princes, with Jamsaheb as the leader, met in a secret conference at Mount Abu under the presidentship of the Resident. The view propagated was that, 'if Travancore can declare its independence, the Kathiawar States, being maritime States, can do likewise... they can rule without any interference from Delhi and develop their ports and they need not depend upon India for anything'. The conference decided to form a 'Union of Kathiawar', comprising as many as seven States, which were Jamnagar, Bhavnagar, Gondal, Porbander, Morvi Dharangadhra and Junagadh. In the event of its Accession to Pakistan, Junagadh 'would enter into an offensive and defensive treaty' with the Union of Kathiawar. Mitter also told Patel, 'the Resident is helping and the Jamsaheb has promised to put a crore of rupees in furtherance of the scheme.... The Resident and the Political Agent are out to Balkanise India'. There was something sinister in granting Junagadh the right to either 'declare separate independence or to join Pakistan'.[5] The move unmistakably implied severance of links with India, Jinnah expected Junagadh to play a role in Kathiawar similar to Bhopal's in Central India.

The situation in Kathiawar was more complex and difficult than the one in Jodhpur. In case of Jodhpur, Patel had to face the challenge of a single ruler; in Kathiawar, seven rulers were uniting to declare their independence. And while the Maharaja, Hanwant Singh of Jodhpur, was young and immature and Patel could treat him as a boy, the Jamsaheb was a tower of strength.

Patel watched the developments here with deep concern and remained waiting for an opportunity to act.

Such an opportunity arrived on 11 May 1947, when Jamsaheb and some other rulers halted for a short while at the New Delhi airport, on their way to some Rajput States to sell their confederation idea. The Jamsaheb's brother, Himatsinhji, informed Patel of this. Patel sent him in his car to bring Jamsaheb to his residence for lunch. Accompanied by Himatsinhji, the Jamsaheb lunched with Patel. The meeting proved momentous. It changed the course of events. Patel's influence on the Jamsaheb was irresistible. The Nawanagar ruler (Jamsaheb) seemed to have been won over by Patel at their very first meeting. Happy over the outcome, Mitter wrote to Patel on 14 May 1947, 'you have converted the Jamsaheb. Now you will have to fashion the Kathiawar and Gujarat units for the Union'.[6]

The decks having been cleared, Patel got into action to face Jinnah's challenge through the unification of the Kathiawar States. Since Gandhi came from Porbander, he was intensely interested in it, and in its achievement was the fulfilment of Gandhi's dream. For Patel, it meant political consolidation of the country in a big way. This unification was highly necessary like the unification of the Rajput States. It was complex, as it involved 222 States of great diversity covering an area of over 22,000 square miles.

Following the transfer of power, there was a wave of agitation all over Kathiawar for responsible government. This had unhealthy repercussions on the maintenance of law and order. Patel was very conscious of the fact that he needed some time to think and hammer out a plan. But events were marching fast. Junagadh had further aggravated the situation. With the influx of refugees from Sind, the communal situation seemed likely to deteriorate and extremist opinions of all kinds appeared to be gaining strength.

Backed by the Kathiawar *Rajakeeya Parishad*, the agitation for responsible government was gathering momentum. In the past, the rulers, particularly, of the smaller States, had depended on the British government for help. Now the States' subjects were able not only to muster their own strength, but to obtain overwhelming support from the rest of the country. The result was that many rulers found themselves unable to maintain order.

Bhavnagar was the first of the bigger States to feel the pressure of the demand for responsible government. The Maharaja went to Gandhi for guidance, who directed the Maharaja to Patel. Patel advised him to yield to the people's wishes. It was agreed that Balwantrai Mehta, the leader of the State's Prajamandal, should be the Premier of Bhavnagar. The Maharaja agreed to accept any privy purse that might be settled by Gandhiji. It was decided that responsible government in Bhavnagar should be inaugurated by the Sardar. This decision had a far-reaching effect on the rulers of the salute States of Kathiawar.

The Government of India could not encourage the idea of responsible government in the smaller States. Even Bhavnagar, with the largest revenue among the Kathiawar States, was without the resources necessary for a modern democratic administration. If therefore, the prosperity and future welfare of Kathiawar was to be assured, the first step should be to consolidate these fragmented areas. How this problem should be tackled was Patel's next consideration.

Hence the State Ministry thought of various schemes. At last, it reached the irresistible conclusion that the only satisfactory solution was the unification of all the States in Kathiawar. Menon discussed with Patel the various schemes which were considered. 'Sardar agreed that, in order to ensure the future prosperity of Kathiawar, we could not do otherwise than amalgamate all the States into one unit.'[7]

By the end of December 1947, Vallabhbhai was resolved on a twin goal for Kathiawar States: union plus democracy. To get closer to it, he accepted an invitation from the Bhavnagar Maharaja to launch the new government in his State, on 15 January 1948, and directed Menon to discuss, immediately after that date, a union with Kathiawar rulers. On the occasion of the inauguration of the Bhavnagar State, Patel addressed a mammoth meeting. During his speech, Patel dropped a hint as to the coming event. He said: 'Little pools of water tend to become stagnant and useless, but that if they are joined together to form big lake, the atmosphere is cooled and there is universal benefit.'[8] The huge crowd hearing him knew exactly what he meant. So did the rulers who by now had arrived in Rajkot to greet Patel and talk with Menon. Patel wished Menon good luck and left for Bombay.

Patel's tactics for Kathiawar differed in two respects from the Orissa and Chhattisgarh States' exercise. Firstly, he obtained the Mahatma's prior blessing for his plan of unification. Secondly, he kept himself in reserve and did not join the negotiations. After the Bhavnagar ceremony, he flew to Rajkot and made a powerful speech. He did not talk directly of the union that Menon was to discuss in that town with the rulers.

The nuts that Menon hoped to crack in Rajkot were wholly different from Cuttack's. Intimidation was unlikely to succeed during five days of intensive negotiation. 'Sophisticated and confident Princes had to be persuaded by argument and the logic of events.'[9]

The logic of events was too plain to be missed by intelligent men. Even so, Menon spelt it out. Democratic rule was irresistible. Elected assemblies in the Kathiawar States were bound to ask for merger with Bombay or for a united Kathiawar. The Government of India would not be able to turn down such a demand. However, the rulers could get good terms if they, rather than elected assemblies, dealt with the Government of India. Menon said: 'His Highness the Maharaja of Bhavnagar has already decided himself in favour of a United Kathiawar State. I may also remind you of the metaphor aptly employed by Sardar Patel on this subject, of how a large lake cools the whole atmosphere while small pools become stagnant and do no good to anyone. I hope your Highness will, therefore, be able to accept the scheme which, while it secures your own essential interests, will also promote a patriotic purpose.' He further added: 'The logic of the facts has to be recognised. It is not possible for 222 States of Kathiawar to continue their separate existence under modern conditions for very much longer. The extinction of the separate existence of the States may not be palatable, but unless something is done in good time to stabilise the situation in Kathiawar, the march of events may bring about still more unpalatable results.'[10]

The young Maharaja of Dharangadhra was the first to join Bhavnagar in support of a Union. Persuading the Jamsaheb of Nawanagar was harder, but once he accepted, Menon's task was easier. On 22 January 1948, Kathiawar's major rulers signed covenant for Union. Later, Menon would recall: 'the poignant spectacle of the rulers parting with their proud heritage. No ruler had thought even a month previously that he would have so soon to part with his State and rulership. Something which had been in their families for generations and which they had regarded as sacrosanct had disappeared as it were in the twinkling of an eye.'

'Though all of them put up a bold front, the mental anguish they were going through was writ large on their faces.... The Maharaja Morvi came to me and asked whether the Government of India would allow him to abdicate and permit his son, who would succeed him, to sign the covenant... Morvi State was well governed and the Maharaja left the largest cash balance in relation to the size of the State, which was only 820 square miles in area.'[11]

The inauguration of the United State of Kathiawar was performed by Vallabhbhai Patel at Jamnagar on 15 February 1948. The oaths of office were administered to the Jamsaheb, as Rajpramukh, to the members of presidium and to the ministers. The same morning, a meeting of the electoral college for the Constituent Assembly had been called and, on the proposal of Balwantrai Mehta, UN Dheber was elected leader. He, thus, automatically became the Premier of the new Kathiawar ministry.

In an inspiring message to the Jamsaheb of Nawanagar, Nehru sending his hearty congratulations, said: 'The consolidation into one administrative unit of the vast number of States with varying number of sovereignty in the Kathiawar peninsula is in itself a great step forward. The fact that a system of responsible government should have been simultaneously agreed upon makes this event one of the most notable in contemporary Indian history. I have every hope that this far-sighted act of statesmanship will be fully justified in the growing economic prosperity and happiness of the people of Kathiawar.'[12]

The Jamsaheb's speech, on this occasion was equally inspiring. In course of his speech, he said: 'The point that I wish to make, on behalf of my order in Kathiawar, is this: it is not as if we were tired monarchs who were fanned to rest. It is not as if we have been bullied into submission. We have by our own free volition pooled our sovereignties and covenanted to create this new State so that the United State of Kathiawar and the unity of India may be more fully achieved and so that our people may have that form of government which is today most acceptable to them and which I hope and pray will prove beneficial to them.'[13]

A United State of Saurashtra thus, came into being after centuries of political fragmentation, no longer a number of separate stagnant pools, but one vast expanse of fresh and limpid water.

By the middle of February 1948— no more than six months after independence—Patel and Menon had presented two accomplished schemes, one where States merged into Provinces and the other where they joined one another in a Union. The two distinct schemes, one executed in the east and the other in the west, set a pattern and created momentum. Before the end of February 1948, the Deccan States were merged with Bombay and two States with Madras. In March 1948, the Gujarat States agreed to merge into Bombay and three small States into Punjab. Other Unions and merger took place in March, April and May

1948. Himachal Pradesh, Rajasthan, Madhya Bharat, Vindhya Pradesh, Matsya, and PEPSU (Patiala and Eastern Punjab States Union) came into being. Thus, the map of India was refashioned.

References

1. VP Menon, *Integration of the Indian States*, Orient Black Swan, New Delhi, 2014, p-161.
2. *Sardar Patel's Correspondence*, vol-V, ed:Durga Das, Navjivan Publishing House, Ahmedabad, 1971, p-475.
3. *Sardar's Letters-Mostly Unknown*, vol-IV ed: Maniben Vallabhabhai Patel, pub:Sardar Vallabhbhai Patel Smarak Bhavan, Ahmedabad, 1977, p-256.
4. Ibid, vol-V, p-17.
5. Ibid, p-20.
6. Ibid, p-19.
7. VP Menon, *Integration of the Indian States,* Orient Black Swan, New Delhi, 2014, p-165.
8. Ibid, p-166.
9. HV Hodson, *The Great Divide:Britain-India-Pakistan*, OUP, 1997, p-501.
10. VP Menon, *Integration of the States*, Orient Black Swan, New Delhi, 2014, p-169-70.
11. Ibid, p-177.
12. Ibid, p-180.
13. Ibid.

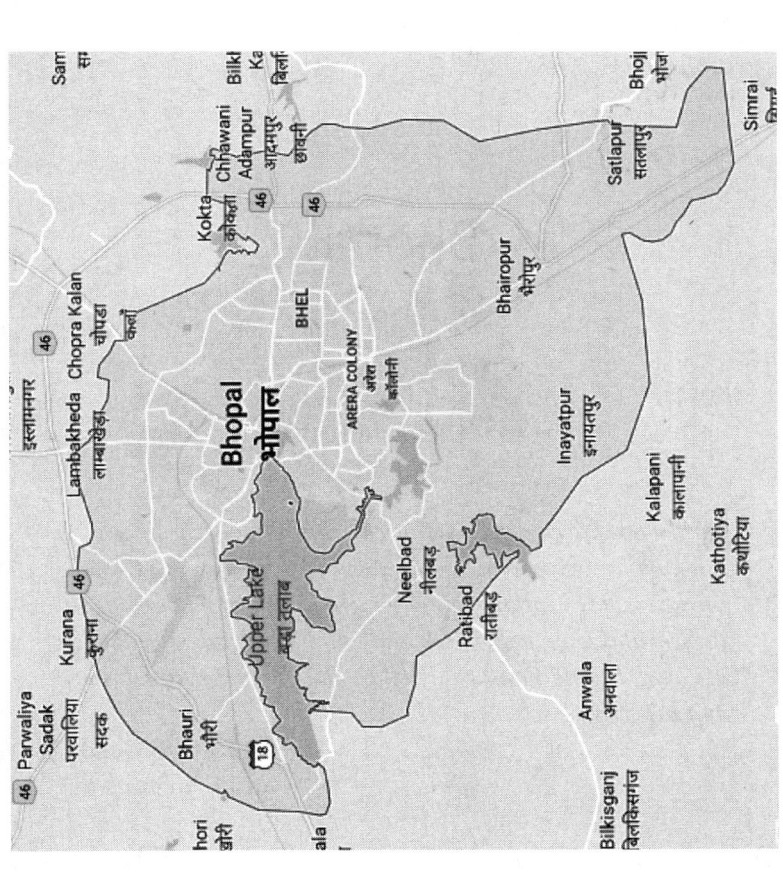

Bhopal

For the last fifteen days I have been occupied with the Princes. It is so taxing. There seems to be no end to the Nawab of Bhopal's intrigues. He is working day and night to cause a split among the Princes and to keep them out of the Indian Union. The Princes are weak beyond measure. They are full of selfishness, falsehood and hypocrisy.

—Sardar Patel to Gandhi
on 11 August 1947

ON 22 MAY 1946, the Cabinet Mission published the Memorandum on *States' Treaties and Paramountcy*, in which they declared that Paramountcy would lapse with India attaining her freedom and all the rights surrendered by the States to the British Crown would revert to them. This void would have to be filled by the States entering into a 'federal relationship with the successor Government or Governments' in British India or by entering into particular political arrangements with it or either of them.¹

The vague phrase 'particular political arrangements' was capable of being variously interpreted and Sir Conrad Corfield, Chief of the Political Department, interpreted it to mean that, on the lapse of Paramountcy, that is, as soon as India became independent, the States would also gain their independence, and would be in a position to negotiate with India or Pakistan on equal terms.²

It was unfortunate that at this time the Nawab of Bhopal was president of the Chamber of Princes. This crafty Prince, under the advice of Corfield, began to organise the Princes into a solid bloc but thanks to the patriotism of some rulers like those of Baroda, Bikaner and Patiala, his schemes were foiled. On Corfield's advice, the Chamber of Princes set up a Negotiating Committee on 10 June 1946 and authorised their Chancellor, the Nawab of Bhopal, to arrange discussions with the Constituent Assembly.

The ruler of Bhopal, Nawab Hamidullah Khan, enjoyed a status and influence with the British and the Princes out of proportion to the State's population, area and revenue. Bhopal's importance was due to its dynamic, articulate and crafty ruler, who was in the forefront of the Princely order by virtue of his personality as a Muslim ruler who could be a most trusted ally of the British.

He ascended the throne in May 1926 and came into prominence at the time of the Round Table Conference in 1931. With British support, he became Chancellor of the Chamber of Princes, first from 1931 to 1932, and again from 1943 till his resignation under force of circumstances in 1947. His second term coincided with the most crucial period of Indian history when the future of a united India was on the anvil.

From the very start of negotiations, the Nawab of Bhopal showed signs of refusal and reluctance to accede. 'The Nawab even threatened to give away the kingdom to his daughter.'³

Initially, he tried to sign the Standstill Agreement without intending to accede to the Indian Government.

Bhopal's Challenge to India's unity was far more pernicious than that posed by CP Ramaswami Iyer or by the Nizam of Hyderabad; whereas his surrender had a great drama. Apprising Gandhi of the dangers inherent in the situation, Patel wrote to him on 11 August 1947: 'For the last fifteen days, I have been occupied with the Princes. It is so taxing. There seems to be no end to the Nawab of Bhopal's intrigues. He is working day and night to cause a split among the Princes and to keep them out of the Indian Union. The Princes are weak beyond measure. They are full of selfishness, falsehood and hypocrisy.' Gandhi's reply showed the great confidence he had in Patel, 'we are faced with difficulty, and difficulties seem to be increasing.... The problem of the States is difficult. But I know you will successfully tackle it'.[4]

Bhopal was sly and aggressive, who surreptitiously but swiftly moved from one Prince to another, tempting one and all to join hands with him in torpedoing Patel's dream of One India. Due to active support of the Political Department and its powerful Secretary, Conrad Corfield, he played the game from a position of advantage. He was also manoeuvring at the behest of Jinnah with the sole aim to dismember India with multiple fractures. Such Balkanisation would have had devastating implications in Indian history. Only Patel seemed to have the strength and political acumen to meet the formidable challenge and avert the catastrophe. He did that with rare boldness and wisdom, and succeeded in making Bhopal lick the dust.

Due to encouragement of Corfield and Jinnah, Bhopal had evolved two objectives—to make efforts to evolve a 'Third Force' out the States, and to secure their Accession to Pakistan, if not immediately but ultimately. Along with the Residents and Agents, he endeavoured to persuade the Hamlets among the Princes to form independent confederations outside the Indian Union. As Jinnah's emissary and one of his closest advisers,

Bhopal was 'not averse to playing an important role in the higher politics of Pakistan'.[5]

Bhopal played an anti-India role in the proceedings of the States' Negotiating Committee on the issue of the Princes joining the Constituent Assembly. The Nawab of Bhopal insisted that the Constituent Assembly should ratify the understanding reached between the two negotiating committees before the States could enter the Constituent Assembly. The Maharaja of Patiala, however, disagreed with the views of Bhopal and urged that the States should join the Assembly. The Nawab of Bhopal made further efforts to dissuade rulers from entering the Constituent Assembly by addressing a personal appeal to them. Here too, Bhopal had to lick the dust when the Maharaja of Patiala announced that he was sending his representatives to the Constituent Assembly because he felt that the stage for the States' participation in the Constitution-making process had definitely come, and that any delay in doing so would be prejudicial not only to his own interests but also to the wider interests of the country. The Maharaja of Bikaner, and other rulers who followed his lead, fully supported the stand taken by the Maharaja of Patiala and decided to send representatives to the Constituent Assembly. Subsequently, the representatives of the States of Baroda, Bikaner, Cochin, Jaipur, Jodhpur, Patiala and Rewa took their seats in the Constituent Assembly. Thereafter, representatives from other States started trickling in to the Constituent Assembly one after another. These developments foiled the designs of Corfield and Jinnah and demorlised Bhopal.

The Nawab of Bhopal had attempted to browbeat weak, vacillating Princes by prophesying 'bloodshed and chaos' in the States if a time-limit on their joining the Constituent Assembly was imposed. He tried to influence them by word of mouth, besides pressing into service his Pakistani-dominated Secretariat, to make them adopt a policy of 'wait and see'. In spite of the shrewdness Bhopal possessed and the patronage he enjoyed of the Political Department, Patel outmanoeuvred him and made him suffer a humiliating defeat at the hands of the Maharajas. And, also through vocal opposition built up within and outside the Chamber by the States Prime Ministers—Dewans Mirza Ismail of Mysore, VT Krishnamachari of Udaipur, Panikkar of Bikaner and BL Mitter of Baroda.

Panikkar and some other Dewans believed that Bhopal was acting 'as an agent of Pakistan' and that 'Bhopal came forward as the standard bearer for Hyderabad', having entered into 'a compact with the Nizam whereby the former (Bhopal) agreed to use the Chamber to rally Hindu Princes to undermine Hindu power in India and the Government of Hyderabad was to finance the devious scheme'.[6] Bhopal had every hope of success. Like Jinnah, he believed that 'a government in India weakened by the hostility of the Hindu Princes to the Congress, would not dare to offend Muslim public opinion and impose its will on Nizam'. Bhopal was of the firm opinion that Hyderabad, as large as England and having a population of 17 million and a revenue of Rs 20 crore, would survive and that his 'tiny island in a Hindu ocean' could do so 'in association with Hyderabad'.[7] Such a dream turned sour with Britain's change of mind—to transfer power on 15 August 1947 and not by June 1948, as decided earlier, and in this regard Patel had played a decisive role. The speed at which events moved left the Princes bewildered. Bhopal suffered, as his isolation increased thereafter. Yet his evil genius was not quite played out—right till he acceded to the Indian Union.

As soon as Lord Mountbatten announced, on 3 June 1947, that the date of the transfer of power could be 15 August 1947, the Nawab of Bhopal resigned his chancellorship of the Chamber of Princes. In his resignation letter, he stated: 'Now that Your Excellency has indicated to us the policy of His Majesty's Government in regard to the future... the Indian States and Bhopal State would, as soon as Paramountcy is withdrawn, be assuming an independent status. I consider it desirable that I should tender my resignation of the office of Chancellor of the

Chamber of Princes with effect from today. Another reason for my resignation is that the Chamber, as now constituted, formed part of a constitutional machinery which in my opinion, will now become *functus officio*.'[8] In another letter to the Viceroy, he stated that: 'The State of Bhopal does not wish to remain associated in any manner whatsoever with the Chamber of Princes or any of its subordinate organisations. It cannot, therefore, be represented by the Standing Committee of that body and will negotiate direct with the successor governments of British India in regard to its interests, and its future relationship with Pakistan and Hindustan.'[9] On the resignation of the Nawab of Bhopal as Chancellor, the Maharaja of Patiala, then Pro-Chancellor, took over the chancellorship.

These two letters of the Nawab of Bhopal clearly indicated that he felt so embittered, and even frustrated, that he refused to attend the meeting of the Rulers and States representatives called by Mountbatten on 5 July 1947, in his capacity as Crown Representative. He dismissed it with the contemptuous remarks that the rulers had been 'invited like the Oysters to attend the tea-party with the Walrus and the Carpenter'. Mountbatten regretted to say, 'I have spent more time on Bhopal's case than on all other States put together... it would be a tragedy if he were to wreck the State by failing to come in now'.[10]

By the first week of August 1947, the Nawab of Bhopal realised that the vast majority of rulers had opted for Accession and that, if he did not come in, Bhopal would be left in an anomalous and difficult position. He wanted to know whether he could sign a Standstill Agreement without acceding. He was told that the Standstill Agreement would not be signed with the rulers who refused to accede. He then sent his Constitutional Advisor, Sir Mohammad Zafrullah Khan, for clarification of the terms of the Instrument of Accession. This could not inspire confidence in Bhopal's intentions, especially so because of Zafrullah's credentials. Zafrullah was an ardent Pakistani, who was soon to represent the Muslims on the Radcliffe Boundary

Commission and later as Pakistan's nominee in the UNO to argue Pakistan's case on Kashmir and Hyderabad. It was made clear to Zafrullah that it would be impossible to make any alternations in the Instrument of Accession and that Bhopal would have to join on the same terms as all other States. At his meeting with Mountbatten, on 11 August 1947, Bhopal sought his help to save his face. He wanted his Accession to be announced ten days after the creation of the Dominion of India—ie. by 25th August. Mountbatten expressed his helplessness unless Patel agreed. Patel was generous to grant Bhopal's request, even when Bhopal had something up his sleeve. At last the Nawab signed the Instrument of Accession.

After the announcement of his Accession on 25 August 1947, Bhopal wrote to Patel on 26 August expressing his gratitude for the spirit of accommodation Patel had shown, and an open confession of his guilt. He wrote: 'I do not disguise the fact that while the struggle was on, I used every means in my power to preserve the independence and neutrality of my State. Now that I have conceded defeat, I hope that you will find that I can be as staunch a friend as I have been an inveterate opponent. I harbour no ill feelings towards anyone, for throughout I have been treated with consideration and have received understanding and courtesy from your side. I now wish to tell you that so long as you maintain your present firm stand against the disruptive forces in the country and continue to be a friend of the States, as you have shown you are, you will find in me a loyal and faithful ally.'[11]

Patel was generous in his reply to the letter of the Nawab of Bhopal. Patel wrote:

'Quite candidly, I do not look upon the Accession of your State to the Indian Dominion as either a victory for us or defeat to you. It is only right propriety which have triumphed in the end, and, in that triumph, you and I have played our respective roles. You deserved full credit for having recognised the soundness of the position and for the courage, the honesty and boldness of having given up your earlier stand which according to us was entirely antagonistic to the interests as much of India as of your own State. I have noted with particular pleasure your assurance of support to the Dominion Government in combating disloyal elements irrespective of caste, creed or religion and your offer of loyal and faithful friendship. During the last few months, it had been a great disappointment and regret to me that your undoubted talents and abilities were not at the country's disposal in the critical times through which we were passing and I, therefore, particularly value this assurance of cooperation and friendship.'[12]

Why was Bhopal playing Jinnah's game? Obviously for a price in return for the services rendered. Bhopal hoped to succeed Jinnah as Governor General of Pakistan. The succession story saw the light of the day immediately after Jinnah's death, on 11 September 1948, when the *Civil and Military Gazette* of Lahore published a news dispatch from its New Delhi correspondent, apparently inspired by the Nawab himself. The news item indicated that the Nawab of Bhopal would succeed Jinnah as Governor-General of Pakistan. The ruling clique of Pakistan looked upon the news with disfavour, characterising it as sinister. Their reaction was that of a usurper coming to Pakistan to become the head of the State. An agitation was whipped up. A procession went through some of the main streets of Lahore staging a protest. A worked-up crowd gathered at the newspaper office on the Mall, and burnt the copies which carried the news item. The Christian News Editor got so many threatening calls that he had to seek police protection.[13]

According to HV Hodson, 'three days before this period of grace expired', Bhopal had a long talk with Patel and then saw Mountbatten, when he explained the reasons for his hesitation: 'He had ambitions to play a big role in the Muslim world in the future, and he feared that if he acceded, Jinnah would denounce him as a traitor to the Muslim cause.' Bhopal had flown to Karachi to meet Jinnah, who though 'sufficiently magnanimous' towards the Nawab, must have by then seen opposition from Liaquat Ali (then Pakistan's Prime Minister) and other Muslim leaders. It was thereafter, on his return from Pakistan, that the State of Bhopal acceded to India and its 'ruler decided not to resign his *gaddi* to his daughter, as he had intended to do in order to take office in Pakistan'.[14]

References

1. KM Munshi, *Pilgrimage to Freedom* vol-I, Bhartiya Vidya Bhavan, Bombay, 1967, p-150.

2. Ibid.

3. VP Menon, *Integration of the Indian States*, Orient Black Swan, New Delhi, 2014, p-XXI.

4. Pyarelal, *Mahatma Gandhi: The Last Phase*, vol-II Navjivan Mudranalya, Ahmedabad, 1958, p-332.

5. Alan Campbell, *Mission with Mountbatten*, Macmillan, 1985, p-147.

6. *KM Panikkar: An Autobiography*, OUP, 1979, p-148.

7. Ibid, p-151.

8. VP Menon, *Integration of the Indian States*, Orient Black Swan, New Delhi, 2014, p-78.

9. Ibid.

10. HV Hodson, *The Great Divide:Britain-India- Pakistan*, OUP, 1997, p-375.

11. VP Menon, *Integration of the Indian States*, Orient Black Swan, New Delhi, 2014, p-108.

12. Ibid.

13. Balraj Krishna, *Sardar Vallabhbhai Patel*, Rupa, New Delhi, 2013, p-371.

14. HV Hodson, *The Great Divide: Britain-India-Pakistan*, OUP, 1997, p-427.

Junagadh

After Partition, we had a huge problem. Those who partitioned the country had mental reservations. They thought that this Partition was not the last word, and they started the game immediately thereafter. Among the Kathiawar States, they went to Junagadh and got its Accession to Pakistan.... We woke up in time and those who tried to play the game saw that we were not sleeping.

—Sardar Patel

THE SARDAR'S warning that it would be suicidal for any State to ignore the compulsions of geography, the vital economic links and the will of the people was fulfilled in case of Junagadh. Up to 14 August 1947, the Dewan of the State kept up the pretense of negotiations with the Indian Dominion. On 15 August 1947, Junagadh announced that it had acceded to Pakistan. This came like a bombshell to all, and particularly to Kathiawar. Junagadh was an important maritime State with close economic, cultural and ethnic links with Kathiawar.

Junagadh was the premier State in the group of Kathiawar States. It lay in the south-west of Kathiawar. It was bounded almost entirely by other Indian States, except for the south and south-west where lies the Arabian sea. The State had no contiguity with Pakistan by land and its distance by sea, from the port of Veraval to Karachi, was about 300 miles. The area of the State was 3,337 square miles and the population (according to the Census of 1941) numbered 670,719, of whom 80 per cent were Hindus. There were several islands of Junagadh territory in the States of Gondal, Bhavnagar and Nawanagar. Similarly, parts of States which had acceded to the Indian Domonion were interspersed with Junagadh's territory. Access to these as well as to certain areas belonging to Baroda State was only possible through Junagadh. Within its borders were Hindu and Jain religious shrines which attracted pilgrims from all over India. Within its area was situated the historic temple of Somnath, which was sacked by Mahmud Ghazni in 1024 AD. Its railways and posts and telegraphs were an integral part of the Indian system. The railway police, telegraphs and telephones were administered by the Government of India.

Junagadh was a Rajput State under the Chudasama dynasty until 1472-73, when it was conquered by Sultan Muhammad Bedga of Ahmedabad. In the reign of Emperor Akbar, it became a dependency of the court of Delhi under the immediate authority of the *suba*[VII] of Ahmedabad. Sometime in 1735, when the Mughal government had fallen into decay, Sherkhan Babi, a soldier of fortune and an officer under the suba, expelled the Mughal governor and established his rule in Junagadh. The last Nawab of Junagadh was a descendant of Sherkhan Babi.

[VII] a territory measure of those times under a military officer

The Nawab, Sir Mahabatkhan Rasulkhanji, was an eccentric of rare variety. His chief preoccupation in life was dogs, of which he owned about 800, each with its human attendant. He carried his love for dogs to such lengths that he once organised a wedding of two of his pets, over which he spent a sum of rupees 20 lakh and in honour of which he proclaimed a State holiday.

The Nawab had all along been paying lip-service to the idea of a united Kathiawar. On 11 April 1947, in reply to some speculations in the Gujarati press regarding the State's attitude towards the future constitutional set-up of India, the Government of Junagadh issued a press note which contained the paragraph: 'What Junagadh pre-eminently stands for is the solidarity of Kathiawar and would welcome the formation of a self-contained group of Kathiawar States. Such a group while providing for the autonomy and entity of individual States and their subjects would be a suitable basis for cooperation in matters of common concern generally and coordination where necessary.'[1]

The clear statement had set all doubts at rest. On 22 April 1947, the Junagadh Government Gazette reproduced a speech of the Dewan, Khan Bahadur Abdul Kadir Mohammad Hussain, in the course of which he categorically repudiated allegations in the vernacular press that Junagadh was thinking of joining Pakistan; that Baluchis and Hurs had been imported into the State forces; and that the local Bahauddin College was to be affiliated with the Sind University.

The Instrument of Accession was sent to the Nawab for signature. When no reply was received by the Government of India till 12 August 1947, telegrams were sent to the Nawab and the Dewan reminding them that the last date for the receipt of intimation of signing of the Instrument of Accession was 14 August 1947. They were requested to immediately reply. Meanwhile, Sir Shah Nawaz Bhutto had taken over as Dewan in May 1947 in place of Abdul Kadir Mohammad, who had gone abroad for medical treatment. On 13 August 1947,

Shah Nawaz Bhutto, the new Dewan, replied that the matter was under consideration. Bhutto was a Muslim League politician from Karachi and father of Zulfikar Ali Bhutto, who later became Prime Minister of Pakistan.

To carry the deception further, Sir Shah Nawaz Bhutto called a conference of leading citizens the same day (13 August). On behalf of the Hindu citizens, a memorandum was presented to the Dewan. The memorandum analysed the dangers that would accrue to the State if it decided to accede to Pakistan. Apart from its geographical position and the fact that the overwhelming majority of the people were Hindus, the premier status of Junagadh in Kathiawar would be lost; the trade routes would be circumscribed; commerce and industry would be crippled and there would be an immense loss of revenue to the State. The memorandum urged that Junagadh should, therefore, accede to India.

Having thus staged a make-believe of consulting public opinion over the issue of accession, the Government of Junagadh, on 15 August 1947, announced their Accession to Pakistan. In this connection, the communique issued by the Government of Junagadh stated: 'The Government of Junagadh has during the past few weeks been faced with the problem of making its choice between Accession to the Dominion of India and Accession to the Dominion of Pakistan. It has had to take into very careful consideration every aspect of this problem. Its main pre-occupation has been to adopt a course that would, in the long run, make the largest contribution towards the permanent welfare and prosperity of the people of Junagadh and help to preserve the integrity of the State and to safeguard its independence and autonomy over the largest possible field. After anxious consideration and the careful balancing of all factors, the Government of the State has decided to accede to Pakistan and hereby announces its decision to that effect. The State is confident that its decision will be welcomed by all loyal subjects of the State who have its real welfare and prosperity at heart.'[2]

In Junagadh's Accession to Pakistan on 15 August, Patel saw 'the first danger sign for splitting India again'. He later admitted, 'After Partition, we had a huge problem. Those who partitioned the country had mental reservations. They thought that this Partition was not the last word, and they started the game immediately thereafter. Among the Kathiawar States, they went to Junagadh and got its Accession to Pakistan... We woke up in time and those who tried to play game saw that we were not sleeping'.[3]

The situation in Junagadh was in marked contrast with that of Jodhpur and one which was much to Patel's disadvantage. In the case of Jodhpur, he had foiled Jinnah's efforts to entice the Maharaja; in Junagadh, he was presented with a *fait accompli* by a Muslim ruler.

The gravity of situation was further increased by Mountbatten recognising Junagadh as 'Pakistan territory' in his report to the King, in which he stated: 'My chief concern as Governor-General was to prevent the Government of India from committing itself on the Junagadh issue to an act of war against what was now Pakistan territory.' Further in the report, Mountbatten exposed what seemed to be his major role in India as her Governor-General: 'But at the same time I was aware that, in the wider aspect, my own physical presence as Governor-General of India was the best insurance against an actual outbreak of war with Pakistan.'[4] He wanted to safeguard Pakistan's position, Mountbatten confessed to Nehru much later. 'Pakistan is in no position even to declare war, since I happen to know that their military commanders have put it to them in writing that a declaration of war with India can only end in the inevitable and ultimate defeat of Pakistan.'[5]

However, Mountbatten's views expressed to the king seemed contrary to the advice he gave to the Princes on 25 July 1947, to recognise 'geographical compulsions which cannot be evaded', as also 'the communal majorities of the ruler's subjects'.[6] Mountbatten had also told the Princes, 'You cannot run away from the Dominion Government which is your neighbour any more than you can run away from the subjects for whose welfare you are responsible'.[7]

In spite of Mountbatten's being Governor-General of India, he made a serious attempt to play a role in Junagadh which was not in India's interest. He had no control over Jinnah's actions, but he thought he could use his position as Governor-General in averting a war with Pakistan by binding India to three conditions: first, reference of Junagadh to the UNO; second, Indian troops should not enter Junagadh territory; and third, offer of holding a plebiscite in Junagadh. Patel was far too clever and strong-willed to fall into a trap laid by Mountbatten, whereas, with this as precedent, Nehru failed in that respect in Kashmir. In Hyderabad too, Mountbatten played a similar role to secure for the Nizam's Association in, not Accession to, India. Association could be terminated, not Accession, with the latter being a permanent commitment.

Patel, reluctantly, agreed to a plebiscite, even when Jinnah had not asked for it. However, he rejected outright the first two. The first would have, by giving Pakistan *locus standi* in Junagadh, internationalised the issue, as it happened later in the case of Kashmir. Patel's terse comment was, 'there was a grave disadvantage in being plaintiff in such cases'.[8] Mountbatten overlooked the fact that in Junagadh's Accession to Pakistan would lie 'Jinnah's tactical shrewdness. He must have seen—or if he did not see, it certainly turned out—that the Accession of Junagadh to Pakistan placed India in an acute dilemma from which any escape could be turned to the advantage of Pakistan'.[9] In fact, 'the Accession of Junagadh to Pakistan was the result of secret negotiations was clear from a number of letters which fell into our (Menon) hands after both the Nawab and the Dewan fled from the State. In one of these, Shah Nawaz Bhutto had written to Jinnah about the interview granted to him by the latter on 16 July 1947, in which Jinnah had advised the Nawab 'to keep out under any circumstances until 15 August and referred to Jinnah's assurances that he would not allow Junagadh to starve as Veraval (port) is not far from Karachi'.[10]

Bhutto was in close contact with Jinnah. Obeying Jinnah's advice, Bhutto did nothing until 15 August. On that day, Pakistan having come into being, Junagadh announced its decision to accede to it. The newspapers of 17 August 1947 brought the news to Patel, who asked the Ministry of External Affairs, which was in Nehru's charge, to discover whether Pakistan intended to accept the Accession. After shirking an answer for almost a month, the Government of Pakistan sent a telegram on 13 September 1947, that the Accession had been accepted.

There was also the danger of Pakistan securing a foothold in Junagadh by landing troops through its port of Veraval, a course she secretly adopted later in Kashmir by sending tribal invaders there. Once Pakistani troops were on Junagadh soil, it would have been difficult for India to dislodge them from there. Patel refused to oblige Mountbatten on two grounds. The first, according to him, was the 'forcible dragging of our eighty per cent of Hindu population of Junagadh into Pakistan by Accession in defiance of all democratic principles'.[11] The second was that Accession to Pakistan would have set up a dangerous precedent. On Campbell-Johnson's admission, it 'would automatically be a direct challenge to the essential validity of the whole Accession policy, with disastrous effects both upon the Kathiawar States and upon the Hyderabad negotiations'.[12] The critics of Patel 'were completely silenced when Junagadh acceded to Pakistan; they realised then the possibilities of disintegration if the policy of Accession had not been implemented'.[13]

Junagadh was a seaboard State, east of Porbandar, in Kathiawar or Saurashtra, the thumb jutting out of western India and containing numerous States and fiefdoms. It's Accession and acceptance by Pakistan represented a blow to the prestige of the Government of India in Kathiawar. It caused the region's Muslims, about eleven per cent of the population, to look to this pocket and to Pakistan's capital, Karachi, rather than to New Delhi for allegiance; it generated in Junagadh's Hindu neighbours the thought to retaliate against the Nawab's regime and also against Muslims all over Kathiawar; and it raised an important question. If the Nawab and his Dewan could deliver Junagadh to Pakistan, could not the Nizam similarly offer Hyderabad to Pakistan?

Kashmir was the Queen. If India argued, as Jinnah was sure it would, that not Junagadh's ruler but its people should choose, he would make the same demand for Kashmir in case the Maharaja joined India. And in Kashmir, an India-or-Pakistan option could easily turn into a poll for and against Islam. This implication was plain, yet on 30 September 1947, Nehru told Liaquat Ali, in Mountbatten's presence, that while India objected to the Nawab's Accession, it would always be willing to abide by the verdict of a general election, plebiscite or referendum in Junagadh. Patel would not have volunteered such a commitment. Emphasising Nehru's words to Liaquat, Mountbatten added an assurance that if the need arose, Nehru would apply the principle to other States too, whereupon, in Mountbatten's words, 'Pandit Nehru nodded his head sadly. Mr Liaquat Ali Khan's eyes sparkled. There is no doubt that both the them were thinking of Kashmir'.[14]

Vallabhbhai made it plain that a plebiscite in Kashmir would be conditional on one in Hyderabad. Not prepared for the latter, Jinnah offered no plebiscite in Junagadh as well.[15] It was up to Jawaharlal, as the External Affairs Minister, to talk with Pakistan on Junagadh but when it came to dealing directly with Junagadh, Patel functioned for India. Jawaharlal was fully included by him and the Cabinet's sanction obtained for all major moves but the direction of policy was in Vallabhbhai's hands. On 19 September 1947, he had sent Menon to Junagadh. Menon found the Nawab—elusive—and Bhutto evasive.

On 24 September 1947, at Patel instance, a brigade consisting of Indian troops and soldiers from some of the Kathiawar States was positioned near Junagadh's frontiers. On

25 September, residents of Junagadh and other parts of Kathiawar gathered in Bombay and formed, with Vallabhbhai's knowledge, a provisional government for Junagadh, the *Arzi Hukumat*, with Samaldas Gandhi, a relative of Mahatma Gandhi, as its president. Rajkot became the *Hukumat's* headquarters.

Four weeks of waiting followed. Patel was giving time to Pakistan to annul the Accession or arrange a plebiscite. Patel had made up his mind that if Pakistan did neither, he would act. Not, to begin with, by sending forces into Junagadh proper, but by tackling three of Junagadh's feudatories, Manavadar, Mangrol and Babariawad. The latter two had already acceded to India, though the Sheikh of Mangrol alleged duress after freely signing the Instrument of Accession. The Nawab of Junagadh and the Government of Pakistan claimed that the feudatories lacked the discretion to accede, but Vallabhbhai disagreed. The Khan of Manavadar had not joined India but he had provoked his neighbours by arresting local leaders; the peace of Gondal State, which adjoined Manavadar, was endangered. On 21 October 1947, the Cabinet authorised the takeover of these three feudatories.

Mountbatten tried to argue against the decision, but when he saw that the Sardar was firm, he urged that the Central Reserve Police rather than the Army be used. But, Vallabhbhai rejected Mountbatten's suggestion. To Patel, the suggestion meant 'taking unnecessary risks; he was firm that the operation should be handled by the Indian Army'.[16] Manavadar was taken over on 22 October 1947, the other two on 1 November.

Meanwhile, over two-and-a-half months' political stalemate and economic stagnation had reduced Junagadh to near bankruptcy, resulting in a steep fall in the State's revenues and leading to a fast deteriorating situation. In view of the prevailing economic crisis, on 27 October 1947, Sir Shah Nawaz Bhutto wrote a pathetic letter to Jinnah, in which he described the disastrous consequences which had followed in the wake of Junagadh's Accession to Pakistan. He wrote: 'Our principal sources of revenue, railways and customs, have gone to the bottom. Food situation is terribly embarrassing though Pakistan has come to our rescue with generous allotment of foodgrains. There has been harsh treatment of Muslims on Kathiawar railway lines who have been subjected to several kinds of hardships and humiliations. Added to this, His Highness and the royal family have had to leave because our secret service gave us information in advance of serious consequences to their presence and safety. Though immediately after Accession, His Highness and myself received hundreds of messages, chiefly from Muslims, congratulating us on the decision, today our brethren are indifferent and cold. Muslims of Kathiawar have lost all enthusiasm for Pakistan.'[17]

The Nawab realised that events were not going as he had anticipated, and he decided to flee. Towards the end of October 1947, he left for Karachi with most of the members of his family, some of his dogs and much of the family jewelry. 'As the party was about to enter the plane, it was found that one of the Begums had forgotten to bring her child but the Nawab refused to wait; the plane took off, leaving the Begum behind to find her way later to the Portuguese settlement in Diu. The Nawab took with him the entire cash balances of the State and all the shares and securities in the treasury.'[18]

On 2 November 1947, the *Arzi Hukumat* captured the town of Nawagadh. Five days later, on 7 November, Bhutto sent the Briton, Harvey Jones, a senior member of the Nawab's Advisory Council, to Rajkot for handing over power to Rajkot and to request Samaldas to take over the reins of government. A day later, on 8 November, Bhutto modified his request: Would the Government of India accept the reins, rather than *Arzi Hukumat*? The new proposal went to NM Buch, New Delhi's Commissioner for the States of Western India and Gujarat. Samaldas voiced no objection. Late that night, Buch passed on the news over the phone to Menon during a dinner at which Nehru and Mountbatten were also present. Prodded by

Mountbatten, Jawaharlal and Menon drafted a conciliatory telegram for Pakistan, stating that the Government of India was acceding to Bhutto's request but would ascertain wishes of the people of Junagadh before accepting the State *de jure*.

It was past midnight. Menon went to 1 Aurangzeb Road, New Delhi, woke Patel up and showed him the draft. 'He was strongly of the opinion that an offer of plebiscite should not be made. He pointed out that the Nawab had already fled, that the administration had broken down, and that as the Dewan had been unable to carry on, he had voluntarily offered to hand the State over to the Government of India. The vast majority of the people in the State were non-Muslims. In these circumstances, to commit ourselves to a plebiscite in regard to Accession was unnecessary and uncalled for. However, after a good deal of further discussion, Sardar finally agreed to the issue of telegram.'[19]

NM Buch and an Indian Army officer, Brigadier Gurdial Singh, entered Junagadh on the afternoon of 8 November 1947, the State's soldiers were disarmed and reigns taken over. Bhutto had left for Karachi the previous evening.

However, Liaquat Ali did not accept the Accession of Junagadh to India. He stated that since Junagadh acceded to Pakistan, neither the Dewan nor the ruler could negotiate a temporary or permanent settlement with India, and that it was a violation of Pakistan territory and a breach of international law. Since Junagadh was the States Ministry's responsibility, Patel had the upper hand in playing a master tactician's game. Understanding Patel, Mountbatten and his advisors had hoped that 'Patel would be satisfied for a decision on the occupation of Junagadh itself to lie in the pending tray until greater problems were safely resolved'.[20] Mountbatten was tactfully left in the dark. By the time he discovered what was afoot, troops were already on the move. According to Campbell-Johnson: 'All these developments were only brought to Mountbatten's notice late in the evening (of 8th November). It is the first time since the transfer of power that the Government have carried out a major act of policy without fully consulting or notifying him in advance of the event. He feels this may be due to Patel's and VP's (Menon) desire to spare him from embarrassment.'[21]

Patel arrived in Junagadh on 13 November 1947, four days after its surrender, and spoke to a large crowd on the grounds of Bahauddin College. After complimenting Bhutto and Harvey Jones for their realism and the Indian forces for their restraint, he touched base on the subject of Hyderabad: 'If Hyderabad does not see the writing on the wall, it goes the way Junagadh has gone.'[22] And then dramatically, 'by way of oratorical flourish, asked the audience to indicate whether they wished the State to accede to India or Pakistan. Over ten thousand hands were immediately raised in favour of Accession to India'.[23]

Patel also did some plain speaking, 'The action of Nawab of Junagadh would be a lesson to those who are persisting in their chimera of attachment to an authority with which they have no natural ties... The State is no property of a single individual. Paramountcy has lapsed—certainly not by the efforts of the Princes, but by those of the people'.[24]

A plebiscite, as Patel had promised, was held on 20 February 1948, after normal conditions were restored—which went overwhelmingly in favour of India. A senior judicial officer of the ICS, CB Nagarkar, who incidentally, was neither Hindu nor Muslim, was asked to supervise it. Out of the total of 201,457 registered voters 190,870 exercised their franchise. Of this number only 91 cast their votes in favour of Accession to Pakistan. A referendum was held at the same time in Mangrol and Manavadar, as well as in Babariawad, Bantwa and Sardargarh. Out of 31,434 votes cast in these areas, only 39 were for Accession to Pakistan. Jossleyn Hennessy of the *Sunday Times* and Douglas Brown of the *Daily Telegraph*, who were in Junagadh at that time, reported that they could find little fault with the manner in which the referendum was conducted.

Patel was the recipient of congratulations from many quarters for his 'crowning success', especially the Princes who eulogised over his 'noble efforts' in achieving 'a unique victory over Junagadh without causing loss of life and property'. All Kathiawar's Princes and people felt grateful to Patel for 'preserving the integrity and unity of Kathiawar by (his) timely action'. [25]

After the Junagadh rally, Patel visited Somnath temple at Prabhas Patnan, with him was NV Gadgil, his colleague in the Cabinet. Both were 'visibly moved to find the temple, which had once been the glory of India, so dilapidated, neglected and forlorn'.[26] Gadgil felt that the temple should be renovated. He mentioned the idea to Patel, who at once agreed and publicly proposed it. The Jamsahab of Nawanagar, who was with them, donated rupees one lakh on the spot, and Samaldas announced that the *Arzi Hukumat* would give Rs 51,000. Gadgil's Ministry, responsible for public works, undertook the task and the Cabinet approved it; but after a discussion between Gandhi and Patel, it was decided that a trust should renovate the temple with funds from the public. The two agreed that India's government was not a theocratic one and did not belong to any particular religion. It was secular and temple should not be built or rebuilt by it. By the time Somnath was renovated, Patel, who had agreed to perform the inaugural ceremony, was dead. In his place President Rajendra Prasad discharged the role, ignoring objections voiced by his Prime Minister, Jawaharlal Nehru.[27]

References

1. VP Menon, *Integration of the Indian States*, Orient Black Swan, New Delhi, 2014, p-115.
2. Ibid, p-116.
3. Sardar Patel, *In Tune with Millions*, vol-III Vallabhbhai Patel Smarak Bhavan, Ahmedabad, 1975, p-4-5.
4. HV Hodson, *The Great Divide:Britain-India-Pakistan*, OUP, 1997, p-430.

5. *Sardar Patel's Correspondence*, vol-I, ed: Durga Das. Navjivan Publishing House, Ahmedabad, 1971, p-220.
6. Alan Campbell Johnson, *Mission with Mountbatten*, Macmillan Publishing Company, 1985, p-192.
7. Ibid, p-141.
8. VP Menon, *Integration of the Indian States*, Orient Black Swan, New Delhi, 2014, p-126.
9. HV Hodson, *The Great Divide:Britain-India-Pakistan*, OUP, 1997, p-430.
10. VP Menon, the *Integration of the Indian States*, Orient Black Swan, New Delhi, 2014, p-118.
11. *Sardar's Letters-Mostly unknown*, vol-V, ed. Maniben, Vallabhbhai Samarak Bhavan, Ahmedabad, 1977, p-74.
12. Allan Campbell-Johnson, *Mission with Mountbatten*, Macmillan Publishing Company, 1985, p-192.
13. VP Menon, *Integration of the Indian States*, Orient Black Swan, New Delhi, 2014, p-102.
14. HV Hodson, *The Great Divide: Britain-India-Pakistan*, Oxford, 1997, p-436.
15. Patel's speech in Junagadh, 13.11.1947, *Sardar Patel,* Birth Centenary, ed. GM Nandurkar, Sardar Vallabhbhai Patel Smarak Bhavan, 1975, p-68.
16. VP Menon, *Integration of the Indian States*, Orient Black Swan, New Delhi, 2014, p-129.
17. Ibid, p-130.
18. Ibid, p-129.
19. Ibid, p-132.
20. Alan Campbell-Johnson, *Mission with Mountbatten*, Macmillan Publishing Company, 1985, p-237.
21. Ibid.
22. Hindustan *Times*, 14.11.1947.
23. VP Menon, *Integration of Indian States*, Orient Black Swan, New Delhi, 2014, p-135.
24. Sardar Patel, *In Tune with Millions*, vol-II, Vallabhbhai Smarak Bhawan, Ahmedabad, 1975, p-62.
25. *Sardar Patel's Correspondence*, vol-VII ed-Durga Das, Navjivan Publishing House, Ahmedabad, 1971, p-392-93.
26. VP Menon, *Integration of States*, Orient Black Swan, New Delhi, 2014, p-135.
27. KM Munshi, *Pilgrimage to Freedom* vol-I, Bhartiya Vidya Bhavan, Bombay, 1967, p-288.

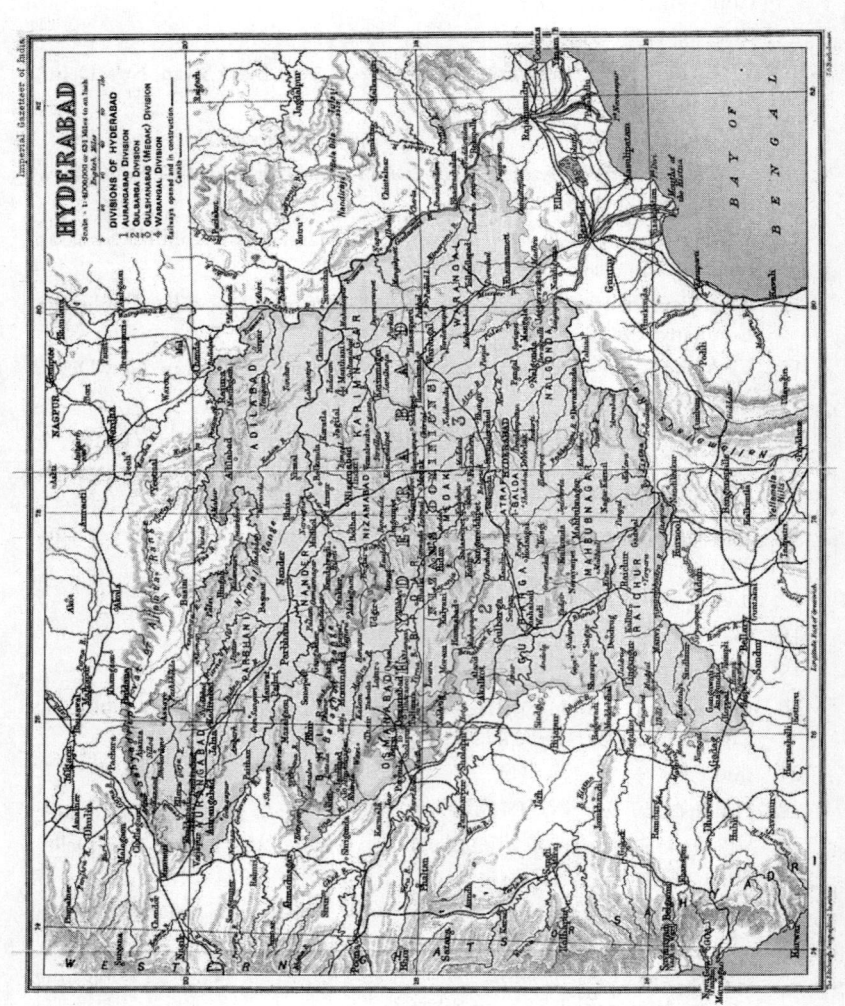

Hyderabad

Patel was the man 'who by his decisiveness resolved the great Hyderabad crisis'. Hyderabad, a State covering 80,000 square miles in the heart of peninsular India, was at that time in the grip of an unscrupulous minority which aimed at secession from India. Had the bid succeeded, India might not have survived as a political unit. This situation needed a man of iron who would not balk at coercive action, and in Sardar, India had, at the vital moment, just the man.

—W Gordon Garham

THE DAYDREAMS of the Nizam and some of his advisors, that Hyderabad was an independent State, had no roots in history. At no time had Hyderabad been an independent State.

The State of Hyderabad was founded by Mir Qamruddin Chin Qilich Khan. He was a son of Aurangzeb's general, Ghaziuddin Khan Feroz Jang. In 1713, six years after Aurangzeb's death, emperor Farrukhsiyar made Mir Qamruddin subedar of the Deccan, with the title of 'Nizam-ul-Mulk' (Regulator of the Realm). Later, emperor Muhammad Shah conferred on him the title of Asaf Jah, by which title the dynasty is still known. By 1724, Mir Qamruddin had made himself virtually independent of Delhi, although he and his successors continued to profess a nominal allegiance to the Mughal emperor right up to 1858, when the British Crown assumed the governance of India.

In 1748, Asaf Jah died. A war of succession between his two sons followed. Joseph-François Dupleix, the founder of French power in India, found an enlarged field for manoeuvre by giving support to the claim of Salbat Jah, one of the two contending heirs to the throne of Hyderabad. Charles Bussey, the brilliant French general, was stationed at Hyderabad to protect Salbat from the Marathas. In return, Dupleix acquired for the French the four districts called the northern Circars (now part of Andhra province – small principalities in coastal regions).

In 1761, Salbat was deposed by his younger brother Nizam Ali Khan, who ordered an invasion of the Carnatic. The Hyderabad forces were repulsed by the British and when peace was concluded by the Treaty of 1766, the Nizam placed himself under British protection. In 1767, in the quest for independence, the Nizam broke his treaty with the British and allied himself with Hyder Ali of Mysore. The joint forces of Hyder Ali and the Nizam, however, were defeated and by the Treaty of Masulipatam of 1768, the British again reimposed their military protection upon the Nizam. From 1768 onwards, a British Resident and a subsidiary force were stationed in Hyderabad.

However, the Nizam was irresponsible in his intrigues. Behind the back of the Resident, he entered into an alliance with the Marathas to oust the British. The plan failed. The East India Company stationed an officer of the King's Army at the Nizam's court with the orders to pursue a policy of increasing the British hold over the Deccan at the cost of Hyderabad and to keep the Nizam helpless.

Between the period when Warren Hastings opened up the prospects of British Power in India and when Wellesley tried to establish British Paramountcy, the conditions in the Nizam's territories were extremely miserable. When Warren Hastings left India in 1784, on a voyage home, he foresaw that the Nizam, once a lower officer of the Mughal Emperor, was destined to be a satellite, either of the rising power of the Marathas or of the East India Company. He described the Nizam's position as follows:

'His dominions are of small extent and scanty revenue; his military strength is represented to be most contemptible; nor was he at any period of his life distinguished for personal courage or the spirit of enterprise. On the contrary, it seems to have been his constant and ruling maxim to foment the incentives of war among his neighbours, to profit by their weakness and embarrassments, but to avoid being a party himself in any of their contests, and to submit even to humiliating sacrifices rather then subject himself to the chances of war.'[1]

In 1799, the Nizam aided the East India Company in the war with Tipu Sultan and after the latter's defeat and death, the British gave a part of its territories to the Nizam. In the following year, the Nizam was obliged to cede a portion of it back to the British in order to meet the cost of the increased subsidiary force.

The death of Nizam Ali Khan and the succession of his eldest surviving son, Sikandar Jah occurred on 7 August 1803, three days after the outbreak of the second British-Maratha War. Before the end of the year, the war was concluded and the Treaty of Deogaon signed. Under this treaty the Nizam, for the help rendered by him to the British, obtained the whole of Berar, west of Wardha.

Sikandar Jah died on 21 May 1829 and was succeeded by his eldest son, Nasir-Ud-Daula. By 1852, the pay of the British contingent had fallen heavily into arrears. The officers and men were put to such a pitiable condition that the only way to relieve them was by making direct payments to them from the company's treasury. The Governor General demanded territorial security from the Nizam in return for these payments. By the Treaty of

1853, the province of Berar, along with certain districts in the Raichur Doab and on the western frontier of Hyderabad, were assigned for this purpose, their administration being taken over by British officers under the control of the Resident[VIII] at Hyderabad.

In 1857, when several parts of the country had risen in revolt against the British, the Muslims in Hyderabad had been eager to join the Great Revolt. The British Residency was twice attacked and the Resident himself was set upon when he was leaving the 'darbar' of the Nizam. For three months, the future of India was tied to the decision of Hyderabad. Had it joined the Great Revolt, Madras, Mysore and Travancore-Cochin would have risen simultaneously. But, it did not so happen.

After the 1857 revolt, the British became more careful. The military contingent which was stationed at Secunderabad was kept ready for any such eventuality. The Resident remained the virtual master of the State, and, as the then Government of India (Queen Victoria's) put it bluntly to the Nizam—that the position of the Resident as representing the Paramount Government of India must always be one of commanding influence and power, and that the Nizam was expected to seek consent and support on all important occasions.

The Resident (Col Cuthbert Davidson), in whom all the real authority was vested, appointed the Chief Minister of the Nizam. Later, he also appointed and removed ministers and enforced constitutional, financial and even administrative reforms. Sir Arthur Lothian, in his postmortem examination of British Policy in Hyderabad, admits that the Residents had, if necessary, to take 'a more intimate part behind the scenes in assisting the proper working of the administration in Hyderabad than in any other State'.[2]

During the one hundred and fifty years since 1798, Hyderabad became progressively more integrated within the

---

[VIII] Which included the tenure of the famous Major-General William Kirkpatrick (1795-1797) and Col James Achilles Kirkpatric, known as the White Mughal (1797-1805), as the early Residents

political and economic structure of India than any of the other States. Its importance, land-locked as it was by the States of Bombay, Madhya Pradesh and Madras, was never overlooked, vital as it was as a link in the unity of India. In 1930, Sir William Barton, an able Resident of Hyderabad, submitted a memorandum containing the following significant observations: 'Flung almost across the Indian peninsula, the great State of Hyderabad holds a strategic position of the first importance both from the political and military point of view. In an emergency, it could practically isolate the South from the North.'[3]

Inspite of Hyderabad's political importance, the Nizam was reminded of his subservience whenever an occasion arose. Lord Reading, in his famous letter of 26 March 1926, addressed to Nizam, refused to treat the Indian Princes as equals, whatever the language of treaties. According to the Viceroy, 'responsibility for the defence and internal security of the country gave the Paramount Power the right to intervene at its discretion in the internal affairs of the State'.[4]

In fact, Hyderabad at no time had relations with any foreign country. The defence of its frontiers was maintained as part of the organic defence structure of British India, the Nizam's army was no more than an appendix of the Indian army. The Government of India, under its last arrangement, called the Indian States Forces Scheme of 1939, increased, decreased, armed and equipped the Nizam's army without the Nizam's consent. Hyderabad could not import weapons of precision or manufacture ammunition.

The internal peace and tranquility of the State was also the responsibility of the Government of India. The arterial communications, the railways as also the postal, telegraphic and telephonic systems, were all laid through Hyderabad and operated upon by the Government of India.

The responsibility assumed by the Government of India required, for its efficient discharge, that the Nizam 'did everything to be done and abstained from every course of action declared dangerous to the common safety or the safety of any other part of India'.[5] By the Government of India Act, 1935, the Political Department of the Government of India was entrusted to the Governor-General as Crown Representative.

The trade and commerce in Hyderabad, in fact its whole economy, was bound up with that of India. The banks in Hyderabad were branches of the British-Indian banks that were scheduled with the Reserve Bank. The State depended for its revenues upon its trade with the rest of the country. It's foodgrains as well as its manufactured and imported articles came from or through the Indian provinces. Its currency, kept alive by the British to feed the vanity of the Nizam, was linked with the Indian currency at a fixed rate of exchange.

The Nizam in 1947, Mir Usman Ali Khan Bahadur, was the seventh in the line. He succeeded to the simhasana on 29 August 1911. In 1918, the title of 'His Exalted Highness' was conferred on him as a hereditary distinction. Shortly thereafter, by an autographed letter from the King, he was granted the title of 'Faithful Ally of the British Government'.

The population of Hyderabad was nearly sixteen million which was closely connected by social, religious and cultural bonds with the rest of India. The population mainly comprised 86 per cent Hindus, 12½ per cent Muslims, 1½ per cent Christians and others. A large number of people spoke Telugu, Marathi and Kannada. Urdu was spoken mostly by the small number of ruling Muslim elite until a new policy of Urduising the State was introduced. The annual revenue of Hyderabad was Rs 26 crore. Its area was over 82,000 square miles. It was this Hyderabad which the Nizam intended to make an independent Islamic State.

Although the population of Hyderabad was over 86 per cent Hindu, the civil services, the police and the army were the close preserve of the Muslims. Even in the representation in the Legislative Assembly, which the Nizam had set up in 1946, the Muslims had the majority over the Hindus in a House of 132.

Nizam's claim for dominion status for his state

Soon after the announcement of Lord Mountbatten's plan of 3 June 1947, the Nizam issued a *firman*[IX] declaring his intention not to send representatives to the Constituent Assembly of either Pakistan or India, and making it clear that on 15 August 1947, he would be entitled to resume the status of an independent sovereign. It had been his ambition to secure Dominion status for his State, on the withdrawal of the British, and treatment thereafter as a member of the British Commonwealth of Nations. When he saw that Clause 7 of the Indian Independence Bill did not permit the grant of Dominion status to an Indian State, he protested against 'the way in which my State is being abandoned by its old ally, the British Government, and the ties which have bound me in loyal devotion to the King Emperor are being severed'.[6]

Mountbatten dispelled all doubts when he told the Nizam's delegation on 11 July 1947, that His Majesty's Government would not agree to Hyderabad becoming a member of the British Commonwealth except through either of the two Dominions of India or Pakistan. This humbled the Nizam's pride, but did not dishearten him as he had other plans up his sleeve: to gain time by engaging India in prolonged constitutional negotiation through Walter Monckton (Nizam's Constitutional Advisor), to make preparations for military confrontation with India by purchase of arms through foreign sources, and to build up the Ittehad-ul-Muslimeen[X] so as to 'arm himself with a view to crushing the Hindu subjects',[7] and to encourage at the same time migration of Muslims from some of the Indian provinces and States to his State.

Earlier, on 8 August 8 1947, it was on Monckton's advice that the Nizam wrote to Mountbatten that he could not contemplate bringing Hyderabad into organic union with either Pakistan or India, but was prepared to enter into a treaty which guaranteed the integrity and independent identity of his State under three

---

[IX] Soverign edict
[X] Ittehad: Coalition of the faithful

conditions: in the event of war between India and Pakistan, Hyderabad would remain neutral; Hyderabad should have the right to appoint Agents-General wherever it thought fit; and if India seceded from the British Commonwealth, Hyderabad would be free to review the situation *de novo*.

Seeing such dangerous trends, Patel could not restrain himself from telling Mountbatten sternly on 24 August 1947, '... I wish to let your Excellency know my mind before you meet the (Nizam's) delegation. I see no alternative but to insist on the Nizam's Accession to the Dominion of India. The least variations in the Instrument of Accession or arrangement regarding the State's association with the Dominion in regard to the three subjects, would not only expose me to the charge of breach of faith with the States that have already joined the Dominion, but would create the impression that advantage lay in holding out rather than coming in, and that, while no special merit attached to Accession, a beneficial position could be secured by keeping out. This is bound to have most unfortunate consequences in our future negotiations for Accession to the Union'. Patel also informed Mountbatten: 'I have authentic information that the recent activities of the Ittehad-ul-Mussalmeen are designed almost to create a feeling of terror amongst the non-Muslim population, so that its agitation in favour of the independence of Hyderabad, with possible alliance with Pakistan, should flourish.'[8]

The developing situation and the attitude of the Nizam was highly distressing and humiliating for Patel. It was humiliating for Patel to let Mountbatten, a foreigner and a Britisher responsible for the partitioning of the country, handle negotiations which primarily concerned him and his Ministry of States. However, he had to swallow his pride by agreeing to this arrangement, which helped Nehru and Patel to set aside their different approaches and overcome, though temporarily, the frequent differences between them. The administrator in Patel saw the problem 'in somewhat simplistic strategic terms', and 'instinctively felt that India could not survive with a hostile force in its belly, as it were'.⁹

On the other hand, Nehru was 'preoccupied with emotional problems of the Muslim minority in India. He was anxious that nothing should be done to hurt their feelings, and he thought that any rough treatment to the Nizam, the premier Muslim ruler, would seriously hurt their feelings'. In order to resolve their difference, 'Pandit Nehru suggested that the matter may be left for negotiations by Lord Mountbatten. Although Sardar felt most strongly on the subject, he agreed to this proposal'.¹⁰ To Patel, this was sheer appeasement, very much in contrast with the treatment meted out to the Maharaja of Jammu and Kashmir by Nehru. Nevertheless, for the sake of harmony and ultimate achievement of what he desired, Patel agreed to Nehru's suggestion but kept the reins in his hand, as Hyderabad, unlike Kashmir, was under the State Ministry's charge.

His firm grip neither allowed Hyderabad to be internationalised, as it happened with Kashmir, nor permitted the slightest shift in his irrevocable attitude. Patel knew his mind better than anyone else. And he also knew the action he was to take in the end. If such action was delayed, it was due to the combined opposition Patel faced, first from Nehru and Mountbatten and later from Nehru and Rajagopalachari and also due to the massive heart-attack he suffered early in March 1948. In order to ensure a close watch on Mountbatten's negotiation, as also to apply a brake on him whenever it became necessary, Patel made his most trusted lieutenant, VP Menon, a co-negotiator.

Meanwhile, Monckton, who was playing a key role from Nizam's side, disclosed his approach in his note of 15 September 1947, to the Nizam's Executive Council: 'My object has been to advise a course calculated to obtain for Hyderabad the maximum degree of real, practical independence, compatible with its prosperity and security... that Hyderabad is landlocked in the belly of Hindustan; that Pakistan is not yet in a sufficiently established state to be able to give effective help; that, if

Hyderabad is to remain independent, she must stand on her own feet.... The guiding principle has been to avoid executing an Instrument of Accession.' Moncton then explained what an agreement of 'Association' as opposed to 'Accession', means: that 'a treaty or agreement, short of Accession, preserves independence in law, whereas Accession destroys it and involves merger or Organic Union; that, when circumstances change, eg. if Pakistan and Hyderabad grew strong enough to warrant it, the treaty can be denounced.... Once a State has acceded to the Dominion, it will find it hard to extricate itself'. Monckton revealed his mind when he said, 'I wanted the negotiations to continue for Hyderabad as long as possible after 15th August.... The longer they continue the better for us... we have breathing space to get ready for the economic and political conflict if it comes.... I know that Patel was and is against any extension of time to Hyderabad and that the Governor-General prevailed over the Cabinet of the Dominion to allow him personally two months' time to see whether he and I, who had known each other intimately for many years publicly and privately, could find a compromise satisfactory to both sides'.[11]

Encouraged by Moncton's note, the Nizam wrote to Mountbatten on 18 September 1947, 'Hyderabad was ready and willing to make such a treaty of Association with India as it would not only secure friendly relations, but would lead to fullest cooperation'.[12] 'Simultaneously with this approach to us', writes Menon, 'the Nizam got into contact with Jinnah with a view to securing the services of Sir Zafrullah Khan as the President of his Executive Council. In this, he was unsuccessful, as Sir Zafrullah Khan had been deputed to lead the Pakistan delegation to the UNO'.[13] After this, an uncertainty hung over Hyderabad. Delegation after delegation, with leaders and members changing now and again, began visiting New Delhi for negotiations with Mountbatten, yet, no agreement was in sight. About mid-October, Patel got completely fed up and wanted to break off the negotiations. This upset Mountbatten. He pleaded,

'It would be a great pity if the negotiations were to break down'.[14] Towards the end of October, the Nizam wrote to say that, 'if negotiations with the Government of India were to break down, he would immediately negotiate and conclude an agreement with Pakistan. Sir Sultan Ahmad told Lord Mountbatten and myself (VP Menon) that the Nizam had sent two persons to Karachi who had returned on 29 October'.[15] Patel felt so annoyed at the Nizam's impertinence that he told Menon that, 'the only decent course for us was to send back the new delegation by the very same plane by which it has arrived'.[16]

Patel's difficulties in dealing with Hyderabad was partly due to Nehru's preference for softer methods and partly due to Menon's persuasion. Apart from Lord Mountbatten's understandable sympathy for the Muslim position in Hyderabad, shared by Pandit Nehru, in anything that concerned Pakistan even indirectly, he was for compromise and conciliation to the maximum extent possible, in order to prevent a confrontation, at least during his time. The Nizam had selected Sir Walter Monckton, a leading British lawyer of his day, as his Constitutional and Legal Adviser in these matters. Monckton wielded considerable influence over Lord Mountbatten, both personally and politically. Lord Mountbatten was very keen to avoid any complications regarding 'his position with Winston Churchill and his political associates. His choice of Lord Ismay as a member of his staff was influenced by the consideration that this would enable him to keep up his links with the Conservative Party, notwithstanding the fact that it was the Labour government[XI] which had selected him for the Indian Viceroyalty.

'This was particularly so since he knew he might have to adopt lines in India which might not fit in with Churchill's way of looking at the Indian problem. Winston Churchill's position

---

[XI] Led by Clement Attlee

regarding Hyderabad was well known, how could a champion of the Empire desert its faithful ally? All these factors placed the Hyderabad problem in a state of flux but nothing made the problem so confusing as the attitude of the Ruler who, despite his shrewdness, intelligence and culture, alternated between Machiavellian tactics and cowardice and could not take a direct stand.'[17]

In view of Lord Mountbatten's influence on Pandit Nehru and even on Gandhi, Patel found himself in a helpless position in settling the problem with his accustomed swiftness. The issue was complicated by the regular contacts of the Nizam with Pakistan, the visits of prominent Hyderabadis to Karachi, the migrations that were taking place from Hyderabad to Pakistan, the regular line of communications which Sydney Cotton (an Australian arms dealer) had established between Karachi and Hyderabad. The patience and resourcefulness of the leading negotiators survived all these in the pathetic hope that all is well that ends well. Formula after formula was devised to meet the situation and, as always happens in such formula-hunting activities, it was Indian interests which were compromised. Patel, to whom the sacrifice of Indian interests was anathema, had to struggle against all these, often only to give in here and there, and found it all a painful and distressing experience. He helplessly submitted, but entertained the hope that one day, they would all have to agree that there was no way out except to adopt a drastic course.

Razakars and Riots

The situation within Hyderabad had worsened with the outbreak of serious communal riots in Secunderabad on 25 August 1947. The police were entirely manned by Muslims. Aravamudh Aiyangar wrote on 29 August: 'Muslims were unwilling to protect the life or property of a Hindu', and 'armed Pathans, Rohillas and Arabs are allowed to roam about without let or hindrance, terrorising the people. This caused an exodus of Hindus... the local Muslim League, which has been well organised and supplied with arms, is only waiting for an opportunity to attack Hindus *en masse*... if Hyderabad joins the Union, there will be mass slaughter on a large scale....' Again he reported on 23 October, '...one Lancaster (bomber plane) landed at Begumpet aerodrome direct from Pakistan. It is suspected that it contained arms and ammunition'.[18]

Earlier, on 19 September 1947, Patel had told Mountbatten, 'The Nizam has mortgaged his future to his own Frankenstein, Ittehad-ul-Muslimeen'.[19] True to this description, the razakar leader, Qasim Razvi, mounted a tirade against Patel. He said on 14 October, 'Patel belongs to the class of Hitler.... Our government is temperamentally like Chamberlin, which has no courage to face the opponent. It is afraid merely by the name of Accession. Mountbatten, like a Daniel, has come in to remove both of these from this intricate position'. Razvi then said, 'why not somebody ask this so called government (of the Nizam), what is there to prevent carrying on negotiations with Pakistan and other Muslim and non-Muslim countries after the Hyderabad Independence Act and His Majesty the Nizam's firman?' And he went on to answer, 'There is nothing to prevent. It is merely the threat of Patel'.[20]

Qasim Razvi was a fanatic with a single-track mind. He believed himself to be a heaven-appointed leader, whose mission was to liberate the Muslims of the Deccan from the Indian Union. But this was only the first step. The next was to be the annexation of the Circars (small principalities in coastal regions), the east coast districts of the Province of Madras, to Hyderabad. His Muslim crusaders were then to march to Delhi to replant the Asafia flag (flag of Hyderabad) on the Red Fort of the Mughals , and never they were to rest till 'the waves of the Bay of Bengal washed the feet of our sovereign'![21] He insisted on the right of the Musalman to enslave the Hindu, who was none but Kafir.

Within less than a year, Razvi had succeeded in becoming an irresistible driving force in Hyderabad, leading even the Nizam to the belief that his cherished aim was almost within his grasp. He had launched insensate attacks against the terror-stricken Hindus of Hyderabad, carried fire and sword to hundreds of harmless and unarmed villages, and at last forced the Government of India to take police action to put an end to his terrorist activities.

Under Razvi, the razakars enveloped themselves in the cloak of holy crusaders. When joining the corps, a razakar took a solemn pledge to sacrifice his life for the Ittehad and Hyderabad when called upon to do so by their leader. In the name of Allah, the pledge ran, 'I do hereby promise to fight to the last to maintain the supremacy of the Muslim power in Deccan'.[22] 'In January 1948, when I (KM Munshi) went to Hyderabad, more than thirty thousand volunteers—men, women and children—were on the rolls of the Corps [the razakar force]. By July-August 1948, over a hundred thousand had been enrolled. The target was five times that number.'[23]

The activities of the razakars were varied. They held demonstrations in Hyderabad and other towns in the districts, denouncing all who opposed them in violent terms. They harassed individuals who favoured Accession to the Union or responsible government in the State. They overawed the public by staging marches on foot or cycles, in buses or lorries. While on the march, they brandished spears and swords and sometimes fired blank shots in the air. The razakars, with or without the cooperation of the Nizam's police, took punitive action against villages on different pretexts. They also raided border villages in the Union in order to inflict reprisals for the act of some unknown suspect.

The razakars ran schools of espionage and propaganda. They infiltrated various territories of the Indian Union and established a network of agents to smuggle arms and recruit Muslim volunteers for the Hyderabad police or the army. Some of the more adventurous spirits among them also spread out in different parts of the country to rouse Muslim feeling against the Union and to encourage an exodus to Hyderabad. The Ittehad leaders maintained that the razakar movement was the spontaneous expression of the unwillingness of the Muslims of Hyderabad to accede to the Union.

The razakars had acquired almost unlimited means at their disposal with the help of the Nizam's government. They used three-ton lorries and dozens of jeeps and one-ton trucks. The Nizam's government obligingly disarmed the Hindus in village after village. The arms so recovered were used by the razakars. The razakars were also found using old firearms supplied by the Nizam's government. They also used modern weapons smuggled into the State by gun-runner Sydney Colton.

The Ittehad had a good publicity machine at its disposal in its psychological war against India. During the year 1948, it published seven daily and six weekly papers in Urdu and the Nizam Radio was at their service. Day after day, they published or broadcast attacks against the Union and often against Nehru and Patel. In the publicity campaign, the speeches of Razvi appeared prominently and frequently. Anti-Indian news items from Pakistan Radio or newspapers describing the imaginary discomfiture of the Indian army on the Kashmir front were also served up for the benefit of the gullible Muslim public of the State. Nawab Deen Yarjung, the Police Commissioner, a trusted man of Nizam, enjoyed the reputation of being a staunch supporter of Razvi and had considerable influence over him.

By 1946, the Ittehad had given up its proselytising activity, but the Nizam government continued to give large grants to mosques, which, in one form or another, went towards decoying helpless Hindus into Islam. The poor Harijans in the villages found it hard to resist such temptation or pressure, with the result the process of conversion continued. A starving Harijan family would permit one of its members to turn Muslim to earn his reward, while the rest of the family, including the convert's wife, would remain Hindu.[24] However, when the pressure was relaxed, the converted generally reverted to their ancestral religion.

When by his firman of 11 June 1947, the Nizam declared his intention of assuming the status of an independent sovereign on 15 August, the State Congress decided to launch what was known as the Accession Styagrah to realise responsible government integrated to the Indian Union. On 15 June 1947, Razvi, by way of challenge to the Congress, had announced what was already an accomplished fact, that the razakars were an armed volunteer corps and that Hyderabad would be independent as from 15 August. He also called upon the Muslims to prepare themselves for all sacrifices. These challenges and counter-challenges were followed by clashes between armed razakars and the unarmed Congress workers. The Nizam's government was a silent but appreciative spectator, for the clashes invariably ended in favour of the razakars.

On 27 July 1947, the Ittehad celebrated Independence Day in Hyderabad City. On 7 August, under the leadership of the State Congress, 'Join the Indian Union' Day was celebrated at 345 centres in the State. During these celebrations, 180 people were arrested and crowds were lathi-charged at several places. Swami Ramanand Tirtha, the President of the State Congress, was also arrested. Congress took up the challenge. It called upon the people to hoist the National Flag on all buildings on 15 August.

After the midnight of the 14th August, when the Bombay-Madras Express was passing through Hyderabad, the Hyderabad station police entered the train and removed the National Flags even from inside the compartments. On Independence Day, the processions and demonstrations flying National Flags were lathi-charged or fired upon by the police and large-scale arrests were made. Armed razakars, cooperating with the police, tore down the National Flag wherever it was found and offered it every kind of insult. Even the flags on the buildings of the Government of India did not escape their fury.

The Accession Satyagrah, launched by the State Congress, spread like a wild fire. About 9,000 people courted arrest. There was a large-scale refusal to pay the compulsory levy on food grains. Thousands of toddy trees were cut down in the villages. Hundreds of village officers resigned. Congressmen, Communists and villagers joined hands in destroying the custom's buildings in border areas. Thousands of students in schools and colleges defied laws.

Razvi also went about his mission with vigour. He declared that Hyderabad was free and independent and threatened direct action against the Nizam's government, if it ever acceded to the Union. A campaign of terrorisation of the villages which had participated in the Accession Satyagrah was launched and large number of Hindus left Secunderabad to find safety in the surrounding Union provinces.

On 27 August 1947, the Nizam by his firman declared that on 15 August, he had assumed the status of an independent sovereign. Immediately a movement was started by Ittehad to refer to him as 'His Majesty'. However, Sir Walter Monckton was emphatic in his view that the Nizam must come to terms with India. This advice brought upon him the wrath of razakars and Razvi. Thereupon, he tendered the resignation of his office to the Nizam. Hearing the news of Monckton's resignation, Lord Mountbatten exclaimed, 'we are sunk. Sir Walter was his trump card'.[25]

The razakars and their leader Razvi had a free run of the whole State and proved themselves so strong as to influence the Nizam in disregarding the advice of men like Nawab of Chhatari, Sultan Ahmad, Mirza Ismail and even Monckton (all confidants of Nizam). From every point of view, the activities of their organisation, Ittehad, were inimical to a state of harmony and peace between the Indian Dominion and the State of Hyderabad. It is not as if the Nizam was a helpless tool in their hands. He was so obsessed by the idea of his own independence, and so convinced of the strength of his own position, and the need for Muslim domination that he submitted to, if not welcomed, their activities when he could have dealt with them with a firm hand. The methods of the razakars were ruthless and their practices revolting.

Standstill Agreement to buy time for independence

Amidst bewildering confusion and deep dangers, Mountbatten, with great effort, managed to get a Standstill Agreement signed on 29 November 1947. By Article II of the Agreement, the Government of India and the Nizam agreed to appoint their agents in Hyderabad and Delhi respectively, and to give them facility for the discharge of their functions. In accordance with Article II of the Standstill Agreement, the Government of India appointed KM Munshi as their Agent-General in Hyderabad. When the Government of India informed the Government of Hyderabad of Munshi's appointment, the Nizam made certain conditions. First of all he wanted Munshi to be no more than a Trade Agent. However, the Government of India did not agree to the proposal of Nizam and said that the functions of the Agent-General were certainly not confined to trade. Next, the Nizam's government raised the questions of the ceremonials to be observed on the occasion of the assumption of charge by the Agent-General. The States Ministry was against this and no ceremonies were observed, nor was there any presentation of credentials when the respective Agents-General assumed their offices.

Immediately after the Standstill Agreement, the Nizam's government issued two ordinances in quick succession. The first imposed restrictions on the export of all precious metals from Hyderabad to India. The second declared Indian currency to be not legal tender in the State. Besides several other violations of the Standstill Agreement, the government in Hyderabad informed the Government of India officially that it was their intention to appoint agents in several other foreign countries. They had already appointed a Public Relations Officer in Karachi without any reference to the Government of India.

Inspite of the hostile attitude of the Nizam, there was divergence of approach on the part of the personalities concerned towards the Standstill Agreement with Hyderabad. 'Nehru felt that the Agreement would purchase communal peace in the

South for at least one year. Lord Mountbatten was sanguine that it would allow heads to cool and hearts to soften and that before the expiry of the Agreement, the Nizam, like all other rulers would accede to India. The Nizam and his advisors conceived the Agreement as providing breathing space in which to secure the withdrawal of the Indian troops from Hyderabad and eventually to build up their position and strength to a stage when they would be able to assert the independence of the State. Sardar was doubtful of the *bona fides* of the Hyderabad Government.'[26]

Purposefully, the Nizam persued a policy of drift, of buying time, which he explained in a cable to Monckton who was in London, on 6 January 1948: 'I agreed with your opinion that no good of our hurrying up, making long term agreement with the Indian Union at the beginning of the year, but to wait and see what further developments arise before we do it, namely, towards the end of the year. Besides, we must see how Kashmir and Junagadh's case is going to be settled by UNO. After that, we can think about our own affair. Is Lord Mountbatten going to get an extension after April next, as was rumoured before? In any case, since he has got no power, what help he can give to us is obvious. In that case, his being in office or not does not affect us materially. So, we must manage our affairs in the best way we can, after taking everything into considerations.'[27] The Nizam's objectives in gaining time were: to further build his armed strength through acquisition of more arms, and completion of new airfields, to initiate 'a large-scale programme of converting Harijans to Islam',[28] and to encourage the Ittehad-ul-Mussalmeen's efforts 'to get Muslims to migrate to Hyderabad' and even 'induce ex-army Muslims or those in active service to join the Hyderabad army'.[29]

Patel had to tell Moutbatten that 'the period of two months, which we have agreed to give the State to make up its mind, is being utilised for preparations rather than for negotiations.... I am convinced that it would neither be proper nor political for us to agree to any arrangement other than Instrument of

Accession already settled between us and other States'.[30] The Nizam, realising that Patel 'will not be bamboozled into a surrender even to the slightest extent', changed his strategy to bank on Nehru, who was more accommodating than Sardar Patel, and pin faith on the chance of having a better reception when C Rajagopalachari becomes Governor-General.

From his sick-bed at Dehradun, where he had retired for convalescence after the heart-attack, in March 1948, Patel watched with exasperating helplessness the growing intransigence of the Nizam, failure of Mountbatten's effort, and a growing feeling in Hyderabad that India was not in dead earnest to take action. When Laik Ali (Prime Minister of Hyderabad) called on him, on 16 April 1948, at Dehradun, Patel told him with stunning bluntness: 'You know as well as I do where power resides and with whom the fate of the negotiations must finally lie in Hyderabad. The gentleman (Qasim Razvi) who seems to dominate Hyderabad, has given his answer. He has categorically stated that, if the Indian Dominion comes to Hyderabad, it will find nothing but the bones and ashes of one and a half crore Hindus. If that is the position, then it seriously undermines the whole future of the Nizam and his dynasty.' Patel made it clear: 'The Hyderabad problem will have to be settled as has been done in the case of other States. No other way is possible. We cannot agree to the continuance of an isolated spot which would destroy the very Union which we have built up with our blood and toil. At the same time, we do wish to maintain friendly relations and to seek a friendly solution. This does not mean that we shall ever agree to Hyderabad's independence. If its demand to maintain an independent status is persisted in, it is bound to fail.'[31]

Many reasons hardened Patel's attitude. On 26 March 1948, Laik Ali had told KM Munshi that the Nizam was willing to 'die a martyr' and that he and lakhs of Muslims who were willing to be killed. Immediately thereafter, Razvi, in a speech on 31 March, indulged in a good deal of sabre-rattling and urged the Muslims of Hyderabad not to sheathe their swords until their objective of Islamic supremacy had been achieved. He exhorted the Muslims to march forward with the Koran in one hand and the sword in the other, to hound out the enemy. The most sinister part of the speech was his declaration that the forty-five million Muslims in the Indian Union would be 'our fifth columnists in any showdown'.

Mountbatten was worried because the question of Accession of Hyderabad had remained unresolved. He had failed to do anything for Britain's 'Faithful Ally', and was worried whether, after he had gone, could Patel be restrained from sending troops into Hyderabad. It was mid-May 1948. In a month's time Mountbatten was to say good-bye to India. He was, therefore, to make one final effort to bring about agreement between Hyderabad and India. Mountbatten's success depended on Patel's acceptance of the plan. So he flew to Dehradun early in June 1948, taking with him Nehru, Rajendra Prasad, Gopalaswami Ayyanger and Baldev Singh—all of whom were confident that Patel would not agree to his plan, as Monckton, who had drafted it, admitted to Mountbatten that 'the terms were now so heavily weighed in Hyderabad's favour that it would be miracle if India accepted'.[32]

Mountbatten's meeting with Patel was momentous. On it hinged the fate of India and of Hyderabad. 'Soon after arrival', records Mountbatten, 'I gave the paper to Patel to read. He grunted, "Impertinence — I will never initial it". I then dropped the subject.... After lunch Sardarji became quite emotional, and spoke of the debt India owed me. "How can we prove to you our love and gratitude? Whatever you ask for, if your wish is in my power, it will be granted." I hardened my heart, for I too was affected, and replied: "If you are sincere, sign this document."

'Sardarji was visibly taken aback. "Does agreement with Hyderabad mean so much to you", he asked in a low voice. "Yes...." Patel initialed the draft.... The others, although astonished, accepted this, and I flew to Delhi very elated at my success.... Monckton could hardly believe his luck and flew back at once to Hyderabad with it.' Mountbatten's elation was however, short lived. 'Then' he admits, 'an astonishing thing happened. The Nizam and his advisors now rejected their own draft.' Monckton was told by Laik Ali, 'We shall fight to the last man'.

'To this' Monckton replied, 'you will be in the first aeroplane to Karachi' (if India sent in her troops). And unhappy Mountbatten records, 'the situation was indeed lost by Hyderabad through the intervention of Qasim Razvi.... But for India, it spelt victory. Now their conscience would be clear if they had to intervene in Hyderabad.'[33]

On 21 June 1948, three days after the breakdown of negotiations with Hyderabad, Lord Mountbatten left India and was succeeded by C Rajagopalachari as Governor-General. It was obvious that the Laik Ali Cabinet, under the control of the razakars, would neither agree to Accession nor to responsible government. The minority community, which was holding a virtual monopoly of all offices under the State government, could not view governance with equanimity. The Nizam and his advisers were possessed by the notion that India was unable to take any action against Hyderabad because it was seriously engaged with Kashmir and other problems.

Tension begain to mount both in Hyderabad and India. Charges of border raids and breaches of Standstill Agreement were made on both sides. After seeing the horrible state of affairs, JV Joshi, a member of the Nizam's Executive Council tendered his resignation letter, addressed to Laik Ali, Prime Minister of Hyderabad. He pointed out that the law and order situation in the Jalna, Aurangabad, Parbhani and Nanded districts in the State had completely broken down; that incidents were not lacking where the police had joined the razakars in looting, arson, murder, rape and molestation of women; and that, in their despair, many Hindus had sought shelter outside the State. To quote his words: 'A complete reign of terror prevails in Parbhani and Nanded districts. I have seen in Loha a scene of devastation which brought tears to my eyes—Brahmins were killed and their eyes were taken out. Women had been raped, houses were burnt in large numbers. My heart wrung in anguish.... Under the circumstances, I cannot continue to lend my name to a Government which is powerless to prevent these heartrending atrocities which I have seen with my own eyes.'[34]

In addition to this, attempts were being made to smuggle arms and ammunition into Hyderabad. Sidney Cotton was engaged in arms airdrops with Karachi as his base. As per information available with the Government of India at that time, in addition to 200,000 razakars with small arms, the State forces numbered 42,000 regulars and irregulars, besides an unascertained number of Pathans, who had previously been imported into the State. The neighbouring provincial governments were extremely concerned about the border raids and in May 1948, it was found necessary to station troops round Hyderabad in order to prevent these incidents and to give some measures of confidence to the people.

Both newspapers and journals started openly accusing the Government of India of inaction in the face of flagrant and repeated violation of Indian territory. The stories brought by evacuees from Hyderabad added considerably to the public indignation. Attacks on trains had created panic and the Government of India had been forced to guard each train with an armed escort. The attitude of the Parliament reflected the general uneasiness in the country.

With Mountbatten's departure, a major roadblock seemed to have been removed. Patel did gain a free hand, but not full freedom. Nehru and Patel differed on the timing of 'Police Action'. With Patel it was *now*; with Nehru it was *later*. Nehru told the Chief Ministers on 1 July 1948, 'we are ready at short notice to invade Hyderabad. But we propose to wait for developments and to avoid such invasion if we can help it, because of the other consequences that it is bound to bring in its train'.[35]

In contrast, Patel was categorical—unwavering and assertive. In his speech at the inauguration of Patiala and East Punjab Union on 15 July 1948, he restated his earlier declaration, 'If Hyderabad did not behave properly, it would have to go the way that Junagadh did. The former Governor-General, Lord Mountbatten, thought that he would be able to secure a peaceful settlement.... Although I was doubtful whether the efforts would succeed, I let him try'.[36]

Patel was now in a new mood, as if he had been unfiltered. This was reflected by what he told KM Munshi over the telephone. Munshi records: 'Next day (the next to Mountbatten's departure) I heard Sardar's voice over the phone, vibrating with good cheer. "Well Munshi, how are you? Is everything all right? What about your Nizam?" "OK, he is all right", I said. Then I told him about Zaheer's, Secretary of the External Affairs of Hyderabad, suggestion—"Settlement". As if he had never heard of any such thing, he said, "what settlement?" His jocular quarries were a sure sign of his mood. He now felt himself to be the master of the game. "The Mountbatten settlement", I said. "Tell him the settlement has gone to England", Patel replied caustically and laughed.'[37] Patel also publicly stated, 'the Terms and talks which Lord Mountbatten had have gone with him. Now the settlement with Nizam will have to be on the lines of other settlements with the States. No help from outside, on which he seems to rest pathetic hopes, would avail him.'[38]

Patel's path was not yet clear. Mountbatten's policy still dominated Nehru's mind. Four days prior to Mountbatten's departure, Nehru had stated, 'We will persue an open-door policy so far as these proposals (offered by Mountbatten) are concerned and the Nizam is welcome to accept them any time he chooses'.[39] This was not acceptable to Patel, as Nehru's outlook indicated three things: first, his unwillingness to act now; second, his unwillingness to shed Mountbatten's influence; and, third, his favouring a policy of drift, which the Nizam had successfully managed with the support of Mountbatten, whose latest proposals had failed, because Jinnah did not want Nizam to settle with India.

Patel was critical of Nehru's outlook in a letter to Gadgil on 21st June 1948: 'I am rather worried about Hyderabad. This is the time we should take firm and definite action. There should be no vacillation; and the more public the action is the greater effect it will have on the morale of our people, both here and in Hyderabad, and will convince our opponents that we mean business... there should be no lack of definiteness or strength about our actions. If, even now, we relax, we shall not only be doing disservice to the country, but would be digging our own grave.'[40]

The Hyderabad situation was climaxing towards confrontation. Meanwhile, Laik Ali (Prime Minister of Hyderabad) kept insisting that the Hyderabad issue be taken to the UNO. On 17 August 1948, he wrote to Nehru, charging India with a series of flagrant breaches of the Standstill Agreement. He complained that there was a total economic blockade of Hyderabad, which was causing serious disruption in the life of the community, and he alleged Indian troops had repeatedly violated Hyderabad territory. Therefore, he informed that Hyderabad had decided to solicit the good offices of the United Nations Organisations in order that the dispute between Hyderabad and India might be resolved and a peaceful and enduring settlement arrived at.

A reply was sent on 23 August 1948, to the effect that the Government of India regarded the differences between them and Hyderabad as a purely 'domestic issue' and, considering Hyderabad's historic as well as present position in relation to India, they could not agree that Hyderabad had any right in international law to seek the intervention of the UNO or any other outside body for the settlement of the issue.

On 28 August 1948, the Nizam's Agent-General in New Delhi informed the Government of India that, as a Hyderabad delegation would be presenting their case to the United Nations, they would be glad of air facilities. After denial of any such air facilities to the Hyderabad delegation from the Indian government side, the Hyderabad delegation, headed by Nawab Moin Nawaz Jung, went to Karachi and from there proceeded to America and presented their case to the Security Council.

To Patel, this was Pakistan's veiled attempt to checkmate India's action in Hyderabad. Patel had written to a friend from Dehradun on 1 July 1948: 'Hyderabad remained unsolved because of my prolonged illness. Nearly four months I have remained out of action.'[41] He was now ready to act—and act quickly and positively. He told Munshi, using the Gujarati idiom: 'The bullock-cart must, sometime or the other, come out of the rut.'[42] He called General JN Chaudhuri to Dehradun. General Chaudhuri was to lead the operations. Patel subjected him to a cross-examination for his personal assurance before he gave the army the word 'Go'. Chaudhuri records what Patel told him:'If I did well, I would take the credit; but if things went wrong, I would be blamed, but whatever I (Gen Chaudhuri) did, I (Gen Chaudhuri) would be supported. This was the wonderful thing about working with Sardar Patel. He gave a feeling of intimacy.'[43] His whole-hearted backing and unflinching faith in men under him not only spurred them into action but helped them to final victory.

Though out of Delhi from the end of April and convalescing, Patel had not been inert over Hyderabad. Making known his support for an economic blockade, he had also persuaded the Cabinet in the middle of May 1948, to authorise preparations for military action.[44] Nehru had warned that sending the Army into Hyderabad could hurt India's military position in Kashmir, and the Chiefs of the Army, the Navy and the Air Force (all Britons) had termed it 'a hazardous military gamble'.[45] Senior Indian officers too seemed to agree that 'Operations against

Hyderabad should be postponed until after the monsoon'.⁴⁶ The defence chiefs feared that 'if we move into Hyderabad, we will be very short of troops for internal security purposes in the rest of the country'.⁴⁷ This was conveyed to Vallabhbhai by Menon.

Patel's response to the warning was in this term, 'It is not, in the final analysis, the action of an Army which maintains law and order—look at the Punjab last August, when 55,000 men could not stop the massacres. It is rather the prestige of the government backed by potential armed action which keeps the people in order. At the moment this prestige is sufficiently high to take action against Hyderabad and maintain order elsewhere at the same time. But if the Government delays action against Hyderabad much longer, then its prestige will fall greatly that no amount of troops will be sufficient for internal security'.⁴⁸

Persuaded by Patel's message, the Defence Committee decided on 13 May 1948 that military preparations should go forward. Still in the country and still the Chairman of the Defence Committee, Mountbatten recorded: 'Pandit Nehru said openly at the meeting, and subsequently assured me privately, that he would not allow any orders to be given for operations to start unless there really was an event, such as wholesale massacre of Hindus within the State, which would patiently justify, in the eyes of the world, action by the Government of India.'⁴⁹

Patel was not willing to give any such assurance. For him Hyderabad's duplicity was reason enough for firm and definite action. The countdown for Hyderabad began, if not on 21 June 1948, the date on which Mountbatten left, then on 5 July, when Patel returned to Delhi. With his espousal, the blockade became official and tighter. Hyderabad played the game by hiring gun-runners who were taking off at night from airports in Pakistan and touching down on landing strips in Bidar and Warangal in Hyderabad. Other developments reinforced the case for intervention.

While Patel pressed for intervention, Jawaharlal, conscious of his word to Mountbatten, tried to avoid and postpone it.

However, the Cabinet was with Patel, and so was the new Governor-General, Rajagopalachari. Finding himself isolated, Nehru yielded and agreed that the Governor-General should ask the Nizam to ban the razakars and invite the Indian Army. Rajaji's letter went on 31 August 1948. A telegram in reply came on 5 September 1948. Banning the razakars was 'impracticable', the Nizam said, and letting Indian troops into his territory was 'out of question'.[50]

There was only one course to take now. But Nehru still had second thoughts. However, for the 'Police Action', Cabinet sanction was essential. Patel faced a formidable task in overcoming Nehru's reluctance to go that far. At one of the meetings of the Defence Committee, of which Nehru was the Chairman, 'there was so much bitterness that Sardar Patel walked out'. Seeing his seat vacant, Menon told a Rotary meeting in Bombay, 'I too walked out five minutes later'.[51] This seemed to have shaken Nehru out of his complacent mood; it mellowed his opposition, though not completely. Later, at a meeting attended by the Governor-General (Rajagopalachari), the Prime Minister, the Home Minister (Patel) and Secretary of the State Ministry (Menon), 'it was decided to order troops into Hyderabad'.[52] Despite such a decision, Patel had yet to face the Hamlet in Nehru.

In the preceding night of the Police Action, the British Commander-in-Chief of the Indian Army, General Bucher, persuaded Nehru that 'even at that late stage, the campaign should be called off as militarily risky and hazardous on grounds of internal security in the whole country'.[53] About midnight on 12 September 1948, after he had spoken to Nehru, Bucher attempted a rare feat in pulling Patel out of bed at that hour and advised him to at least postpone the action for fear of air attacks on Bombay and Ahmedabad. Patel reminded Bucher, 'how London had suffered during the Great War, and coolly assured him that Ahmedabad and Bombay both could stand up to an attack if it came'. Bucher, writes Munshi, 'was hesitant throughout. He overestimated the capability of the Hyderabad army, underestimated that of his own troops, and knew not the ability of Sardar… to deal with the problems of internal law and order. Like most Englishmen, he was unable to realise that no price was too high to be paid for eliminating the razakar menace which threatened the very existence of India'.[54] Patel had reportedly told Nehru, when contacted on telephone, 'to forget about it and go to sleep as he himself was doing'. In view of HVR Iyengar, then Home Secretary, Government of India, 'the verdict of history will be that the Sardar was right',[55] a verdict which Nehru wholeheartedly agreed with later.

Operation Polo

The Indian troops marched into Hyderabad in the early hours of 13 September 1948. The operation was named 'Operation Polo'. It lasted barely 108 hours. The Nizam was reduced to a bundle of nerves; Razvi, the fire-spitting and sabre-rattling hero, looked woebegone in a military barrack. For its remarkable speed and astonishing success, the army earned a handsome tribute from Patel, who wrote to Bucher: 'I should like to send you and officers and men under your command my sincerest felicitations on the successful conclusion of the Hyderabad operations. The speed and the skill of these operations cannot fail to extort admiration even from our severest critics, and I have no doubt that history will record these operations as a masterpiece of efficiency, organization and all-round cooperation. The Indian Army has added one more chapter to its glorious record of achievements, and I should like to convey to you and through you to all those who have had a hand in these operations my personal thanks for the part which each one has played in it. We are really proud of them all.'[56]

On 17 September 1948, Laik Ali and his Cabinet tendered their resignations. The Nizam sent for KM Munshi (who had been under house arrest ever since the Police Action began) and informed him that he had given orders for his army to surrender;

that he (the Nizam) would be forming a new government; that Indian troops were free to go to Secunderabad and Bolarum, and that the razakars would be banned. Munshi communicated this to the Government of India. In reply, 'I (Menon) conveyed to Munshi that the Military Commander would be in charge of the administration and that the question of the formation of a new Cabinet did not arise'. Munshi was asked 'not to commit from the Government of India's side in any manner, but to leave it to the Military Governor to deal with all further problems under the orders of the Government of India'.[57]

Major-General JN Chaudhuri took charge as Military Governor on 18 September 1948. Simultaneously with the occupation of Hyderabad, Lt General Rajendrasinhji issued a proclamation asking the people to remain calm and not to give way to panic. The people were asked to render every assistance to the Military Governor's administration and not to obstruct it in any way, and peace and protection were guaranteed to all law-abiding citizens. The members of the Laik Ali ministry were placed under house arrest. Leading razakars were apprehended. Qasim Razvi was arrested on 19 September 1948.

The Nizam withdrew the Hyderabad case from the UNO on 23 September 1948, where Patel had sent, as a leader of the Indian delegation, the last Dewan of Mysore Ramasamy Mudaliar, whom he had selected on merit, brushing aside party considerations, uninfluenced by the fact that throughout his political life he had been an opponent, and 'whose very religion was enmity to the Congress'.[58] Patel complimented Mudaliar, 'I should like to say how much I appreciated the skill and ability with which you represented India's stand on Hyderabad before the Security Council'.[59]

India's success was a personal triumph for Patel. Patel's work for unifying India was completed by what Hyderabad's ruling clique saw as 'take over', its Hindu majority as liberation and Vallabhbhai himself as the quelling of a rebellion. The Nizam's surrender fulfilled Vallabhbhai's dream of a unified

India, thirteen months after the goal of independence had been realised. The climax of Patel's striving was also the culmination of the process of history that brought Muslim rule over a Hindu majority to an end. Operation Polo did not only remove the cancer from the belly of India, but it also belied the hopes of the prophets of doom.

Nehru was most happy with the outcome. His fears and doubts had been belied. He wrote to the Chief Ministers on 21 September 1948: 'What has happened in Hyderabad has created a situation which should lead to a stabilisation of the communal situation in India, or rather to a progressive elimination of the communal....' He wrote again on 4 October, 'I have a feeling that India turned the corner more specially since these Hyderabad operations. We are on the upgrade now. The atmosphere is different and better....'[60]

Patel visited Hyderabad in the last week of February 1949. Nehru had preceded him. Patel was the first Indian to have been received by the Nizam at the aerodrome. Patel's courteous treatment of the defeated Nizam not only dispelled the latter's fears, but cemented a friendship between the two. To the people of Hyderabad, Patel spoke in sincere, plain, straightforward language. He told the Osmania University students, 'Now we must draw a curtain on the past. Everyone in the country should join together in making India a great country. People must maintain complete communal amity, for, we have all been born and brought up on the Indian soil, and we have to live and die together on the same soil'.[61]

While addressing the public at Fateh Maidan, Patel told the people of Hyderabad that they were 'now a part of India—in fact, the heart of India'. He asked them to appreciate the realities of the post-Partition situation. He said: 'India has become two. Those who were responsible for starting the agitation for the two-nation theory have got what they wanted. But there are still some in the country who cherish the same ideals. To them I will say that their rightful place is in the other country. It is better for such people to go to Pakistan, for their God is there.... I warn such people that if they ever dreamt that they can get any assistance from outside, or that others outside can interfere in the affairs of Hyderabad, they are insane. The affairs of Hyderabad are an internal problem for the people themselves to decide.' Patel was however, generous in his advice to the Muslims of Hyderabad: In the poisoned atmosphere of the past, many people did things that they should not have done.... The dust of the turmoil is now settling down. The turbid waters are now getting clearer. These people should refrain from raising the dust again, and making the water muddy again. They should forget the past. They should purify the atmosphere by going along the right path.[62]

The Nizam wrote an amiable letter to Patel after the latter returned to New Delhi. He wrote: 'I was glad to get an opportunity of making my acquaintance with you... and hope that this will prove to be a happy augury for the future of the premier State of Hyderabad....' Patel's large-hearted reply was: 'I was happy to learn that your Exalted Highness had adapted yourself so readily to the changed conditions. As I told your Exalted Highness, while error is human failing and divine injunctions all point to forgetting and forgiving, it is the duty of human beings to contribute their share to this process by sincere repentance and by employing the period that is left in discharging their duties to their people and to their God.' A grateful and an extremely happy Nizam again wrote to Patel on 12 May 1949: '...your great personality is valuable asset for India at this crucial period when the whole world is in turmoil.'[63]

Surrender of the Nizam had double significance for Patel. On the personal level, it was his crowning glory: vindication of what he had stood for and unwaveringly advocated, despite the opposition he had from Mountbatten and Nehru. On the national level, it was a historic achievement: the integration of 554 Princely States. Writing in the *Christian Science Monitor*, W Gordon Graham called Patel the man 'who by his decisiveness resolved the great Hyderabad crisis', and significantly observed:

'Hyderabad, a State covering 80,000 square miles in the heart of peninsular India, was at that time in the grip of an unscrupulous minority which aimed at secession from India. Had the bid succeeded, India might not have survived as a political unit. This situation needed a man of iron who would not balk at coercive action, and in the Sardar, India had, at that vital moment, just the man.'[64]

An equally glowing tribute came from General Bucher who was gracious in his ungrudging admission, 'I take no credit to myself for the success of the Hyderabad operation. In all the circumstances from the beginning to end, I was not prepared to say, "Go", until every possible development had been thought out and guarded against. The Sardar was, in my opinion, a very great man indeed.... Undoubtedly, he was right when he decided that either the Government of Hyderabad must accept the Indian Government's conditions, or else the State would have to be entered in order to eliminate the razakars'.[65]

Patel's quick, bold step and instant success had two implications. First it killed for good the British policy of creating Hyderabad as the 'Third Dominion'. According to Munshi, 'Sir, Arthur Lothian, who retired as Resident of Hyderabad on 26th November 1947, was a great protagonist of Hyderabad as the Third Dominion. It is even possible that he himself had presented the idea to the Nizam in the first place; at any rate, Sir Conrad Corfield, the Adviser to Crown Representative, was its active sponsor'.[66] Secondly, as Patel put it, 'Hyderabad was an ulcer which had been operated upon'.[67]

The Police Action not only performed such operation, but saved India from Balkanisation and thereby ensured unification of India into a single, homogeneous country. Hyderabad's integration prevented its becoming a Islamic State, as Munshi puts it: Their object, scarcely concealed, was to establish Islamic domination, with or without the aid of Pakistan, first of Hyderabad, then of the South and ultimately of the whole of India.[68] 'Political integration of India, achieved during a short period of a year and half, was a unique achievement. At no time in the history of India, which was divided into hundreds of small units, was the country fused into an integrated whole so swiftly and so successfully and without use of force.'[69]

References

1. Edward John Thompson, *Making of the Indian Princes*, Oxford University Prass, 1943, p-1.
2. Sir Arthur Lothian, *Kingdom of Yesterday*, John Murray, 1951, p-80.
3. KM Munshi, *The End of Era*, Bhartiya Vidya Bhavan, 1957, p-xxii.
4. Ibid.
5. Ibid.
6. VP Menon, *Integration of Indian States*, Orient Black Swan, New Delhi, 2014, p-286.
7. *Sardar Patel's Correspondence*, vol-VII, letter dated August 31, 1947, from Aravamudh Aiyangar, Member, Nizam's Executive Council, to Gopalaswami Ayyangar, p-56.
8. Ibid, p-109.
9. *For a United India: Speeches of Sardar Patel* (1947-50), compiled by Publication Division, Ministry of Information & Broadcasting, Government of India, p-11.
10. HVR Iyengar (ICS): *The Indian Express*, On working Together, September 18, 1969.
11. *Sardar Patel's Correspondence*, vol-VIII, p-67.
12. VP Menon, *Integration of the Indian States*, Orient Black Swan, New Delhi, 2014, p-291.
13. Ibid.
14. Ibid, p-295.
15. Ibid, p-297.
16. Ibid.
17. V Shankar, *My Reminiscences of Sardar Patel*, the Macmillan Company of India Limited, 1974, p-118.
18. *Sardar Patel's Correspondence*, vol-VII, p-46, 53-54, 87.

19. Ibid, p-111.
20. Ibid, p-80-81.
21. KM Munshi, *The End of An Era*, Bhartiya Vidya Bhavan, Bombay, 1990, p-36.
22. Ibid, p-37.
23. Ibid.
24. KM Munshi, *The End of An Era*, Bhartiya Vidya Bhavan, Bombay, 1957, p-39.
25. Ibid, p-59.
26. VP Menon, *Integration of the Indian States*, Orient Black Swan, New Delhi, 2014, p-304.
27. *Sardar Patel's Correspondence*, vol-VII, p-134.
28. Ibid, p-118.
29. Ibid, KM Munshi's letter of May 17, 1948 to the Nizam, p-158.
30. Ibid, p-110.
31. Balraj Krishna, *Sardar Vallabhbhai Patel*, Rupa Publications, New Delhi, 2013, p-345.
32. Ibid, p-346.
33. *This was Sardar*, Commemorative volume, vol-I, Sardar Vallabhbhai Patel Smarak Bhavan, Ahmedabad, 1974, p-244-45.
34. VP Menon, *Integration of the Indian States*, Orient Black Swan, New Delhi, 2014, p-334.
35. *Jawaharlal Nehru: Letters to Chief Ministers* (1947-63), vol I, ed-Madhav Khosla, Penguine, p-147.
36. *For a United India : Speeches of Sardar Patel* compiled by Publication Division, Ministry of Information & Broadcasting, Government of India, p-40.
37. KM Munshi, *The End of An Era*, Bhartiya Vidya Bhavan, Bombay, 1990, p-177.
38. For a United India, Ibid, p-41.
39. Balraj Krishna, *Sardar Vallabhbhai Patel*, Rupa, New Delhi, 2013, p-348.
40. *Sardar Patel's Correspondence*, vol VII, Ed–Durga Das, Navjivan Publishing House, Ahmedabad, 1971, p-217.
41. *Sardar's Letters-Mostly Unknown*, vol-V, ed. Maniben Vallabhbhai Patel, Pub–Sardar Vallabhbhai Smarak Bhavan, Ahmedabad, p-307.

42. KM Munshi, *The End of An Era*, Bhartiya Vidya Bhavan, Bombay, 1990, p-217.
43. *General JN Chaudhuri, An Autobiography* as narrated to BK Narayan, Vikas, New Delhi, 1978, p-146.
44. HV Hodson, *The Great Divide:Britain-India-Pakistan*, OUP, 1997, p-491-2.
45. Ibid, p-491.
46. Ibid, p-492.
47. Ibid, p-492.
48. Ibid.
49. Ibid.
50. Rajmohan Gandhi, *Patel: A Life*, Navjivan Publishing House, Ahmedabad, 2013, p-481.
51. Balraj Krishna, *Sardar Vallabhbhai Patel*, Rupa, New Delhi, 2013, p-350.
52. *The Times of India*, August 6th, 1958.
53. HVR Iyengar, *The Indian Express*, On working Together, September 18, 1969.
54. KM Munshi, *The End of An Era*, Bhartiya Vidya Bhavan, Bombay, 1990, p-239, 237.
55. HVR Iyengar, *The Indian Express*, On working Together, September 18, 1969.
56. *General Sir Roy Bucher: Letter to Balraj Krishna*, December 19, 1968.
57. VP Menon, *Integration of the Indian States*, Orient Black Swan, New Delhi, 2014, p-340.
58. *KM Panikkar: An Autobiography*, Oxford University Press, 1977, p-154.
59. *Sardar Patel's Correspondence*, vol VII, Navjivan Publishing House, Ahmedabad, p-647.
60. *Jawaharlal Nehru: Letters to Chief Ministers* (1947-1963), vol-I ed. Madhav Khosla, Penguine Books, p-206-7.
61. *Said the Sardar*, speeches published by Hyderabad State Congress, p-1,5.
62. Ibid.
63. *Sardar Patel's Correspondence*, vol – VII, Navjivan Publishing House, Ahmedabad, p-309-10, 315.
64. W Gordon Graham, *The Christian Science Monitor*, February 1, 1951.
65. *General Sir Roy Bucher, Letter to Balraj Krishna*, December 19, 1968.

66. KM Munshi, *The End of An Era*, Bhartiya Vidya Bhavan, Bombay, 1990, p-34.
67. Sardar Patel *In Tune with Millions*, vol–II, Sardar Vallabhbhai Patel Smarak Bhavan, Ahmedabad, 1975, p-276.
68. KM Munshi, *Pilgrimage To Freedom*, vol-I, Bhartiya Vidya Bhavan, 1967, p-171.
69. Ibid, p-172.

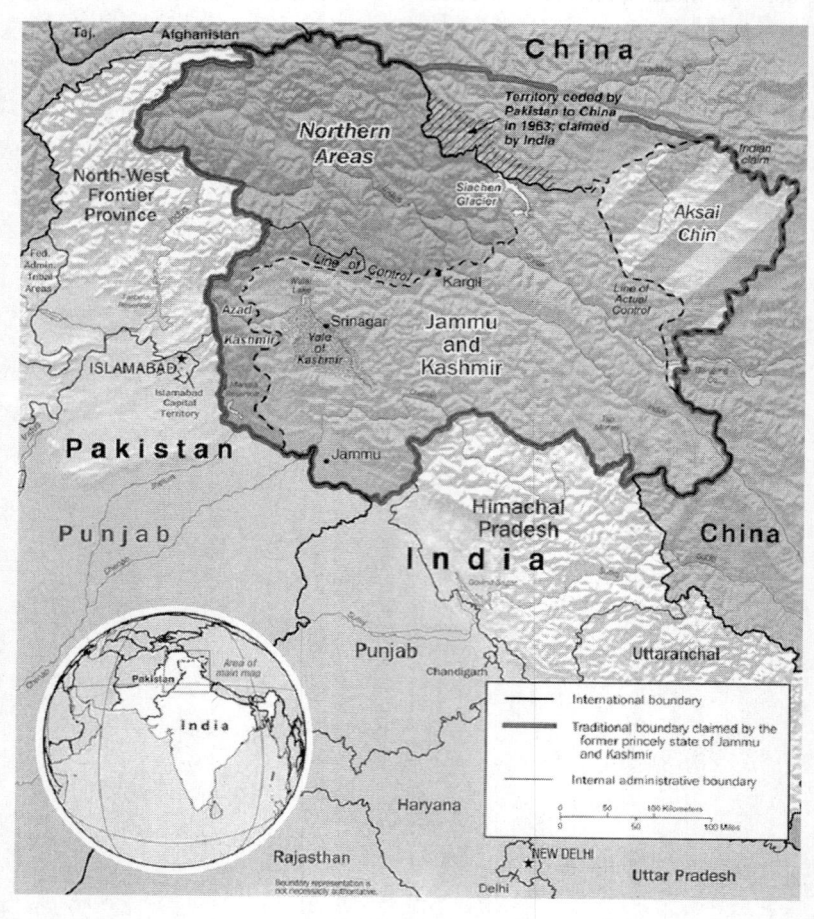

Jammu and Kashmir

The present issue relates to Kashmir. This raises all manner of connected issues — international, military and others — which are beyond the competence of the States Ministry as such. That is why it has to be considered by the cabinet as a whole frequently and various ministers separately or together. And that is why I have to take personal interest in this matter as PM to bring about coordination in our various activities.

—Nehru to Patel

THE HISTORY of Jammu and Kashmir, as a separate State, starts from 1846. Till fourteenth century it was ruled by a series of Buddhist and Hindu dynasties, whose historical mention is found in the celebrated versified chronicle known as *Rajatrangini* (Kalhana, 12th CE). It was during this epoch that old remains of Kashmir at places like Anantnag, Bijbehara, Pandrattan, Sankaracharya, Pattan and Martand were constructed.

Thereafter, a Muslim dynasty was established which continued to rule till 1587, when Akbar invaded Kashmir and made it a part of the source of revenue of the Mughal Empire. In 1752, Kashmir passed from the feeble control of the Mughal emperor into the powerful grasp of Ahmad Shah Abdali of Afghanistan, and for the next sixty-seven years it was held for the Pathans by a series of governors who were more or less independent of their kings. In 1819, it was conquered by Maharaja Ranjit Singh, the great Sikh ruler. Till 1846, it remained under the Sikhs and was administered by their rulers.

In the latter half of the eighteenth century, Jammu was ruled by a Dogra chief of Rajput descent, named Ranjit Deo. He died in 1780 and there ensued a quarrel for succession. This gave the Sikhs the opportunity of turning Jammu and the neighbouring hill tracts into a dependency. The three great-grand nephews of Ranjit Deo, namely Gulab Singh, Dhyan Singh and Suchet Singh entered the service of Maharaja Ranjit Singh. They rendered such a distinguished service that later in 1818, Ranjit Singh conferred the principality of Jammu on Gulab Singh with the hereditary title of Raja; Bhimber and Chibal including Poonch on Dhyan Singh; and Ramnagar on Suchet Singh. Both Dhyan Singh and Suchet Singh were subsequently killed.

With the death of Ranjit Singh in 1839, the Sikh power started disappearing. In 1846, at the close of the first Sikh war, Gulab Singh appeared on the scene as mediator between the English and the Sikhs. In the negotiations that followed, the Sikh Maharaja was called upon to pay an indemnity to the East India Company of Rs 1 crore, in addition to a large territory in the Punjab. As the indemnity was beyond his means to pay, he ceded all his hill territories from Beas River to the Indus, including Jammu and Kashmir. But Lord Hardinge, then Governor-General, considered the occupation of the whole of this territory inadvisable on the ground that it would increase the extent of the British frontier and the military establishment for guarding it; also because it would create new conflicting interest.

Also, most of the parts of the districts (with the exception of the small vale of Kashmir) were unproductive. On the other hand, the ceded tract comprised the whole of the hereditary possession of Gulab Singh, who being eager to obtain an indefeasible title to them, came forward and offered to pay the war indemnity on condition that he was made an independent ruler of Jammu and Kashmir. A separate treaty embodying this arrangement was concluded by the English with Gulab Singh at Amritsar on 16 March 1846.

The Treaty of Amritsar marks the commencement of the history of the Jammu and Kashmir State as a political entity. The treaty put Gulab Singh, as Maharaja, in possession of all the hill country between the Indus and Ravi, including Kashmir, Jammu, Ladakh and Gilgit. It excluded Lahoul, Kulu and some other areas including Chamba which, for strategical purposes, was considered advisable to retain by the English and for which a remission of Rs 25 lakh was made from the one crore demanded, leaving Rs 25 lakh as the final amount to be paid by Gulab Singh. Gulab Singh had some difficulty in obtaining actual possession of the province of Kashmir. The last Governor appointed by the Sikhs successfully resisted Gulab Singh for a while and it was not until the end of 1846 that Maharaja Gulab Singh, with the aid of British troops, was established in Kashmir.

No subsidiary force was imposed on Gulab Singh. Political relations between the Government of India and the State commenced in the year 1849 and were conducted by the Punjab Government, through the Maharaja's agent at Lahore. No representative of the Government of India was located in the State and it was not until the year 1852 that the first Officer on Special Duty in the State was appointed. This Officer resided in Kashmir during the summer months only. Maharaja Gulab Singh died in 1857 and was succeeded by his son Ranvir Singh. The channel of political relations with the State, however, continued as usual until 1877, in which year the Officer on Special Duty was placed under the Government of India, with instructions to correspond direct with them on all matters of political importance. In 1885, after the death of Maharaja Ranvir Singh and the accession to the gaddi by Maharaja Pratap Singh, the designation of the Officer on Special Duty was changed to 'Resident in Kashmir' who was permanently located in Srinagar.

Gilgit

Gilgit was part of the territories of Jammu and Kashmir. A political agent in Gilgit was first appointed in the year 1877 but he was withdrawn in 1889. It comprised: (1) Gilgit Wazarat (2) the State of Hunza and Nagir (3) the Punial Jagir (4) Governorships of Yasin, Kuh-Ghizr and Ishkoman and (5) Chilas. In 1935, Soviet Russia had taken virtual control of Sinkiang in Turkestan, a move which had made necessary for the Government of India (the ruling British) to take over the administration of the Gilgit sub-division from the Jammu and Kashmir State. They did so by taking the Gilgit region on a sixty-year lease from the Maharaja of Jammu and Kashmir and undertook the sole responsibility for the administration and defence of the area. Under this lease, the Gilgit sub-division was administered by a British Assistant Political Agent of the Indian Political Service. The Gilgit Scouts, commanded by British officers who were specially chosen for a responsible and somewhat delicate task, had also been built up. When Lord Mountbatten's plan of transfer of power was announced on 3rd June 1947, the Political Department retroceded the area to the Maharaja and the Gilgit Scouts were also handed over to him.

J&K after Transfer of Power announcement

Lt General Maharaja Sir Hari Singh, who was the ruler of Jammu and Kashmir at the time of the transfer of power, ascended the gaddi on 23 September 1925.

After announcement of the 3rd June plan, when Mountbatten was discussing the policy of accession of the Indian States to one Dominion or the other, he became particularly concerned about

Kashmir. Kashmir was a State with the biggest area in India, with a population predominantly Muslim, ruled by a Hindu Maharaja. On the other hand, the Government of Pakistan was sure to eye Kashmir not only because its ruler was Hindu and population Muslim, but also because of the National Conference, the only political organisation of the people of the State, which was closely associated with the All India States People's Conference and was known to be definitely in favour of acceding to India.

Sheikh Abdullah, a former school teacher, had started an organisation, the Muslim Conference, in 1930, to establish responsible government. This naturally led to conflict not only with the Maharaja but also the Hindu minority. Communal riots took place and gradually the Sheikh realised that he could fight the ruler for democratic rights of the people only if this organisation ceased to be communal. Thus, in 1938, the Muslim Conference was transformed into the National Conference. This not only drew a number of Hindus into the new organisation but also opened the door for cooperation with the All India States People's Conference, which for all practical purposes, was a branch of the Indian National Congress, working for the establishment of responsible government in the princely States all over the country.

This cooperation brought the Sheikh into contact with Jawaharlal Nehru who, besides being keenly interested in the struggles of the people against their Princes, also took pride in being a Kashmiri. Gradually, the Sheikh became a trusted friend of Nehru. It is to be mentioned here that when Sheikh Abdullah was arrested by the Maharaja in 1946, Nehru tried to enter Kashmir to assist the Sheikh in his trial but was stopped and arrested at Kohala bridge. At Maulana Azad's request, Nehru was released and returned to India. On this very occasion, Jinnah had issued a statement describing the Sheikh's movement as 'an agitation carried by a few malcontents who were out to create disorderly conditions in the State'.[1]

While Jinnah's attitude towards the Sheikh lost him the support of the all-powerful National Conference, it did not gain him the goodwill of Maharaja Hari Singh. The Maharaja, by nature, was a man of self-interest. Knowing full well that both India and Pakistan needed him, he decided to use their rivalry to secure an independent status for his State. Lord Mountbatten, on the other hand, wanted the Maharaja to decide soon, as he knew that Kashmir was bound to become a bone of contention between the two new dominions and might lead to war.

Mountbatten visited Kashmir in June 1947 and spent four days discussing the situation and arguing with the Maharaja but the Maharaja, on one pretext or the other, evaded discussing the question of accession. Mountbatten told him that independence was not, in his opinion, a feasible proposition and that the State would not be recognised as a Dominion by the British government. He assured the Maharaja that, so long as he made up his mind to accede to one Dominion or the other before 15 August, no trouble would ensue, for whichever Dominion he acceded would take the State firmly under its protection as part of its territory. He went so far as to tell the Maharaja that, if he acceded to Pakistan, India would not take it amiss and that he had a firm assurance on this from Sardar Patel himself. Lord Mountbatten went further to say that, in view of the composition of the population, it was particularly important to ascertain the wishes of the people. The Maharaja appeared incapable of making up his mind and so, Lord Mountbatten asked for a meeting with him and his Prime Minister on the last morning of his visit. At the last moment, the Maharaja sent a message to say that he was confined to bed and begged to be excused.[2]

Immediately after the transfer of power on 15 August, Lord Ismay went to Srinagar. Lord Mountbatten had asked him to persuade the Maharaja to take one course or the other as soon as possible, but nothing came out of Lord Ismay's efforts.[3]

It has been alleged that Sardar Patel was not anxious about Kashmir's accession to India. This is disapproved by Patel's letter of 3 July 1947, to the Maharaja. He wrote, 'I fully appreciate the difficult and delicate situation in which your State has been placed but as a sincere friend and well wisher of the State, I wish to assure you that the interest of Kashmir lies in joining the Indian Union and its Constituent Assembly without any delay. Its past history and traditions demand it, and all India looks up to you and expects you to take that decision. Eighty per cent of India is on this side'.[4] The Maharaja did not reply. His wily Prime Minister, Ramchandra Kak, wrote saying that, 'the matter you mention is a complicated one'.[5]

Standstill Agreement and Pakistan's attack

While the negotiations were still going on, the Government of Jammu and Kashmir announced its intention of signing Standstill Agreements with both India and Pakistan. Pakistan signed a Standstill Agreement. 'But we (India) wanted to examine its implications. We left the State alone. We did not ask the Maharaja to accede, though at that time, as a result of the Radcliff Award,[XII] the State had become connected by road with India. Owing to composition of the population, the State had its own peculiar problems. Moreover, our hands were already full and, if truth be told, I (VP Menon) for one had simply no time to think of Kashmir.'[6]

The signing of Standstill Agreement was merely a deception by Pakistan to put the Maharaja to sleep and then make a surprise attack. As early as 27 September, Nehru informed Patel that the Muslim League in the Punjab and the NWFP were making

---

[XII] The Radcliffe Line was the boundary demarcation line between India and Pakistan published on 17 August 1947 upon the Partition of India. Before his appointment, Cyril Radcliffe had never visited India and knew no one there. To the British and the feuding politicians alike, this neutrality was looked upon as an asset. To avoid disputes and delays, the division was done in secret. The final Awards were ready on 9 August but not published until two days after the partition. Radcliffe justified the casual division with the truism that no matter what he did, people would suffer. Radcliffe 'destroyed all his papers before he left India', on 15 August, before the Award was announced

preparations to enter Kashmir in considerable numbers, and in view of Patel's contacts with the Maharaja, he suggested that there was no other option for the Maharaja but to release Sheikh Abdullah and the National Conference leaders, to make a friendly approach to them, seek their cooperation and make them aware of the attitude of Pakistan and then to declare adhesion to the Indian Union. The Maharaja had already come to know about Pakistan's preparation and despite his deep suspicions about the Sheikh's intentions, he freed him. Meanwhile, Major-General Janak Singh was replaced by Mehrchand Mahajan as Prime Minister of Jammu and Kashmir.

The all-out invasion of Kashmir started on 22 October 1947. The main raiders' coloumn had approximately 200 to 300 lorries, and consisted of about 5,000 frontier tribesmen. The raiders continued to advance and on 24 October, they captured the Mahura Power House which supplied electricity to Srinagar. The raiders had announced that they would reach Srinagar on 26 October, in time for the Id celebration at the Srinagar mosque. The armed tribesmen were led by Pakistani officers. They penetrated deep into Kashmir, looting houses, abducting women, burning villages and committing wholesale massacre of both Hindu and Muslim women and children. Jinnah was in such a hurry that he had stationed himself at Abbotabad, ready to enter the Kashmir capital as conqueror.

As mentioned earlier, soon after the announcement of transfer of power, the Gilgit Agency had been retroceded to the Maharaja. The Maharaja then appointed a Governor for the area. The Governor, accompanied by Major General HL Scott, Chief of Staff of the Jammu and Kashmir Army, reached Gilgit on 30 July 1947. On arrival, they found that all the officers of the British Government had opted for service in Pakistan. There was no civil staff available to take over from these officers. The Gilgit Scouts also wanted to go over to Pakistan. In addition to the Scouts, 6-J&K Infantry Battalion (half of them Sikhs and half Muslims) were the only State force units available.

On the evening of 24 October, the Government of India received a desperate appeal for help from the Maharaja. They also received from Field-Marshal Auchinleck[XIII] information regarding the raiders' advance and probable intentions. On the morning of 25 October, a meeting of India's Defence Committee, presided over by Lord Mountbatten, was held. The committee considered the request of the Maharaja for arms and ammunition as also for reinforcement of troops. It was agreed to send VP Menon, Secretary in the States Ministry, to fly to Srinagar immediately in order to study the situation on the spot and to report to the Government of India.

After seeing the situation at Srinagar, VP Menon felt that the first thing to be done was to get the Maharaja and his family out of Srinagar. The reason for this was obvious. The raiders were close to Baramula. The Maharaja was quite helpless and if the Government of India decided not to go to his rescue, there was no doubt about the fate that would befall him and his family in Srinagar. There was also a certainty that the raiders would loot all valuable possession in the palace. In these circumstances, Menon advised him to leave immediately for Jammu and to take with him his family and his valuable possessions. The Maharaja took Menon's advice and left Srinagar. The events unfolded in the following manner.

At midnight on 31 October, the Governor's residence was surrounded by the Gilgit Scouts. The next morning, the Governor was put under arrest and a provisional government was established by the rebels. The Muslim elements (including officers) in the State forces garrison had deserted, the non-Muslim elements were largely liquidated. Those who survived escaped to the hills and then joined the State force garrison at Skardu. On 4 November 1947, Major Brown, the British Commandant of Gilgit Scouts ceremonially hoisted the Pakistan

---

[XIII] Supreme Commander of all British forces in India and Pakistan until late 1948

flag in the Scout's lines and in the third week of November, a Political Agent from Pakistan established himself at Gilgit.[7]

On his return from Srinagar, on 26 October, VP Menon reported his impressions about the grave situation in Kashmir to the Defence Committee. He emphasised the supreme necessity of saving Kashmir from the raiders. Lord Mountbatten was, however, of the opinion that it would be improper to move Indian troops into Kashmir—at the moment it was an independent country—as Kashmir had not yet decided to accede to either India or Pakistan. He said that *if the Maharaja acceded to India, only then* it would be possible to send troops to Srinagar. This was the only basis on which Indian troops could be sent to the rescue of the State from further pillaging by the aggressors. 'He further expressed the strong opinion that in view of the composition of the population, accession should be conditional on the will of the people being ascertained by a plebiscite after the raiders had been driven out the State and law and order had been restored. This was readily agreed to by Nehru and other ministers.'[8]

'Soon after the meeting of the Defence Committee, on 26 October, I (VP Menon) flew to Jammu, accompanied by Mahajan. On arrival at the palace, I found it in a state of utter turmoil, with valuable articles strewn all over the palace. The Maharaja was asleep. He had left Srinagar the previous evening and had been driving all the night. I woke him up and told him of what had taken place at the Defence Committee meeting. He was ready to accede at once. He then composed a letter to the Governor-General, describing the pitiable plight of the State and reiterating his request for military help. He further informed the Governor-General that it was his intention to set up an interim government at once and to ask Sheikh Abdullah to carry the responsibilities in this emergency with Mehrchand Mahajan, his Prime Minister. He concluded by saying that if the State was to be saved, immediate assistance must be available at Srinagar. He also signed the Instrument of Accession (26 October 1947).

Just when I was leaving, he told me that before he went to sleep, he had left instructions with his ADC that, if I came back from Delhi, he was not to be disturbed as it would mean that the Government of India had decided to come to his rescue and he should therefore, be allowed to sleep in peace, but if I failed to return, it would mean that everything was lost and, in that case his ADC was to shoot him in his sleep.'[9]

'With the Instrument of Accession and the Maharaja's letter, I flew back at once to Delhi. Sardar was waiting at the aerodrome and we both went straight to a meeting of the Defence Committee, which was arranged for that evening, 26 October. There was a long discussion, at the end of which it was decided that the accession of Jammu and Kashmir should be accepted, subject to the proviso that a plebiscite would be held in the State when the law and order situation allowed. It was further decided that an infantry battalion should be flown to Srinagar the next day, 27 October. The decision had the fullest support of Sheikh Abdullah, who was in Delhi at that time, and who had been pressing the Government of India on behalf of the All-Jammu and Kashmir National Conference for immediate help to be sent to the State to resist the tribal invasion.'[10]

Even after the decision was taken at the meeting of the Defence Committee, the Chiefs of Staff of the Indian Army, Navy and Air Force were apprehending risks involved in the operation. But Nehru, inspite of risks of massacre in Srinagar and communal holocaust in India, asserted that there was no alternative to sending troops. The Indian troops were airlifted to Srinagar on 27 October 1947, and operation was launched on subsequent days. The Defence Headquarters, consisting of British and Indian officials, worked tirelessly since 26 October. The lack of adequate lines of communication and of intelligence of the enemy strength and dispositions made planning very difficult. In the early hours of the morning of 27 October 1947, over a hundred civilian aircraft and RIAF planes were mobilised to fly troops, equipments and supplies to Srinagar.

The RIAF and civilian pilots and ground crews rose to the occasion and worked heroically to make the airlift a success. The enthusiasm with which the airforce personnel, civilian and military, worked that morning was phenomenal. Some of the pilots did several sorties in the course of the day. Nor should one forget to mention the civilian airline companies, but for whose wholehearted cooperation, the airlift could not have been possible. Lord Mountbatten, who had been Chief of Combined Operations and Supreme Allied Commander, South Asia, said that in all his war experience he had never heard of an airlift of this nature being put into operation at such short notice and he complimented all concerned on the astonishing performance.

The first available unit for the airlift was the Ist Battalion of the Sikh Regiment, which was stationed on internal security duties in the Gurgaon district near Delhi. The Commander of this battalion was Lt Colonel Dewan Ranjit Rai. The tasks assigned to him were to secure the airfield in Srinagar, to render assistance to the Government of Kashmir in maintaining law and order in Srinagar and, if possible, to drive away any tribesmen[XIV] who might have entered the city. As only meagre information was available as to the strength of the enemy, for a while it was not known whether the first airlift had fallen into their hands. For his own sortie, Lt Colonel Rai was told to circle above Srinagar and, if there was any doubt, not to land but to fly back to Jammu. At 10.30 am, after a tense suspense, a wireless flash

---

[XIV] Also called Kabails. They were tribal militias from the Frontier Tribal Areas adjoining the British North-West Frontier Province. Eyewitness accounts say, the bulk of the Frontier tribesmen–Wazir, Mahsud, Turi, Afridi, Mohmand, the Malakand Yusufzais–came into Kashmir via the longer Lohar Gali route in lorries and trucks. Around 2,000 tribesmen stormed Muzaffarabad that morning and easily scattered the Kashmir State army deployed there. Others came through the Pakistani town of Garhi Habibullah to the west, and the Kashmiri city of Muzaffarabad to the east. Margaret Bourke-White was a correspondent and photographer with American magazine LIFE, when the raids happened. Her book, *Halfway to Freedom, 1949*, gives a vivid account. Another high-profile account is from Shaukut Hayat Khan' book, *The Nation that Lost its Soul!*

from Srinagar airfield announced the safe landing of the first of the Indian troops. Lt Colonel Rai heaved a sigh of relief as the airfield was now in the hands of the Indian troops.

Lt Colonel Rai found on landing that the enemy was at Baramula, the strategic bottle-neck which opens into the Srinagar valley. Once the raiders were allowed to enter and fan out into the Srinagar valley, all would be lost. Rai, therefore, decided to advance to Baramula with a view to stopping the raiders there. The transport was provided by Bakshi Ghulam Mahomed, who was number two in the National Conference. When Lt Colonel Rai contacted the so-called raiders, he found them to be an organised body of men armed with light and medium machineguns and mortars, and led by commanders who knew modern tactics and the use of ground. Rai also discovered that the strength of the raiders was far more than his and he, therefore, decided to withdraw to Pattan on the main Baramula-Srinagar road, 17 miles from Srinagar. While conducting the withdrawal, he was killed in action. By his initiative and determination, this gallant officer helped to check the advance of the raiders on Srinagar. He was posthumously awarded *Mahavir Chakra*.

Jinnah always felt that the very name of Pakistan would have a false ring without Kashmir, in as much as the letter K in Pak was meant to stand for Kashmir. In utter desperation, he characterised Kashmir's accession to India as 'fraud and violence', and giving up the subterfuge of unauthorised invasion by tribesmen, wanted the regular Pakistan army to enter Kashmir and fight the Indians out of it. However, Supreme Commander Auchinleck told him that this would lead to a regular war between the two dominions and consequently the British military officers serving on both sides would have to withdraw from it.

For the first time Jinnah realised that he had his way as long as it was a triangular fight, with the British aiding him. And that in a duel, he had no chance against his erstwhile target. He had no alternative left but to invite Indian leaders to a conference in Lahore. 'Lord Mountbatten was eager that the invitation should be accepted and that he and Nehru should go to Lahore, but Sardar was strongly opposed to either of them making the visit. He said that, as Pakistan was the aggressor in this case, it was not right to follow a policy of appeasement by running after Jinnah. If Jinnah wanted to discuss the matter, he should come to Delhi. Nehru was inclined to agree with Lord Mountabatten. He argued that we had not gone to Kashmir for territorial acquisition and if we could find a peaceful solution of the problem, we should not stand on prestige.'[11]

Ultimately it was Mountbatten who, along with Lord Ismay, went to Lahore on 1 November, after the Gilgit occupation, and had a long discussion with Jinnah. In regard to Jinnah's statement made to him—that Kashmir's accession to India was brought about by violence—Mountabatten sarcastically replied that he agreed that it was so, since the violence had come from the tribesmen for whom Pakistan was responsible and the Maharaja was compelled to accede to India to obtain help against the invaders. Jinnah then proposed that both sides should withdraw at once. When Mountbatten asked him how the tribesmen could to be called off, Jinnah said that all he (Jinnah) had to do was to give them an order to come out and to warn them that if they did not comply, he would send large forces along their lines of communications. Mountbatten was naturally surprised by Jinnah's admitting that the tribesmen were at his beck and call and expressed mild astonishment at the degree of control that he (Jinnah) appeared to exercise over the raiders.[12]

On his part Mountbatten proposed that a plebiscite should be held in Kashmir and that the United Nations Organisation might be asked to provide supervisions for it. Jinnah strongly opposed it, and when Mountbatten asked why he was against plebiscite, he said with the troops of the Indian dominion in military occupation of Kashmir and with the National Conference under Sheikh Abdullah in power, such propaganda and pressure would be brought to bear that the average Muslim would never have the courage to vote for Pakistan.[13]

Jinnah pressed for a plebiscite to be held under the joint control of and supervision of the Governors-General of India and Pakistan. Both Lord Mountbatten and Lord Ismay were at pains to explain to Jinnah that the fact that he was also President of the Muslim League, that gave him a special position in Pakistan which Lord Mountbatten did not enjoy in India. Jinnah might, therefore, be able to offer joint control, but Lord Mountbatten being a strictly constitutional Governor-General, was in no position to accept the offer. The conversations were inconclusive, Lord Mountbatten returned to Delhi.[14]

While fighting was on, there were two meetings between Nehru and Liaquat Ali Khan, the first one in Delhi on 26 November, and the second in Lahore on 9 December. Kashmir was discussed at length but no progress was made. Ultimately, on 30 December 1947, the Government of India, *in spite of strong opposition by Mahatma Gandhi*, made a formal reference to the Security Council of the United Nations, accusing Pakistan of aggression against Kashmir. Nehru referred the issue of Kashmir to the United Nations Security Council only on the suggestion of Mountbatten. But, as predicted by the Mahatma, India was awarded 'monkey justice' by the Security Council. What was meant to be the Jammu and Kashmir Question referred by India was turned into the Indo-Pakistan Question by the Security Council. Great Britain, at the instance of the United States of America, sided with Pakistan. They ignored the fact of Pakistan's aggression and raked up, just as Pakistan wanted, all its grievances against India. They accepted Jinnah's allegation that 'India was out to throttle and choke the Dominion of Pakistan at birth'. England had divided British India between the two dominions on the basis of Jinnah's two-nation theory, and its statesmen now had every desire to extend the principle to Kashmir, a large majority of people there being Muslim.[15]

Nehru was also to regret this decision later as, instead of taking note of the aggression by Pakistan, the Security Council, guided by Britain and the United States, tended to side with

Pakistan. Nehru, who had expected to get justice from the United Nations, was to express his disillusionment in a letter to Vijaylakshmi Pandit in February 1948: 'I could not imagine that the Security Council could possibly behave in the trivial and partisan manner in which it functioned. Those people are supposed to keep the world in order. It is not surprising that the world is going to pieces. The United States and Britain have played a dirty role. Britain probably being the chief actor is behind the scenes.'[16]

The United Nations, through one of its resolutions, passed on 31 December 1948, asked both India and Pakistan to accept ceasefire. As regards accession, it was left to be decided by plebiscite under UN supervision after Pakistan had first withdrawn its troops from Kashmir, including the area which was still under its control, and which later came to be known as Azad Kashmir. As Pakistan failed to vacate the occupied territory, the question of implementing the plebiscite part of the UN resolution, did not arise.[17]

Dubious Sheikh

The complexity of Kashmir did not end here. When the interests of England and America began to flag, China came forward in support of Pakistan's claim over Kashmir. Another player, which made Kashmir an unending drama was the ambition of Sheikh Abdullah who wanted to become the all-purveying monarch of the State. He had been loyal only to his ambition in the fulfilment of which he had counted every personal relationship as nothing. He had begun his political career as a Muslim communalist against the Hindu Maharaja. However, he soon realised he could not succeed without help from outside the State. The only choice left to the Sheikh was to turn himself into a nationalist and change his Muslim Conference to National Conference and seek help of the Congress. Nehru had a soft corner in his heart for Kashmir. This is because his grand father had left Kashmir about a century and half ago for Allahabad and for Jawaharlal distance must have added greater charm to a beautiful land. Abdullah's association must have filled his heart with hope of recovering Kashmir. Thus, the friendship that came to be formed between the Sheikh and Nehru was one of pure convenience on the part of the former and went deep in the case of the latter.

Although the Sheikh was determined to replace Maharaja Hari Singh, he also knew that to begin with, he would have to lull his suspicions and gain his confidence. In this connection, the letter that he wrote to him on his release is of interest, showing as it does the working of his mind. After attributing the regrettable happenings of the past to 'machinations of interested people' he wrote, 'In spite of what has happened in the past, I assure your Highness that myself and my party have never harboured any sentiment of disloyalty towards your Highness as person, throne or dynasty. The development of this beautiful country and the betterment of its people is our common aim and interest and I assure your Highness the fullest and loyal support of myself and my organisation. Not only this, but I assure your Highness that any party, within or without the State which may attempt to create any impediments in our efforts to gain our goal will be treated as our enemy and will be treated as such'.[18]

However, it took hardly a week for the Sheikh to start the process of fulfilling his ambition. He used a Kashmiri brahmin, Dwarkanath Kachru, for the purpose. On 4 October 1947 Kachru wrote to Nehru, 'Sheikh Sahib feels that unless there is transfer of power to a substantial degree, the National Conference may find itself in a difficult position. To fight the League, to maintain law and order inside the State and to carry the masses with them, it is highly essential that a settlement with the National Conference should be brought about simultaneously with the accession to the Union'.[19]

It would appear that within a week, the Sheikh had understood that it was easier for him to work upon the trusting Nehru than upon the hardheaded Patel, as is revealed by the last paragraph of Kachru's letter, 'I need hardly repeat that you realise the whole position much better than most of us but I hope your colleagues will also take a similar view of the situation here'.[20]

Patel at once understood the game and wrote to Nehru, strongly protesting against the unwarranted comment against him. Patel wrote to Nehru, 'para 19 of Kachru's letter has a fling which is obviously aimed at me. I do not think that anything which could have been done for Kashmir has been left undone by me, nor I am aware of any difference between you and me on matters of policy relating to Kashmir. Still it is most unfortunate that persons down below should think that there is a small gulf between us. It is also distressing to me'.[21] Ignoring the attempt of the Sheikh to create difference between Nehru and Patel, Mehrchand Mahajan was forced to make a substantial gesture to win Sheikh Abdullah's support. However, since the Pakistani forces had already entered Kashmir, Mahajan was compelled to suggest to Sheikh Abdullah that it was not the proper time to think of any constitutional issue.

Sheikh Abdullah was as much opposed to accession to Pakistan as the Maharaja himself, in fact, even more. Sheikh Abdullah was well aware that as a Muslim, he would be as much welcome to India as the Maharaja would be in Pakistan. He, therefore, strongly pressed the Maharaja to accede to the Indian Union. Knowing fully Abdullah's close association with Nehru, the Maharaja would have turned a deaf ear to his importunity, had Jinnah not precipitated the issue of accession by raiding Kashmir, forcing the Maharaja to accede to India. The Maharaja was aware of personal advantages accruing to him if he joined Pakistan. The Maharaja signed the Instrument of Accession and with it signed away his own future. Thus, in his contest with the Sheikh, he had been worsted.

Sheikh, after his release, had been placed at the head of a provisional government. Because of his letter written to the Maharaja, in which he had pledged his loyalty in high spirits, the Maharaja must have expected at least minimum loyalty from him. But as early as 7 November 1947, Dalip Singh, Agent to the Government of India in Jammu and Kashmir, informed Patel that, 'H.H. personally disliked Sheikh Sahib and Sheikh Sahib's endeavours to try and maintain authority in Jammu without reference to H.H. are merely causing friction and tension'.[22]

To end the trouble between the Sheikh and the Maharaja, Patel proposed that an interim government on the model of Mysore be formed. The Maharaja agreed but the Sheikh raised all sorts of objections. Premier Mehrchand Mahajan, in his letter 21 November 1947, wrote to Patel, 'There should not be further delay in the formation of an interim government' and added, 'Sheikh Sahib, I suppose is in no hurry about it, having got dictatorial powers which are being exercised in a dictatorial manner regardless of all rules and forms of law'.[23]

Even Nehru approved of the Mysore model[XV] but, in one of his letters to the Maharaja, impressed upon him the importance of Abdullah. 'If there is going to be a plebiscite, then obviously we have to work in such a way as to gain the goodwill of the majority of the population of the State, which means chiefly the Muslims. The policy recently pursued in Jammu province has alienated the Muslims there very greatly and has created a great deal of ill-feeling in certain parts of the country. The only person who can effectively deal with the situation is Sheikh Abdullah.'[24]

Sheikh Abdullah, however, was not agreeable to a select Mysore model without suitable alterations to his advantage. He particularly wanted to have complete control over the Dogra army which was under the control of Maharaja; wanted to get rid of Mehrchand Mahajan, an ex-Chief Justice of Punjab High Court and a stickler for rules and regulations. Nehru had to fall

---

[XV] The process of transition by which Mysore became an integral part of Indian Union was smooth and easy. In August 1947, the Maharaja executed both Instrument of Accession and the Standstill Agreement. In June 1948 he executed revised Instrument of Accession giving the Central Legislature power to legislate on all matters in the federal and concurrent legislative lists, except relating to duties and taxation

in line with the Sheikh's wishes and N Gopalaswami Ayyangar, a member of the Constituent Assembly and minister without portfolio, who was used to assist on the Kashmir issue, wrote to the Maharaja accordingly. On receiving a copy of the above letter, Patel wrote to Ayyangar, 'The proposals which you have made may ease matters from the point of view of Sheikh Abdullah, but whether they would ease matters from the point of view of the Maharaja is difficult for me to say. We have to bear in mind that it was he (Sheikh Abdullah) who suggested to the Maharaja to agree to the Mysore model and unless the Maharaja can be persuaded to agree to alter it, I feel that we cannot insist on him to accept any change. We have also to take into account that it is the Maharaja who has entered into commitment with Mahajan and, therefore, it is for him to decide whether or not he could release himself from that commitment. All we can do is to persuade him to agree to this position'.[25]

Nehru refused to let Patel handle Kashmir issue

Ayyangar continued to negotiate and the Maharaja too persisted in declining to accept any modifications of the Mysore model. Patel found himself in a difficult position and frankly told Ayyangar that negotiations should be left to be conducted by him (Patel) as the one in charge of the States Ministry. As Ayyangar was acting under the instructions of Nehru, the latter had to tell Patel that he was personally interested in Kashmir and that Nehru should be left free to handle its affairs. Referring to the correspondence that had passed between Patel and Ayyangar, Nehru wrote to Patel, 'I must confess that I am surprised to read this. I do not appreciate the principle which presumably the States Ministry has in view in regard to its work. That ministry, or any other ministry, is not an *imperium in imperio*, jealous of its sovereignty in certain domains and working in isolation from the rest. If that was so, then the government would not be a close-knit organism working together with a common purpose, and the PM would have no function to perform. But I do not wish to consider the wider question of principle at this stage though it may have to be discussed later.

'The present issue relates to Kashmir. This raises all manner of connected issues—international, military and others—which are beyond the competence of the States Ministry as such. That is why it has to be considered by the Cabinet as a whole frequently, and various ministers separately or together. And that is why I have to take personal interest in this matter as PM to bring about coordination in our various activities.'[26]

Patel's instant reaction to this forthright letter was to tender his resignation. The draft of a letter from him to Nehru, found in his papers, is dated 23 December 1947, which said, 'your letter makes it clear to me that I must not or at least cannot continue as a member of the government and hence I am hereby tendering my resignation. I am grateful to you for the courtesy and kindness shown to me during the period of office which was a period of considerable strain.'[27] However, after the intervention of the Mahatma, the letter did not reach Nehru.

Perhaps, the story of Kashmir would have been different if only that State Ministry had been allowed to remain within Patel's jurisdiction. It was taken away from him by Nehru at the instance of Sheikh Abdullah. But for Jawaharlal Nehru, says KM Munshi, 'who under the influence of Sheikh Abdullah, took away the portfolio of Kashmir from the Sardar's States Ministry, Kashmir would never have become the problem that it has been'.[28]

The Sardar seriously doubted the rightness of Nehru's policy towards Kashmir and refused to share his (Nehru's) abounding confidence in the Sheikh. He was, however, not alone in entertaining such misgivings. Some of the members of the Union government wondered what precisely could be the ultimate aim of the Sheikh concerning that State. Even Gandhiji writes to Pyarelal, 'If Sheikh Abdullah is erring in the discharge of his duty as the chief of his cabinet or as a devout Muslim, he should certainly step aside and give place to a better man'.[29] One must remember, Gandhi did not favour the Kashmir issue being taken to the United Nations where he was certain that India would get only what he called, 'monkey justice'. 'The Sardar endorsed this view and held that if Pakistan had a grievance, it was open to that country to go anywhere it chose. He felt that India's precipitate action in rushing to the world body was a great mistake.'[30]

Betrayal by Sheikh Abdullah

Sheikh was determined to pursue his ambition to have absolute control over Kashmir. India's going to the United Nations with Kashmir further emboldened him and he began to act more arbitrarily than before. He now started a tirade against the Maharaja and also indulged in propaganda against India and its leaders. At a press conference on 29 September 1948, after strongly criticising the Maharaja, Abdullah referred to the Hindu fanaticism of East Punjab and to certain people in India whom he believed wanted to surrender Kashmir to Pakistan. When Patel drew Nehru's attention to the Sheikh, the latter explained away the conduct of his protégé in this manner, 'Sheikh Abdullah is, I am convinced, a very straight and frank man. He is not a very clear thinker, and he goes astray in his speech as many of our politicians do. He is, of course, obsessed with the idea of meeting the challenge of Pakistan and keeping his own people influenced by Pakistan's propaganda. I made it clear to him that while I entirely agreed with this, the approach should be different'.[31]

On Nehru's suggestion, Patel started persuading the Maharaja to leave Kashmir and allow Yuvraj Karan Singh to act on his behalf. After lot of persuasion, Hari Singh wrote to Patel on 6 May 1949, that he was agreeable to absent himself from the State for a period of three or four months, but wanted to be assured that this step was not a prelude to any idea of abdication. However, the step did become a prelude to his abdication and he was never allowed to return.

Nehru had agreed to Mountbatten's suggestion for a plebiscite because he had felt sure that with Abdullah in sole charge of the government, the bulk of the Muslim population of the State would vote for accession to India. But Abdullah, in fact, did not want a plebiscite. The Sheikh knew that the moment the accession to India was finalised by a plebiscite, held under the supervision of the UN, he would be deprived of his trump card in dealing with the Indian government. If Kashmir had to go to India at all, he must have thought, then it must go as a *gift from him* and he would gift it on his own terms. Writes BN Mullik, then Director, Intelligence Bureau, 'If a plebiscite had been held in Jammu and Kashmir sometime in 1949, there was a good chance that the majority of the people would have voted for India, because the wounds inflicted by the Pakistani raiders on the peaceful people of Kashmir were still fresh in their minds and India was held in much respect as their saviour.... However, the strongest opposition to the plebiscite came from Sheikh Abdullah himself. His contention was that he alone represented Kashmir and whatever he decided was good enough for the Kashmiris and it was not necessary to have a plebiscite to find out what the people wanted.... So the Indian government was on the horns of a dilemma. It had accepted the UNCIP's (United Nations Commission for India and Pakistan) resolution about a plebiscite and could not go back on it. On the other hand, its greatest supporter in Kashmir, Sheikh Abdullah, resolutely set his face against a plebiscite'.[32]

The Maharaja's exit paved the way for his exile from the State. Around August 1949, BN Mullik spent ten days in the valley and worked his assessment of the situation. According to Mullik, 'He (Sardar) suspected that Sheikh was not genuine and was misleading Pandit Nehru... He (Sardar) apprehended that Sheikh Abdullah would ultimately let down India and Jawaharlal Nehru, and would come out in his real colours... Events as they turned out subsequently, proved that the Sardar was right and I was not. Within three years, we found ourselves fighting against

Sheikh Abdullah. Sardar Patel was dead by then... Probably, things would not have come to this pass at all if the Sardar was still alive, because Sheikh Abdullah had a very wholesome respect and fear of him'.[33]

Developments in Kashmir were alarming. Rising above personal discouragements, and even affronts, Patel served the interest of the country by playing the role of an honest broker; to bring about stability and harmony in the State through reconciliation between Abdullah and Maharaja. It was easier for him to handle the Maharaja, but not Abdullah. His fears proved true when Abdullah was explosive at a press conference on 29 September 1948, of which Patel complained to Nehru, 'we, the Maharaja and Sheikh Abdullah himself came to settlement last March (1948). That settlement has not only been faithfully adhered to by the Maharaja, but in certain respects he has acquiesced in departures from the settlement to the advantage of Sheikh Abdullah'. Patel further pointed out, 'I am not aware of any single instance... in which the Maharaja has obstructed or resisted any of the popular reforms. As a constitutional head, he may have asked for reconstruction in one or two matters, but this could hardly be treated as the subject of a grievance. It is undignified and constitutionally improper for a Prime Minister (Abdullah) to attack the constitutional head of his administration, knowing full well that the latter is not in a position to defend himself or to retaliate. On the top of it, to insinuate that he is trying to retain power, or that he has strong friends in India, or that he could buy friends is, in my opinion, to say the least, most unfortunate'.[34]

Patel also wrote to Abdullah the same day in an effort to bring him to the path of reasonableness, 'I had hoped... with practically no resistance or obstruction from the Maharaja in regard to the many schemes of reforms which you have introduced and are introducing, you would now accommodate yourself to your new constitutional relationship with him. I had never imagined that you would ventilate your grievance in public, and I had thought that at least in fairness to ourselves, and having regard to the agreed arrangements between ourselves, if you had any grievance, you would first come to States Ministry and seek a satisfactory solution through our medium'. Patel argued with Abdullah, 'No one knows better than you today the Maharaja is powerless to resist your wishes. Even if he feels inclined differently, on merits, he has to endorse your wishes if you pressed them. It is within my knowledge that he has deferred to your wishes in matters which concerned him intimately.... I am therefore, unable to comprehend your reference to his trying to retain power'.[35]

By the first week of October 1948, Abdullah had grown so bold as to become a law unto himself, and he demanded, '...the choice is between the Maharaja and the people, and if the choice is not soon made, it might lead us into trouble both militarily and politically. The only alternative is that His Highness should abdicate in favour of his son'.[36]

Patel minced no words in reminding Abdullah, 'you seem to be in peculiar position of having been misunderstood, apart from many others, by all three of us — Jawaharalal, Gopalaswami (Minister without portfolio in Nehru's cabinet who was asked to assist him in handling Kashmir) and myself. Jawaharlal has written to me and, I believe, spoken to you also, taking exception to your attitude at the press conference. Similarly, Gopalaswami has done the same and spoke to you the very next day.... There is no disposition on your part either to understand our point of view or to strike a new line as demanded by the changed situation. I am quite convinced that the grossly prejudiced view, which you have taken of the matters referred to is not likely to mend matters; instead it is likely to make them worse and more complicated'. Patel further told Abdullah, 'you do not seem to realise that both you and we ourselves owe the technical correctness of our position in regard to Kashmir to the Maharaja's signing the accession and his calling upon you to form the Ministry. Without that, neither we or you would have been where we are… I am also surprised that you, who had a different attitude towards his Highness when you were in jail, as is typified in your letter to him, a copy of which is with me, should now speak in such terms'.[37]

Such advise cut no ice with Abdullah. He continued to be high-handed, uncompromising, overbearing and dictatorial. He could do so, as he knew Nehru would not let him down because of his hatred for the Maharaja. Patel failed to save the Maharaja, as Nehru ultimately came round to Abdullah's view—which he expressed in his letter of 17 April 1949 to Patel, '…it was highly desirable that the Maharaja should take some kind of leave and not remain in Kashmir'.[38] In glaring contrast, Abdullah was growing bolder with his despotic utterances. In an interview with Michael Davidson of *The Scotsman*, he said, 'Accession to either side cannot bring peace. We want to live in friendship with both Dominions. Perhaps, a middle path between them… an independent Kashmir must be guaranteed not only by India and Pakistan, but also by Britain, the United States and other members of the United Nations'.[39]

After seeing the report of Abdullah's interview with Davidson, Patel was so disturbed that he wrote to Gopalaswami on 1 May 1949, 'you have probably seen the interview by Sheikh Sahib to Michael Davidson which was published in *The Scotsman* of 14 April 1949. A vehement exponent of accession to India seems to have been converted to an independent Kashmir'.[40] The same day, Gopalaswami wrote back to Sardar, 'It is a most astonishing performance. Kachru, who is going to Kashmir tomorrow, has just been to see me, and I am sending a message through him to Sheikh Abdullah. I have asked him to tell the latter that I condemn the Sheikh's action and that I feel that what he has told Michael Davidson and what the latter has published will have the most serious and mischievous consequences both in India and abroad. I have asked him to inform the Sheikh that, reading between the lines, I suspect a plan, the first step of which is this blessing by the Premier of Kashmir to the idea of an independent Kashmir, and this public expression of his conviction that accession to India will not bring peace, and the final step of which may well be perhaps one of the greatest betrayals in history. He will also be told that India will expect him publicly to repudiate some of the things attributed to him by Michael Davidson. It is all so distressing'.[41]

Patel was simply complying with Nehru's wishes when he undertook the painful task of the Maharaja leaving the State on 29 April, about which he wrote to Nehru on 11 May: '...I explained to him the whole position and commended to him my view that, in the circumstances of his relations with the Ministry and the situation created by the reference to the UNO and the plebiscite issue, it should be best for him to absent himself from the State for sometime and to make the Yuvraj Regent.' Nehru added further poignancy to the Maharaja's sense of shock and bewilderment by suggesting to Patel, 'I do not think any period should be fixed for the Maharaja's absence from Kashmir. The matter had been left vague'. The Maharaja could not help telling Patel, 'I would not be human if I did not express my sense of keen disappointment and bewilderment at having been called upon to make such a sacrifice of personal prestige, honour and position... while Sheikh Abdullah has been allowed to depart from time to time as suited his inclinations, from the pledged and written word, to act consistently in breach of the loyalty which he professed to me prior to his release from jail and the oath of allegiance which he took when he assumed office, and to indulge openly along with his colleagues in a campaign of vilification and found calumny against me, both inside the State and outside. I should have had to be driven from position to position—each of which I thought I held on the advice of the State Ministry'.[42]

Inclusion of Article 370 in the Constitution

Patel was officiating for Nehru during the latter's absence in Europe in October-November 1948, when the Constituent

Assembly debated some amendments to article 370. Abdullah could not contain his anger over the Assembly's right to do so. To him, Article 370 was to be 'an executive act of the Government of India as distinguished from Parliament to "exclude altogether the Parliament of India from having any say regarding the Constitution of Jammu and Kashmir" and that only the State Assembly could "revise or annul any action taken by the Government of India."'[43] In that burning anger, Abdullah cast aside the respect the House commanded of each member and walked out in protest with the threat that he was going back to Kashmir. It was a virtual boycott. Patel could not take up the cudgels with Abdullah, as the debate was on. Later he sent Mahavir Tyagi to the railway station to deliver a stern message. Abdullah had settled down in his compartment when Tyagi stepped in to tell him, 'Sheikh Sahib, the Sardar says you could leave the House but you can not leave Delhi.'[44] Evidently, Patel alone, not Nehru, could strike such fear in Abdullah, and he alone could have tamed the 'Lion of Kashmir'.

The uncermonious manner in which Kashmir had been taken away from his charge had caused Patel considerable pain. As a result, he had adopted a bystander's attitude, though offering help whenever called upon and he rendered such help as a matter of duty to the country. He avoided a direct clash with Nehru for two reasons: Nehru's sentimental love for Kashmir and his nearness for Sheikh Abdullah; also to ensure his own freedom in handling Hyderabad. Patel, therefore, witnessed with acute sorrow Abdullah's high-handedness in getting rid of the Maharaja's Prime Minister and constitutional advisor, Mehrchand Mahajan, and thereafter, sending the Maharaja himself into an indefinite exile. Both were with Nehru's support, no matter if they lacked constitutional validity.

What mattered most to India was Article 370. Its genesis lay in Nehru's agreeing to Abdullah's having a separate Constitution for the State. Even President Rajendra Prasad was 'taken back',[45] when Abdullah conveyed to him Nehru's acceptance of such a proposal. A day or two prior to Nehru's departure for Europe, Abdullah arrived in New Delhi for its implementation. Nehru entrusted the drafting of the Article to KM Munshi, Ayyangar and Abdullah. According to Munshi, 'Abdullah was unhappy with the Article we drafted, and though he was scheduled to support the Article before the Constituent Assembly', Munshi feared he might be absent from the proceedings.[46] Instead, Abdullah chose to lodge his protest in person with a walkout.

Nehru left India at a very crucial moment, when there persisted lot of confusion and bitterness due to this Article. However, Nehru entrusted Ayyangar with completing this difficult task, get it adopted by the Constituent Assembly. Prior to that, the Article had to have the approval of the Congress Parliamentary Party. At the meeting, the issue raised 'a storm of angry protests from all sides and Gopalswami Ayyangar found himself a lone defender, with Maulana Azad an ineffective supporter.'[47] Ayyangar got so unnerved that he appealed to Patel to come to his rescue. Patel, out of sheer magnanmity to save the ugly situation from getting out of hand, came forward to support Ayyangar. With great difficulty he got the party's approval the very next day, and thus, paved the way for its presentation to the Constituent Assembly. Patel, however, told Ayyangar the bitter truth which others feared to utter in public. 'Whenever Sheikh Sahib wishes to back out, he always confronts us with his duty to people. Of course, he owes no duty to India or to the Indian Government, or even on a personal basis to you and the Prime Minister who had gone all out to accommodate him.'

After Patel's death, Abdullah had no qualms even to state: 'We shall not hesitate to secede from India if we are not assured a place of honour and dignity in terms of the safeguards provided for the people of the State under Article 370 of the Constitution.'[48]

Instead of plebiscite, the Sheikh arranged to have a Constituent Assembly. Elections to this body were held in September 1951. In the Kashmir valley, where Muslims were in majority, Sheikh Abdullah could have got all his candidates elected without any difficulty, but from Jammu, which was a Hindu-majority area, most of the elected members would have been opposed to the Sheikh, although they were as much in favour of accession to India as Abdullah's own followers from the valley. In view of this, as stated by BN Mullik, 'nomination papers of most of those who could form an opposition were rejected'. Mullik further says, 'The result of this election satisfied the Sheikh's vanity, as he used to declare openly that he was Kashmir and anybody who was opposed to his views did not have any place in the valley. So, to him, an opposition party in the Constituent Assembly was unthinkable'.[49]

Having cleared the decks, Abdullah was now poised for his next assault: to send the Maharaja into exile, which he achieved with remarkable ease and speed with Nehru's help. Soon Nehru himself became a victim in 1953, when Abdullah challenged Nehru's authority and conspired to become Sultan-e-Kashmir. Before the Maharaja's abdication, Abdullah secured the exit of Mahajan from Dewanship, so as to weaken the position of the Maharaja by denying him the support of a trusted legal advisor.

The Constituent Assembly confirmed Kashmir's accession to India, abolished the office of the Maharaja, replacing it by a Sadar-e-Riyasat (governor) and decided to have a separate flag for the State. Sheikh Abdullah became the Prime Minister of Kashmir and Yuvraj Karan Singh was elected Sadr-e-Riyasat. The Constitution, which finally emerged at the instance of the Sheikh, kept 'Kashmir as autonomous as possible with only a tenuous bond through accession on defence, communications and foreign affairs'.[50]

Provisions of Article 370

The sum and substance of Article 370 is that with regard to Jammu and Kashmir, in addition to Defence, Foreign Affairs and Communication, the Union Parliament can make laws on items in the Union and Concurrent Lists but *only with the concurrence* of the State government. This puts the Jammu and Kashmir State on a special footing. While the Union Parliament has unfettered powers to make laws for all the States in respect of items included in the Union and Concurrent Lists of the Constitution, it can do so with regard to Jammu and Kashmir *only with the consent of the State government.*[51]

The Constituent Assembly of Jammu and Kashmir ratified the State's accession to India in February 1956. With this ratification, the issue of accession was finally settled but the issues with regard to Jurisdiction of Parliament to subjects other than Defence, Foreign Affairs, Communication were kept flexible. The President could, with the concurrence of the State government, extend provisions of the Indian Constitution to the State of Jammu and Kashmir.[52]

The proposals to extend more items of the Indian Constitution to Jammu and Kashmir were discussed by the representatives of the Union government and the State government. At that time, Sheikh Abdullah was the Prime Minister of Jammu and Kashmir. The understanding reached during this discussion is known as the Delhi Agreement (1952). In pursuance of this agreement, the then President of India issued a number of provisions of the Indian Constitution for J&K. This provision was amended from time to time, extending more provisions of the Indian Constitution to the State. Separately, the Constitution of Jammu and Kashmir was amended in 1966 to change the denominations of Sadre-e-Riyasat to that of Governor and of Prime Minister to the Chief Minister.[53] Important among the provisions of the Indian Constitution extended to the State of Jammu and Kashmir included Article 356 and the Jurisdiction of the Supreme Court, the Election Commission, and the Comptroller and Auditor General.

The political parties in Jammu and Kashmir, particularly the National Conference, have been raising voice against the extention of the Indian constitutional provisions in the State. They claim that such extended provisions are erosion of the

State's autonomy. During Assembly debates, the National Conference leaders put forward a number of provisions of the Constitution extended to the State of Jammu and Kashmir during the period between 1953-1975 which, they claim, 'eroded the autonomy of the State':

- By the 1954 Presidential order, the operations of Customs, Central Excise, Civil Aviation, Post and Telegraph were extended.
- In 1958, All India Services—IAS, IPS was introduced. Functions of Comptroller and Auditor General were extended.
- In 1959, the legislative entry relating to Census were applied, making way for conducting of census of 1961 under Central law.
- In 1960, J&K was brought under the jurisdiction of Supreme Court. The jurisdiction of Election Commission of India was extended.
- In 1964, Article 356 and 357 of the Constitution were applied, making way for the introduction of President's Rule and Emergency.
- In 1965, a number of legislative entries relating to welfare of Labour, Trade Unions, Social Security and Social Insurance were applied.
- In 1966, provisions relating to direct elections to Lok Sabha were applied.
- Since 1953, about 337 laws relating to Charter Accounts Law, Coinage Act, Conservation of Foreign Exchange and Prevention of Smuggler Activities Law, Contempt of Courts Law, Customs Law, Copyright Act, Dangerous Drugs Act, Delimitation etc have been extended to Jammu and Kashmir State.
- Moreover, the Visa-type 'Permit Systems' was abolished.[54]

Thus today, Jammu and Kashmir State has a Constitution of its own which is an unfortunate by-product of Article 370. No other State of the Indian Union has a separate Constitution.

All other States have uniform structure; it is laid down in part IV of the Constitution of India.

Article 35A of the Constitution of India

One more constitutional fact cannot be overlooked which assumes significance, particularly, in the light of the fact that Article 370 does not protect the laws enacted by the Assembly of Jammu and Kashmir or rules, regulations framed by the Government of Jammu and Kashmir, from being declared *ultra vires* of the Constitution of India, if it is found unconstitutional. Therefore, the then Government of India, headed by Pandit Jawaharlal Nehru, as its Prime Minister, in the year 1954 got a new Article 35A incorporated in the Constitution of India whereby protecting the legislations enacted by the Assembly of Jammu & Kashmir, which reads:

> 35A: Saving of laws with respect to permanent residents and their rights—notwithstanding anything contained in this Constitution, no existing law in force in the State of Jammu and Kashmir, and no law hereafter enacted by the Legislature of the State,—(a) defining the classes of persons who are, or shall be, permanent residents of the State of Jammu and Kashmir; or (b) conferring on such permanent residents any special rights and privileges or imposing upon other persons any restrictions as respects—(I) employment under the State Government; (II) acquisition of immovable property in the State; (III) settlement in the State; or (IV) right to scholarships and such forms of aid as the State Government may provide, shall be void on the ground that it is inconsistent with or takes away or abridges any rights conferred on the other citizens of India by any provision of this part.

A perusal of Article 35A would clearly show that any law made by the State of Jammu & Kashmir or its legislative Assembly in respect of definition of classes of persons, permanent residents of the State of Jammu & Kashmir, conferring on such permanent residents any special rights and privileges or restrictions in respect of employment under the State Government, acquisition of immovable property in the State, settlement in the State, right to scholarships and such other forms of aid as the State government may provide, cannot be declared void on the ground of its being inconsistent or on the ground of curtailment of any rights conferred to the citizens of India by Part III of Constitution of India.

How Article 35A was added

Article 35A was incorporated not by any constitutional amendment by the Indian Parliament but by a Presidential Order issued by the President of India, exercising power under Article 370 (I) (d). Most legal luminaries opine that this act of the then Government of India is highly unconstitutional and contrary to established democratic norms.

Article 370 read with Article 35A of the Indian Constitution

Article 370 was incorporated in the Constitution of India as a 'temporary provision' which is evident from reading of Part XXI of the Constitution of India which consists of Articles 369 to 392. Thus, Article 370 is a temporary and transitional provision incorporated in the Constitution of India by the Constitution framers.

However, by way of 13th amendment Act 1962, the word 'and special' has been added in the heading of Part XXI to the Constitution of India. It shows that at the time of coming into force of Constitution of India, Article 370 was not a special provision. It has been special only after the 13th amendment.

However, it was unanimously agreed by the members of the Constituent Assembly that Article 370 may continue to remain incorporated till Jammu & Kashmir adopts its Constitution. Therefore, Article 370 was incorporated to the Constitution of India as transitional provision between the date of coming into force of the Indian Constitution and till the date of framing and adoption of Constitution by the Constituent Assembly of J&K. This is also evident from the debate of the Constituent Assembly and the proceedings recorded thereto. Therefore, after coming into force of the Constitution of State of Jammu & Kashmir, Article 370 ought to have been deleted which has not been done, so far. Hence, it is a debatable point whether Article 370 ought to have been in operation or not after the Constitution of the State of Jammu & Kashmir coming into force.

Constitution of Jammu and Kashmir

The Constituent Assembly of Jammu & Kashmir adopted its Constitution on 7th November 1956. The Premble of the Constitution states: We, the people of the State of Jammu and Kashmir, having solemnly resolved, in pursuance of the accession of this State to India which took place on the sixth day of October, 1947, to further define the existing relationship of the State with the Union of India as an integral part thereof, and to secure to ourselves – justice, social, economic and political; liberty of thought, expression, belief, faith and worship; equality of status and opportunity and to promote among us all; fraternity assuring the dignity of the individual and the unity of the Nation.

Article 3, contained in the part III of the said Constitution further states, 'Relationship of the State with the Union of India: —The State of Jammu and Kashmir is and shall be an integral part of the Union of India.'

India's Fundamental Rights can't be implemented in J&K

Due to existence of Article 370 and 35A, fundamental rights provided under the Constitution of India cannot be implemented in the State of Jammu & Kashmir.

Due to these two articles, there is helplessness in granting relief to those Hindus who have migrated from West Pakistan to Kashmir after partition of India who have not been given voting rights, status of residents or any other right which is guaranteed by Part III of the Constitution of India. The helplessness to provide relief to such persons has been expressed even by the Supreme Court in the case of Bachan Lal Kalgotra & Others versus Jammu & Kashmir, in 1987. The observations of the Supreme Court were:

> The petitioners have a justifiable grievance. We are told that they constitute nearly seven to eight per cent of the population of the State of Jammu & Kashmir. Surely, they are entitled to expect to be protected by the State of Jammu & Kashmir. In the peculiar context of the State of Jammu & Kashmir, the Union of India also owes an obligation to make some provision for the advancement of the cultural, economic and educational rights of these persons. We do hope that the claims of persons like the petitioner and others to exercise greater rights of citizenship will receive due consideration from the Union of India and the State of Jammu & Kashmir. We are, however, unable to give any relief to the petitioners.

Nehru disillusioned

Inspite of all favour extended by Nehru to Sheikh Abdullah, the latter betrayed Nehru's confidence, as soon as he felt that he had achieved what he wanted. Nehru had himself come round to Patel's viewpoint later in 1962, when he told BN Mullik of Abdullah's 'communal activities throughout the period he had acted as the National Conference leader. It was the Pakistani aggression which had mellowed him a little for a short time, because the tribals had committed gruesome atrocities on Muslim populations in the valley. But, as soon as he became Prime Minister, he came out in his true colours once again and started anti-Hindu activities... his entire outlook and behavior was based on the fact that the Kashmir valley had a Muslim majority'.[55]

Sheikh Abdullah, perhaps, had some inkling about Nehru's disillusionment and he also feared that the Indian government might go to the extent of taking some action against him. This led him to establish contact with Pakistan through one Pir Maqbool Gilani. The Intelligence Bureau received information that 'an emissary (from Pakistan) was on his way to Tanmarg (near Gulmarg) to meet Sheikh', writes Mullik, himself in charge of the IB. 'Suspicions deepened when the Sheikh suddenly left for Tanmarg on the morning of 8 August 1953. So, the day was automatically determined by the Sheikh's own action, as any further delay might be attended with unforeseen results.'[56] That day, Sheikh Abdullah was arrested and exiled from Kashmir and Bakshi Ghulam Mohammad succeeded him as Prime Minister.

Reference to UNO was blunder on the part of Nehru

The Government of India has been subjected to criticism for some of its decisions on Kashmir, such as the promise to hold a plebiscite, to take the matter to the UN, and accept ceasefire.

As against the first decision, it has been argued that the signing of the Instrument of Accession by the Maharaja should have been considered enough, as has been done in the case of so many other States. The suggestion to hold plebiscite had come from Mountbatten and the critics say that Nehru should not have agreed to it. As a matter of fact, Mountbatten had himself declared in the Conference of the Princes addressed by him on 25 July 1947, that it was for each prince to decide to which of the two dominions he would like to accede. Moreover, when he had gone to Kashmir in June 1947, it was not to advise Maharaja Hari Singh to hold plebiscite but merely to urge upon him to take a quick decision to avoid complications between India and Pakistan on the Kashmir issue. This being so, if the Maharaja had decided to accede to India at that time, Mountbatten and Nehru would have, as a matter of course, treated the accession as final. It, therefore, appears that Mountbatten raised the question of plebiscite only because the accession followed on the heels of the invasion of Kashmir by Pakistani tribesmen.

Mountbatten might also have been consciously or unconsciously influenced by the two-nation theory, but Nehru professed to being a thorough nationalist and he could have objected to Mountbatten's suggestion on the ground that as a Congressman and secularist, he could not treat Kashmir any differently from any other princely State simply because a majority of Kashmir's population was Muslims. But Nehru failed to do so. He must have agreed to plebiscite owing to his blind faith in Mountbatten and Sheikh Abdullah. Nehru's decision to refer the Kashmir issue to the UNO stunned all others as this decision was taken without consulting his Cabinet colleagues.

DP Mishra writes, 'On 26 October 1947, when India accepted Kashmir's accession, I happened to be in Delhi. When I met Patel in the evening, he told me how he had been busy for the whole day with Kashmir's accession. Next morning, as I was leaving Delhi by the State plane from Safdarjung, Indian troops were flying for Srinagar from Palam. Soon after, I heard Nehru's voice on All India Radio, Nagpur, committing the Government of India on the holding of a plebiscite in Kashmir. From my talk with Patel, I had received the impression that the signature of the Maharaja had finally settled the Kashmir issue, I was surprised by Nehru's announcement. When I visited Delhi next, I pointedly asked Patel whether the decision to hold a plebiscite in Kashmir was taken at a meeting of the Cabinet. He sighed and shook his head. It was evident that Nehru had acted on Mountbatten's advice and had ignored his colleagues'.[57]

It was Mountbatten's brainwave to approach the UNO. As mentioned earlier, he had first discussed it with Jinnah when he had met him in Lahore, on 1 November 1947, without any consultation with Nehru. Although Jinnah had rejected his proposal, Mountbatten persuaded Nehru to go down this path. The insistence by Mountbatten was the result of his desire to bring about a ceasefire, if not a solution, because he wanted to avoid trouble between the two Commonwealth countries. His desire to have ceasefire was fulfilled, but Nehru's wisdom has been questioned.

Lieutenant-General BM Kaul says, 'we were politically unwise in accepting the ceasefire in view of our success at the time in Uri, Tithwal and Kargil sectors'.[58] In Kaul's opinion, 'as reprisal against Pakistan's invasion of Kashmir, India could have attacked the bases of the invaders and this would have led to an all-out war between the two countries in 1947'. He adds, 'India could have defeated Pakistan decisively on ground of its own choice, instead of getting involved in a pointless war at a high altitude'. Kaul further states that, 'Nehru was convinced at the time that such a step was unnecessary as, according to him, Pakistan would collapse financially soon if it fought against a strong country like India for more than few months'.[59]

Patel, however, was of a different view. He did not believe in carrying out the Kashmir operations half way through. He would have preferred the Indian Army not to halt at Uri but to advance beyond—possibly up to Muzaffarabad. General SSP Thorat confirms that, 'our forces might have succeeded in evicting the invaders, if the Prime Minister (Nehru) had not held them in check and later ordered the ceasefire... obviously, great pressures must have been brought to bear on him by the Governor General... Panditji was a great personal and family friend of Lord Mountbatten'.[60] Capture of Domel and Muzaffarabad, which Nehru had considered of primary importance, could have been possible only if the Indian Airforce had carried the war further afield and bombarded the bases. Mountbatten would not let that happen, while Patel could not force his way as he could in Junagadh earlier, and in Hyderabad later.

One, however, gets an indication of Patel's mind while he was acting as Prime Minister. He sent for Air Marshal Thomas Elmhirst, Chairman of the Chiefs of Staff Committee, with whom he wanted to discuss a point relating to the Kashmir War. Elmhirst writes, 'He was not well, and the meeting was in the sitting room of his home, and we were alone. He (Patel) said something to this effect, "If all the decisions rested on me, I think that I would be in favour of extending this little affair in

Kashmir to a full-scale war with Pakistan... let us get it over once and for all, and settle down as a united continent.'" According to Elmhirst, Patel was 'obviously a man of action, of few words, frank, straightforward and unequivocal... whose intelligence, firmness and strength of character I much admired'.[61]

Patel proved vindicated, both in regard to the reference to the UNO and the plebiscite issue. Ayyangar admitted to Patel in his letter of 5 June 1948, 'The ways of the Security Council have been extraordinary, and in dealing with the Kashmir question, it has behaved in a manner which has surprised even a person like me.... As you say, we have entangled ourselves with a set of persons who will not see things straight'.[62] Even Nehru, in a letter to Patel from Paris, on 27 October 1948, lamented over foreigners' attitude towards Kashmir. '...this business of a plebiscite and the conditions governing it, fills people's mind. Of course, people cannot get rid of the idea that Kashmir is predominantly Muslim and, therefore, likely to side with Muslim Pakistan.'[63] In August 1949, when the American Ambassador and the British High Commissioner wanted to see Nehru with a view to persuading him to accept arbitration by Admiral Nimitz[XVI] of the US Kashmir Commission, Nehru confessed to Patel: 'All this barrage is, I suppose, meant to sweep us away.'[64] Nehru veered round to Patel's original view, which Patel had made clear in a letter to Nehru, written on July 1950, where he had declared that in the circumstances prevailing in Kashmir and 'in the world situation today, a plebiscite is unreal'.[65]

What would have been the fate of Kashmir under Patel? This has been speculated upon by, among others, Jayaprakash Naryan and MN Roy— one socialist, the other communist, but both pro-Nehru and inveterate opponents of Patel. Narayan thought that the Kashmir issue, being left to Nehru, 'proved to be

---

[XVI] Chester William Nimitz played a major role in the naval history of World War II as Commander in Chief, United States Pacific Fleet

unfortunate for the nation. Because of Panditji's mishandling, the issue no longer remained an internal affair, as it should be, but is smouldering as an international issue in the United Nations and its Security Council, making it possible for Pakistan to rake it up every now and then. Many a veteran leader in the country maintain that, had the matter been handled by Sardar (and it fell within his domain), he would have found a satisfactory solution, and thus prevented its becoming a perennial headache for us and a cause of bitterness and animosity between India and Pakistan'.[66] HV Kamath, then MP, says that Patel once told him that, 'If Jawaharlal and Gopalaswami (Ayyanger) had not made Kashmir their close preserve, "separating it from my portfolio of Home and States", he would have tackled the problem as peacefully as he had already done in Hyderabad'.[67]

MN Roy's speculation over Patel's attitude towards Kashmir was, 'I am inclined that it was as realistic as his attitude towards partition. Nevertheless, once the dye was cast by the gambler's megalomania, the Sardar had no choice but to play the game. But one could be sure that he loathes the stupidity clothed in the glamour of popular heroes'.[68] What would have been Patel's attitude? An attempt has been made to find out an answer in the postscript. As regards Mountbatten's role in the issue of Kashmir, why blame a foreigner who could not be true to India when, as goes the Indian saying, our own coin was defective. The truth is that while in Pakistan, Jinnah alone took decisions till September 1948, on India's side, too many cooks spoiled the Kashmir broth.

References:

1. DP Mishra, *Living An Era*, Vol II, pub-Vikas Publishing House, New Delhi, 1978, p-27.
2. VP Menon, *Integration of the Indian States*, Orient Black Swan, New Delhi, 1956-revised edition 2014, p-354-55.

3. Ibid, p-355.
4. Durga Das (ed), *Sardar Patel's Correspondence*, Vol I, Navjivan Publishing House, Ahmedabad, 1971, p-33.
5. DP Mishra, *Living An Era*, Vol-II, Vikas Publishing House, New Delhi, 1978, p-27.
6. VP Menon, *Integration of the Indian States*, Pub – Orient Black Swan, New Delhi, 1956-revised edition 2014, p-355.
7. Ibid, pp-363-64.
8. VP Menon, *Integration of the Indian States*, Orient Black Swan, New Delhi, 1956-revised edition 2014, p-359.
9. Ibid.
10. Ibid, p-360.
11. Ibid, p-363.
12. DP Mishra, *Living An Era*, Vol II, Vikash Publishing House, New Delhi, 1978, p-29-30.
13. Ibid p-30.
14. VP Menon, *Integration of the Indian States*, Orient Black Swan, 1956-revised edition 2014, p-364.
15. DP Mishra, *Living An Era*, Vol II, Vikash Publishing House, New Delhi, 1978, p-30.
16. S Gopal, *Jawaharlal Nehru- A Biography*, Vol-2, Harvard University Press, 1980, p-27-28.
17. Ibid, p-31.
18. Durga Das (ed), *Sardar Patel's Correspondence*, Vol I, Navjivan Publishing House, Ahmedabad, 1971, p-130.
19. Ibid, p-55.
20. Ibid.
21. Ibid, p-56.
22. Ibid p-87.
23. Ibid p-96.
24. Ibid, p-103.
25. Ibid, p-107.
26. Ibid, p-121.

27. Ibid, p-122.
28. Kulapati's Letter, *Bhavan's Journal*, 26 February 1967, p-14.
29. *Mahatma Gandhi, The Last Phase*, Pyarelal, Vol-II, p-500.
30. VB Kulkarni, *The Indian Trimvirate*, Bhartiya Vidya Bhavan, 1969, p-393.
31. Durga Das (ed), *Sardar Patel's Correspondence*, Vol II, Navjeen Publishing Ahmadabad, 1972, p-233.
32. BN Mullik, My years with Nehru, Allied Publisher, New Delhi, 1971, p-7-8.
33. BN Mullik, *My Years with Nehru: Kashmir*, Vol II, Allied publishers, New Delhi, 1971, p-14-17.
34. BN Mullik, *My Years with Nehru*, Allied Publishers, New Delhi, 1971, p-23.
35. Durga Das (ed), *Sardar Patel's Correspondence*, Vol I, Navjivan Publishing House, Ahmedabad, 1971, p-227.
36. Ibid, p-228-230.
37. Ibid, p-238.
38. Ibid, p-241-45.
39. Ibid, p-263.
40. Balraj Krishna, *Sadar Vallabhbhai Patel*, Rupa Publications, New Delhi, 2013, p-399.
41. Durga Das (ed), *Sardar Patel's Correspondence*, Vol I, p-266.
42. Ibid, p-267.
43. Ibid, p-266-69.
44. Valmiki Choudhary, *President and the Indian Constitution*, Allied Publishers, New Delhi, 1965, p-257-58.
45. Mahavir Tyagi: Interview with Prakash Vir Shastri (MP) in *Swatantra Jyoti*, Sardar Patel, Number 1973, p-27.
46. Valmiki Choudhary, *President and Indian Constitution*, Allied Publishers, New Delhi, p-298.
47. KM Munshi, in his letter to Balraj Krishna, dated 17 December 1968.
48. V Shankar, *My Reminiscences of Sardar Patel*, Vol II, Macmillan Co of India, New Delhi, 1974, p-61.
49. Jagmohan, *My Frozen Turbulence in Kashmir*, Allied Publishers, New Delhi, 1991, p-107.
50. BN Mallik, *My Years with Nehru*, Allied Publishers, New Delhi, 1971, p-24.

51. Jagmohan, *My Frozen Turbulence in Kashmir*, Allied Publishers, New Delhi, 1991, p-232.
52. Ibid.
53. Ibid.
54. Jammu and Kashmir Legislative Secretariat — Assembly Debate on Autonomy Report, 9th Session, 8 and 10 April 2000, and 20, 21, 22, 24 and 26 June 2000.
55. BN Mullik, *My Years with Nehru*, Allied Publishers, New Delhi, 1970, p-102.
56. Ibid, p-44.
57. DP Mishra, *Living An Era*, Vol II, Vikas Publishing House, New Delhi, 1978, p-40.
58. BM Kaul, *Confrontation with Pakistan*, Vikas Publishing House, New Delhi, 1971, p-9.
59. Ibid, p-6.
60. Lt Gen SPP Thorat, *From Reveille to Retreat*, Allied Publishers, 1986, p-101.
61. Elmhirst, Air Marshal Thomas, Letter to Balraj Krishna, 18 January 1969.
62. Durga Das (ed), *Sardar Patel's Correspondence*, Vol-I, p-201-02.
63. Ibid, p-249.
64. Ibid, p-294.
65. Ibid, p-317.
66. Jayaprakash Narayan, *Bhavan's Journal*, Sardar Patel: A Reappraisal, 16 January 1982, p-63.
67. HV Kamath, *Bhavan's Journal*, Sardar Vallabhbhai Patel: Some Memories, 16 January 1982, p-63.
68. MN Roy, *Men I Met*, Lalvani Publishers, Bombay, 1968, p-17.

Patel's Historic Letter of 7 Nov 1950 to Nehru

Mature and farsighted advice on Chinese Diplomacy

IT WAS the lack of foresight and imperviousness to Sardar Patel's wise counsel which brought India into mortal conflict with China.

The relations between the two countries have now become so estranged that it will be difficult to discover a *modus vivendi* between them within any foreseeable future, especially when thousands of square kilometres of Indian territory have been forcibly occupied by China. The far-reaching consequences of countenancing China's seizure of Tibet were little appreciated in India's External Affairs Ministry. The belief that the then unscalable barrier of the Himalayas would ensure protection for India from the expansionist designs of China was held with the intensity of an obsession. The fact that in modern times there are no natural frontiers was ignored with impunity. It was not realised then, nor is it being realised even now, that neither slogans nor conventional wisdom are a substitute for a sound foreign policy. We have the testimony of outstanding statesmen that no country can afford to be unselfish in its external policies. What is right is the protection of the interests of one's own country.

The tragedy of Tibet would have perhaps been less poignant if the makers of India's foreign policy had seen its pitfalls in good times. Sardar Patel's detailed demi-official letter of 7 November 1950 to Nehru must be studied with care, not only because it gives us a deep insight into his statesmenship, but also because the subsequent humiliation and defeat which India suffered at the hands of China could have been avoided if the measures indicated in it had been adopted by the then Indian government.

Besides making a number of proposals, the Sardar had suggested to the Prime Minister that they should meet early for discussing the problem. 'To my knowledge', says KM Munshi, 'the meeting suggested by the Sardar did not take place. Comment is hardly necessary.'[1]

It was not the Deputy Prime Minister (Patel) alone who held views on Tibet and China different from those of Nehru. Many members of his Cabinet including C Rajagopalachari, NV Gadgil and KM Munshi, expressed grave doubts about the soundness of the views adopted by the Government of India.

Indian military experts were also profoundly disturbed when China overran Tibet in 1950. They drew up a scheme in 1951-52 for constructing roads right up to the borders of Ladakh to facilitate the defence of Indian borders. Unfortunately, neither the Indian Ambassador to China, KM Panikkar, nor the policy makers in New Delhi attached any importance to such precautionary measures. Despite his scholarship and knowledge of history, Panikkar failed to fathom Peking's perfidy. In fact, he is stated to have declared that the attitude adopted by China towards Tibet was inevitable, right and just. When military authorities reminded Panikkar that the Chinese must have had reasons for accessing the peaks of the Himalayas, he offered no direct reply. Instead, he told them that the Indian military authorities' way of thinking was exactly like that of the British Army officers. After receiving this undeserved rebuke, the experts gave up the matter in despair.[2]

NV Gadgil, on whose narration this account is largely based, says that India could do precious little militarily when China annexed Tibet, but he holds that the tragic events of 1962 could perhaps have been averted if she had taken a firm stand on the sovereignty of Tibet. Nor was the scheme prepared by the Indian military experts taken into consideration. 'Why it became still-born', says Gadgil, 'is known only to Parmeshwar (God) above and Nehru below'.[3]

In his preparatory note to the Sardar's letter to Nehru on Tibet, reproduced in the *Bhavan's Journal*, KM Munshi says: During the Cabinet meeting on the Tibetan question, all of us acquiesced in what Jawaharlal Nehru had already done, only one or two of us venturing to voice feeble criticism. Among them was Shri NV Gadgil for whom there was a snub,'Don't you realise that the Himalayas are there?' I timidly ventured to say that in the seventh century the Tibetans had crossed the Himalayas and invaded Kannauj.[4]

Munshi has not stated what reaction this reminder evoked from the Prime Minister, but students of constitutional history cannot fail to observe with regret that there was no free interchange of ideas or views in the Union Cabinet even on the issues attesting the fate and future of the country so long as Nehru presided over it. A few days after the ineffective Cabinet meeting mentioned by Munshi, the Prime Minister received the Sardar's letter setting out his views on Tibet.

Patel pointed out that both the Indian government and its representative at Peking (now Beijing) had been thoroughly deceived by China about its intentions towards Tibet. Its action in taking possession of that poorly-defended country was 'little short of perfidy'. The tragedy of the Tibetans was aggravated by the fact that they had reposed great confidence in this country to safeguard their territorial integrity. 'They chose to be guided by us' wrote the Sardar, 'and we have been unable to get them out of the meshes of Chinese duplicity or Chinese malevolence'. India's remonstrations with Peking over its aggressive action against Tibet were feeble and apologetic. The Chinese were indeed totally unimpressed with the Indian protest and retorted by saying that their 'action in Tibet' had become necessary as an insurance against what they called the Anglo-American machinations in that country. Their excuse was an insult to one's intelligence and the fact that they refused to accept Indian assurances was a clear proof that their so-called friendship for this country was a fraud and sham.

The Sardar reminded the Prime Minister that, in spite of his (Nehru's) direct approaches to the Chinese and assurances to them that no Anglo-American strategy or diplomacy was involved in Tibet, they refused to believe in this country's *bona fides*. Similarly, they were unimpressed with India's sincere efforts to secure the membership of the United Nations Organisation for China. In spite of such proofs of friendship for them, they remained unconvinced and regarded Indians 'as tools or stooges' of the British and the Americans. 'In Peking', the Sardar wrote, 'We have an Ambassador who is eminently suitable for putting across the friendly point of view. Even he seems to have failed to convince the Chinese. Their last telegram to us is an act of gross discourtesy, not only in the summary way it disposes of our protest against the entry of Chinese forces into Tibet but also in the wild insinuation that our attitude is determined by foreign influences'.

The Sardar was convinced that with the occupation of Tibet by the Chinese, the Himalayas had ceased to offer an effective protection to India against their expansionist ambitions. Their territorial claims over the neighbouring countries were enormous. He mentioned Burma (now Myanmar) among the countries against which Peking had its designs. 'Chinese irredentism', he wrote, 'and communist imperialism are different from the expansionism or imperialism of the Western powers. The former has a cloak of ideology which makes it ten times more dangerous'. What with the racial composition of the population inhabiting the north and the north-eastern regions of India, he expressed grave apprehensions about their security and suggested effective action for safeguarding Indian interests there. 'During last three years', he told Nehru, 'We have not been able to make any appreciable approaches to the Nagas and other hill tribes in Assam. European missionaries and other visitors have been in touch with them, but their influence was in no way friendly to India or Indians'.

He also drew the attention of the Prime Minister to the internal situation. He recalled what the communists had done in Telangana and Warangal and said that the fall of Tibet now gave them 'a comparatively easy means of access to Chinese communists and through them to other foreign communists'.

In these circumstances, it was necessary that 'we must have a clear idea of what we wish to achieve and also the methods by which we should achieve it'. *He wondered whether India should continue to advocate the admission of China into the United Nations Organisations after the Tibetan episode. He asked for a thorough review of the country's armed strength,* bearing in mind the fact that it had now to defend itself, not only against a hostile Pakistan but also against an aggressive China.

It was indeed necessary to take a long range view of its defence requirements. 'My own feeling is', wrote this discerning statesman, that 'unless we assure our supplies of arms, ammunitions and armour, we would be making our defence position perpetually weak and we would not be able to stand up to the double threat of difficulties both from the west and north-west and north and north-east'. He also indicated the need for the disposition of the Indian troops in a manner that would be conducive to an effective defence of the vulnerable parts of the country's frontiers. *The aim was to guard 'important routes or areas which are likely to be the subject of dispute*'. He further stressed the need for strengthening the intelligence services of the armed forces with a view to collecting useful information about the Chinese threat to the Indian borders and to the country's internal security. Besides, effective political and administrative measures should be taken to ensure that India's position in Nepal, Bhutan, Sikkim, Darjeeling, and the tribal territory in Assam was not jeopardised.[4]

Patel like Nehru, was conditioned by the Gandhian principles, but he never succumbed to idealism when dealing with the affairs of state. We cannot but marvel at the sagacity and far-sightedness shown by him in anticipating the Chinese peril with such precision. It is India's misfortune that his historic warning to Nehru given with all the weight and authority of a Deputy Prime Minister, went virtually unheeded. Even if a part of the scheme recommended by him had been implemented, the Chinese would perhaps have regarded prudence as the better part of valour and would not have ventured to attack India with such savage fury in 1962. Patel would probably have perused the matter and helped the country to become militarily strong if death had not claimed him exactly one month and eight days after he wrote that memorable letter.

Earlier, in 1901, British India's confrontation over Tibet had been with Russia; now it was with China.[xvii] Curzon, the then Viceroy, had firmly clarified the British position vis-a-vis Tibet

---

[xvii] Before 1941, Russia was Great Britain's enemy and thus Russia was British India's enemy. China was a friend of Britain as well as the USA and a part of the Allies, thus British India's friend. China was then afraid of Japan, its traditional enemy.

When Germany attacked Russia in 1941, Stalin walked over to the Allies and when WWII ended in 1945, China no longer had to fear Japan. The US and UK went back to being enemies of a communist Soviet Union. China, as a communist nation. was in the Soviet camp, no longer friends with the UK-USA. Post 1947, it could very easily give the excuse of 'Anglo-American machination' to support its expansion plans in the region

Sradar Patel pointed out: the communist mentality of 'whoever is not with them being against them', this is a significant pointer, of which we have to take due note. Any student of geopolitics would know, for territory, China's face-off had to be with free India, which the powers in India refused to recognise

which approximated Patel's thinking, though Curzon's language was of an imperialist and empire-builder. Like Curzon, Patel did not desire occupation of Tibetan territory; and his view was that of Curzon's who had stated:Of course, we do not want their territory. It would be madness for us to cross the Himalayas and occupy it. But, it is important that no one else should seize it; and that it should be turned into a sort of buffer State between the Russian and Indian Empires. If Russia were to come down to the big mountains, she would at once begin intriguing with Nepal... Tibet itself, not Nepal, must be the buffer that we endeavour to create.[5]

References:

1. KM Munshi, *Pilgrimage to Freedom*, Bhartiya Vidya Bhavan, Bombay, vol-I, 1967, p-181.

2. VB Kulkarni, *The Indian Triumvirate*, Bhartiya Vidya Bhavan, Bombay, 1969, p-394-95.

3. NV Gadgil, *Under the Shadow of the Red Fort* (in Marathi), p-94-95.

4. *Bhavan's Journal*, February 26, 1967, p-15.

5. For the full textof Sardar Patel's letter of 7 November 1950, to Jawaharlal Nehru, see the attached letter which appeared in the *Bhavan's Journal*, 26 February 1967, p-15-20.

6. Judith M Brown, *Modern India : The Origins of an Asian Democracy*, Oxford University Press, 1985, p-128.

Letter to Nehru, on China

D.O. No. 821-DPM/50
7th NOV 1950
NEW DELHI

My Dear Jawaharlal,

Ever since my return from Ahmedabad and after the Cabinet meeting the same day, which I had to attend at practically 15 minutes notice and for which I regret, I was not able to read all the papers, I thought I should share with you what is passing through my mind.

I have carefully gone through the correspondence between the Extremal Affairs Ministry and our Ambassador in Peking and through him the Chinese Government. I have tried to peruse this correspondence favorably (sic) between our Ambassador and the Chinese Government as possible, but I regret to say that neither of them comes out well as a result of this study. The Chinese Government has tried to delude us by professions of peaceful intentions. My own feeling is that at a crucial period they managed to instill into our Ambassador a false sense of confidence in their so-called desire to settle the Tibetan problem by peaceful means.

There can be no doubt that during the period covered by this correspondence, the Chinese must have been concentrating for an onslaught on Tibet. The final action of the Chinese, in my judgment, is little short of perfidy. The tragedy of it is that the Tibetans put faith in us; they chose to be guided by us; and we have been unable to get them out of the meshes of Chinese diplomacy or Chinese malevolence. From the latest position, it appears that we shall not be able to rescue the Dalai Lama.

Our Ambassador has been at great pains to find an explanation or justification for Chinese policy and actions. As the External Affairs Ministry remarked in one of their telegrams, there was a lack of firmness and unnecessary apology in one or two representations that he made to the Chinese Government on our behalf.

It is impossible to imagine any sensible person believing in the so-called threat to China from Anglo-American diplomacy or strategy. This feeling, if genuinely entertained by the Chinese in spite of your direct approaches to them, indicates that even though we regard ourselves as friends of China, 'THE CHINESE DO NOT REGARD US AS THEIR FRIENDS'. With the Communist mentality of 'whoever is not with them being against them', this is a significant pointer, of which we have to take due note.

During the last several months, outside the Russian camp, we have been practically alone in championing the cause of Chinese entry into the UNO and in securing from the Americans, assurances on the question of Formosa. We have done everything we could to assuage Chinese feelings, to allay its apprehensions and to defend its legitimate claims in our discussions and correspondence with America and Britain and in the UNO. In spite of this, China is not convinced about our disinterestedness; it continues to regard us with suspicion and the whole psychology is one, at least outwardly, of scepticism, perhaps mixed with a little hostility.

I doubt if we can go any further than we have done already to convince China of our good intentions, friendliness and goodwill. In Peking we have an Ambassador who is eminently suitable for putting across the friendly point of view. Even he seems to have failed to convert the Chinese. Their last telegram to us is an act of gross discourtesy not only in the summary way it disposes of our protest against the entry of Chinese forces into Tibet but also in the wild insinuation that our attitude is determined by foreign influences. It looks as though it is not a friend speaking in that language but a 'POTENTIAL ENEMY'.

With this background, we have to consider what new situation we are now faced with as a result of the disappearance of Tibet, as we knew it, and the Chinese expansion almost upto our gates. Throughout history, we have been seldom worried about our North-East frontier. The Himalayas have been regarded as an impregnable barrier against any threat from the North. We had a friendly Tibet, which gave us no trouble. The Chinese were divided. They had their own domestic problems and never bothered us about our frontiers.

In 1914, we entered into a convention with Tibet, which was not endorsed by the Chinese. We seem to have regarded Tibetan autonomy as extending to (an) independent treaty relationship. Presumably, all that we required was the Chinese counter-signature. The Chinese interpretation of suzerainty seems to be different. We can, therefore, safely assume that very soon they will disown all the stipulations which Tibet has entered into in the past. That throws all frontier and commercial settlements with Tibet, in accordance with which we had been functioning and acting during the last half a century, into the melting pot.*[xviii]*

China is no longer divided. It is united and strong. All along the Himalayas in the North and North-East, we have on our side of the frontier a population not ethnologically or culturally different from Tibetans or Mongloids. *The undefined state of the frontier and existence on our side of a population with affinities to Tibetans or Chinese has all the elements of potential trouble between China and us.* Recent and bitter history also tells us that communism is no shield against imperialism, and that COMMUNISTS ARE AS GOOD OR AS BAD IMPERIALISTS AS ANY OTHER.

Chinese ambitions in this respect not only cover the Himalayan slopes on our side but also include important parts of Assam. They have their ambitions in Burma also. Burma has the added difficulty that it has no McMahon Line around which to build up even the semblance of an agreement. Chinese irrentism and communist imperialism are different from the expansionism or imperialism of the Western Powers. The former has an ideological cloak, WHICH MAKES IT TEN TIMES WORSE.

Racial, national or historical claims lie concealed in the guise of ideological expansion. The danger from the North and North-East, therefore, becomes both communist and imperialist. While our Western and North-Western threat to security is still as prominent as before, A NEW THREAT HAS DEVELOPED FROM THE NORTH AND NORTH-EAST.

Thus, for the first time after centuries, India's defence has to concentrate on two fronts simultaneously. Our defence measures have, so far, been based on calculations of superiority over Pakistan. We shall now have to reckon with communist

---

xviii As long ago as in 1950, Patel had clearly spelt out the Indian position vis-à-vis Tibet. The italicising is to draw attention to how futuristic his warnings were. —Editor

China in the North and North-East, A COMMUNIST CHINA WHICH HAS DEFINITE AMBITIONS AND AIMS AND WHICH DOES NOT IN ANY WAY SEEM FRIENDLY TOWARDS US.

Let us also consider the political conditions on this potentially troublesome frontier. Our Northern or Northeastern approaches consist of Nepal, Bhutan, Sikkim, Darjeeling and tribal areas in Assam. *They are weak from the point of view of communications. Continuous defensive lines do not exist.* There is an almost unlimited scope for infiltration. Police protection is limited to a very small number of passes. There, too, our outposts do not seem to be fully manned. Our contact with these areas is by no means close and intimate.

The people inhabiting these portions have no established loyalty or devotion to India. Even the Darjeeling and Kalimpong areas are not free from pro-Mongoloid prejudices. *During the last three years, we have not been able to make any appreciable approaches to the Nagas and other hill tribes in Assam.* European missionaries and other visitors have been in touch with them, but their influence was in no way friendly where Indians were considered. There was political ferment in Sikkim some time ago. It is quite possible that discontent is smoldering (sic) there.

Bhutan is comparatively quiet, but its affinity with Tibetans would be a handicap. *Nepal has a weak oligarchic regime based almost entirely on force; it is in conflict with a turbulent element of the population*, as well as with enlightened ideas of modern age. In these circumstances, to make people aware of the new danger, or to increase the defensive strength is a very difficult task indeed; and that difficulty can be got over only by enlightened firmness, strength and a clear line of policy.

I am sure the Chinese and their source of inspiration, Soviet Russia, would not miss any opportunity of exploiting these weak spots, partly in support of their ideology and partly their ambition. In my judgment, therefore, *the situation is one in which we cannot afford to be either complacent or vacillating. We must have a clear idea of what we wish to achieve and the methods by which we should achieve it. Any lack of decisiveness in formulating our objectives or pursuing our policy to attain them is bound to weaken us and increase the threats.*

Along with these external dangers, we shall now have to face serious internal problems as well. Hitherto, the Communist Party of India has found some difficulty in contacting communists abroad, or in getting supplies of arms, literature etc. from them. They had to contend with the difficult Burmese and Pakistan frontiers in the East or with the long seaboard. They shall now have a comparatively easy means of access to Chinese communists, and through them to other foreign communists. Infiltration of spies, fifth columnists and communists would now be easier.

The whole situation thus, raises a number of problems on which we must come to an early decision so that we can, as I said earlier, formulate the objectives and methods of our policy.

It is also clear that the action will have to be fairly comprehensive, involving not only our defence strategy and state of preparations, but also problems of internal security. We shall also have to deal with administrative and political problems in the weak spots along the frontier to which I have already referred.

It is, of course, impossible for me to exhaustively set out all the problems. I have, however, given below some of the problems which, in my opinion, require early solutions, around which we have to build our administrative or military policy measures.

a. A military and intelligence appreciation of the Chinese threat to India, both on the frontier and internal security.

b. An examination of our military position and such re-disposition of forces as might be necessary, particularly with the idea of guarding important routes or areas which are likely to be the subject of dispute.

c. An appraisement of the strength of our forces and, if necessary, reconsideration of our retrenchment plans for the Army in the light of these new threats.

d. A long term consideration of our defence needs. My own feeling is that unless we assure our supplies of arms, ammunition and armour, we should be MAKING OUR DEFENCE POSITION PERPETUALLY WEAK and would not be able to stand up to the double threat of difficulties both from the West and Northwest, North and Northeast.

e. The question of the Chinese entry into UNO. In view of the Chinese rebuff, and the method it has followed in dealing with Tibet, I doubt whether we can advocate its claims any longer. The UNO would probably threaten to virtually outlaw China in view of its active participation in the Korean War. We must determine our attitude on this question also.

f. The political and administrative steps which we should take to strengthen our Northern and Northeastern frontiers. This would include the entire border i.e. Nepal, Bhutan, Sikkim, Darjeeling and the tribal territory in Assam.

g. Measures of internal security in the border areas, such as UP, Bihar, Bengal and Assam.

h. Improvements of our communications, road, rail, air and wireless in these areas and with the frontier outposts.

i. Policing and intelligence of frontier outposts.

j. The future of our mission at Lhasa and the trade posts at Gyangtse and Yatung and the forces we have in operation in Tibet to guard the trade routes.

k. The policy in regard to the McMahon Line.

It is possible that a consideration of these matters may lead us into wider questions of our relationship with China, Russia, America, Britain and Burma. This however would be of a general nature, though some may be important. For instance, we might have to consider whether we should not enter into closed association with Burma in order to strengthen the latter in its dealings with China.

I do not rule out the possibility that, before applying pressure on us, China may do the same to Burma. With Burma, the frontier is entirely undefined and the Chinese territorial claims are more substantial. In its present position, Burma might offer an easier problem for China and, therefore, might claim its first attention. I suggest that we meet early to have a general discussion on these problems and decide on such steps as we might think to be immediately necessary and direct quick examination of other problems with a view to taking early measures to deal with them.

Yours,
Vallabhbhai Patel

Administrative Unifier and a Great Administrator

SARDAR PATEL has been, without doubt, the greatest statesman-administrator of independent India that our country has produced during the last four centuries. The Sardar, already past seventy, had less than five years to accomplish his mission and that makes his achievement the more remarkable. The British had taken a hundred years to extend their direct rule over India, and still, with only paramountcy over a third of it. Never before in the history of India since the Mauryan bureaucracy, did we have a uniform system of administration, from which no part of the country was excluded. Nor was the country ever before unified as an unrestricted democracy. Even at the last election under British rule (1946), only about ten per cent of India's population had the franchise.

To comprehend what the Sardar achieved as unifier and as a principal contributor to the building of India's democratic constitutional structure, one must understand what exactly he added as a superb administrator. His immense contributions in meeting the formidable problems created by the violent upheaval accompanying the partition, and the extraordinary energy with which he attended to the complex and sensitive business of the partition council is just one example.

While conserving the frame of the administration in British India, built through the experience of a century and a half, he had the creative imagination and the will to extend it to the princely States. It was India's good fortune, at the most crucial stage of its modern history, to have in Sardar Patel a combination of the vision of a statesman with the sagacity and practical outlook of an administrator, without which the Indian administrative system might not have been revitalised, and its standards might well have fallen below what the critical times and the new nation required.

To build up the India of his dreams, the Sardar felt the need for an efficient and enthusiastic Civil Service. The Indian Civil Service under the British Raj had earned renown for the ability and versality of its members, but following the country's partition and its independence in 1947, nearly 700 European and Muslim officers, out of a total of 1,150 had left the service. There was, thus, a serious depletion in the ranks of senior officers. The burden of running the administration of a problem-ridden country fell upon a small number of officers. But they accepted their responsibility cheerfully because they were sustained by the knowledge that their labours would now be devoted to the service of their motherland. They were no longer torn between two loyalties, as their predecessors had been under the British regime. As AD Gorwala, a distinguished retired civil servant, has put it, 'in the double duty of the past to the British Crown and to the Indian people, there was room for confusion', but now in free India, 'by the grace of God', there was none.[1]

Patel's intervention, in the Constituent Assembly, proved necessary for the acceptance of two Articles relating to the Services. One, Article 311, made it difficult for politicians to punish officials. The other, Article 314, guaranteed the terms and privileges of members of the Indian Civil Service in accordance with an assurance that Vallabhbhai had given shortly before independence. Both provisions attracted criticism. Many members of the Assembly had been imprisoned during the freedom struggle by the officials whom the Article would protect. Ananthasayanam Ayyangar, a future Speaker of the Lok Sabha, said of Article 314: This is an extraordinary guarantee... This guarantee asks us to forget that those persons who are still in the service—400 of them—committed excesses.[2]

The Sardar hammered Ayyangar and in the process spelt out his idea of the Minister-Secretary relationship: I am distressed that a senior member like Mr Ayyangar considers and expresses the opinion that the members of the Indian Civil Service are enemies of our country. If that is so, it is his business to move a resolution to dispense with them and run the administration in a vacuum.

'I wish to record in this House that if during the last two or three years most of the members of the Services had not behaved patriotically and with loyalty, the Union would have collapsed.

'If you [believe this] and decide not to have this Service, I will take the Service with me and go. They will earn their living. They are capable people.

'Today my Secretary can write a note opposed to my views. I have given that freedom to all my Secretaries. I have told them: "if you do not give your honest opinion, then please you had better go."

'Do not take a lathi and say: "We are supreme Parliament." Have you supremacy to go back on your word?'[3]

All opposition collapsed after this. His stout defence of the men of the ICS and his role in the founding of its successor agency, the Indian Administrative Service, and of the Indian

Police Service, earned him the title of the civil servnts' 'patron saint'.[4] The civil servant's industry, ability and, in some cases, independence, had impressed Vallabhbhai, but he also saw the all-India services as a protection against separatism: they gave the Centre a lever against the provinces. The foundation for his relationship with the Services was laid early in 1947, when he called over 30 senior officials to 1-Aurangazeb Road, New Delhi, and invited them to join him and his colleagues in serving the country.[5] The gesture moved the officials and removed their fears.

From the day the Civil Service was thrown open to the Indians, it attracted to its ranks some of the ablest men in the country who made their mark in the various branches of the administration. 'The first Indian to enter the ICS was Satyendranath Tagore, a brother of the poet. Seven years after Tagore's admission in 1864, four more Indians, namely, Surendranath Banerjea, Romesh Chandra Dutt, Beharilal Gupta and Shripad Babaji Thakur, followed his example.'[6]

Sir Surendranath Banerjea, who belonged to the second batch of Indians that entered the Service, would probably have won many administrative laurels had not his brilliance cost him his job.[7] Two more names of brilliant civil servants may be mentioned by way of illustration. The achievement of KPS Menon, both in the academic and the administrative domain, were impressive. He appeared for the ICS examination in 1921 and outshone all his competitors, Indian and British, by standing first. He won signal success in his career when barely within three years of his service, he was admitted to the sanctum of the Foreign and the Political Department of the Government of India. Sir Girija Shankar Bajpai was much senior to Menon, but like him, he made his mark as an officer of outstanding ability and rose to great positions of trust and responsibility both under the British regime and in free India. Endowed with a masterful personality and equipped with a brilliant intellect, he made his presence felt wherever he went. Of him, Menon has said: 'One might say of

Bajpai, as Dryden said about Shakespeare, that he laid waste his whole territory simply by occupying it so conclusively.'[8]

The Sardar was determined to harness the abilities of these talented men to the service of their motherland. He was indeed the only senior Congress leader who not only appreciated and admired their capabilities, but also won their confidence by fighting for their rights, privileges and immunities. He realised that the problems of the country, which were of such heart-breaking complexities, could be dealt with effectively only with their expert assistance. The partition had inflicted a grievous wound on the Indian body politic. Equally disastrous was the impact of the war on the country's economy. The integration of the princely States, a large number of which had long been governed according to medieval standards, posed a serious administrative problem. The economy of the country needed to be galvanised to meet the aspirations of the masses for better way of life. The problem of national defence also called for urgent and expert consideration.[9]

Creation of IAS and IPS

Amidst deepening crisis in the Interim Government, the Secretary of State in His Majesty's Government decided in October 1946 to stop further recruitment to the Indian Civil Service, with the indication of the possibility of termination of his connection with the Services earlier than the date of constitutional changes. Such a step had dangerous implications. A breakdown prior to the transfer of power in the already depleted Services, with some members showing anti-India bias and some others pro-League, endangered the country's administrative unity. The British had built their Empire on the foundations of such unity through the 'Steel Frame'. Such a 'frame' was all the more needed in a newly-born democratic India, yet, riddled with fissiparous tendencies. Patel felt more than any other leader that only a single, all-India Administrative Service and Indian Police Service could help him preserve what the British had built and through which they had ruled over India.

Patel was quick to act. He called a conference of the provincial Chief Ministers (then called Prime Ministers) in New Delhi in October 1946 and spoke with them with such stern confidence: The sooner the Secretary of State's control is ended and the present structure wound up, the better.[10] After a tour of India, Leonard Mosley had confirmed, and Patel was aware of, that 'emotionally, the majority of British Civil Servants in India were pro-Muslim'.[11] To meet boldly the new challenge, Patel ordered the immediate replacement of the ICS with a new Indian Administrative Service and the Indian Police with the Indian Police Service.

Patel's decision was not to the liking of the Chief Ministers. They favoured provincial (State) civil servants who could be under their complete control in order to ensure their pliability. According to BK Nehru, a senior member of the ICS, 'It was only he (Patel) who could force down the throats of unwilling and very powerful heads of provincial governments the concept of the all-India service'. BK Nehru admits that Patel, 'with his much longer vision and his greater grasp of the essential requisites for the Rule of Law', successfully convinced the Constituent Assembly, on 10 October 1949 by saying, 'the Union (of India) will go, you will not have united India, if you do not have a good all-India Service which has independence to speak out its mind'. Patel considered 'an efficient, disciplined, contented service... a *sine qua non* of sound administration under a democratic regime'.[12]

Time being short, no competitive examination for recruitment could have been held earlier than in July 1947. Patel could not wait that long. A beginning had to be made by recruiting the first batch from amongst demobilised Armed Force personnel, who joined the newly-started IAS training school in Metcalfe House in New Delhi in April 1947. That was a bold step. Britain hadn't yet decided whether and when to abdicate power, least of all announce a date of transfer of power. Patel's move was to prevent any possible breakdown in the administration. The Service's continuity was to ensure not only that, but equally so to maintain law and order, already strained to a break-point.

Patel told the probationers of the first batch, on 21 April 1947, that 'the days of the ICS of the old style are going to be over', and that the formation of the IAS in its place was 'both significant and epoch-making—an unmistakable system of the transfer of power' from foreign to Indian hands. The IAS, he said, 'marks the inauguration of an all-India Service officers entirely by Indians and subject completely to Indian control', and 'the Service will now be free to, or will have to, adopt its true role of national Service without being trammeled by traditions and habits of the past'. Patel offered the probationers a few words of paternal advice: The days when the Service could be masters are over... Perhaps, you are aware of a saying regarding the Indian Civil Service—that, it is neither Indian nor civil, nor imbued with any spirit of service... your predecessors had to serve as agents of an alien rule; and even, against their better judgment, had sometimes to execute the biddings of their foreign employers ... A Civil Servant cannot afford to, and must not, take part in politics. Nor must he involve himself in communal wrangles. To depart from the path of rectitude in either of these respects is to debase public service and to lower its dignity.[13]

As an administrator in charge of Home, Patel's immediate task was to grapple with the problems the country was facing, political as well as administrative. Patel had, as Girija Shankar Bajpai, Secretary General to the Government of India and the seniormost ICS, assessed it, 'a double task: conservative, in the good sense of the word, in what had been provinces in the old India; creative in the Indian States. Neither was easy. To the ordinary stresses of a transition caused by the withdrawal of trained personnel, which had wielded all power for a hundred years, was added the strain of Partition and the immense human upheavals and suffering that followed it'. Bajpai thought: The fate of our new State hung in the balance during those perilous months... that, despite some oscillation, the scales stayed steady was due not only to the faith of the people in its leaders, but to the firm will and strong hand of the new Home Minister—Sardar Patel.[14]

Patel's unique success as a great administrator was due to his two strengths, his head and heart: the former gave him the strength of mind and an iron will; the latter, a considerate, accommodating spirit. He was neither a hidebound person, nor an ideologue. He was a stern realist. His flexibility helped him adopt a strategy that suited a particular situation, without changing his basic concepts. He realised, more than his colleagues, that in the solution of administrative problems, only the Civil Servants could act as his faithful agents—not the politicians.

Patel's realism was acknowledged by British historian Judith Brown: Patel, as Home Minister in the Interim Government, was well aware that in the turbulent days of 1946-47, the ICS, whatever its previous image in the eyes of Congressmen, was a bastion against chaos and disintegration of Government... Patel was partly instrumental in persuading other Congressmen that continuity in administration must be maintained, clearly the Service was a source of stability.[15] He, therefore, turned to those members of the ICS who had opted to serve free India. He needed them as much as they needed him. The British had left them orphaned while Prime Minister Nehru and pro-left Congressmen openly aired hostility towards them as a class.

Patel's concept of the Civil Service emerged from the belief he held and which he once expressed to his Home Secretary, HVR Iyengar: It would be a bad day if people did not look up to officials holding high positions. Ministers come and Ministers go, but the permanent machinery (the Civil Service) must be good and firm, and have the respect of the people.[16]

A Great Administrator

As an administrator, Patel was a class by himself. He conducted his work mostly from his residence—not by reading files till midnight, but by giving decisions on briefings by his Secretaries.

His method of settling official matters was short and swift, involving the minimum of time and achieving the maximum results. His Secretaries visited him with their briefs to obtain orders. Though verbal, he always stood by them. He had a photographic memory.

The officers working with the Sardar found that he listened, was not omniscient, said little, said it clearly, decided quickly, delegated freely, inserted no second thoughts and took responsibility. In addition, he was accessible to his officials and often in direct touch with them. He was in short, the Civil Servant's ideal minister.[17]

In his working with Patel, Iyengar had an intriguing experience. One day he had discussed with Patel an important issue concerning a political leader who had threatened a fast-unto-death and with dire consequences if his conditions were not accepted immediately. Iyengar carried in his pocket the letter he had received from the leader concerned, in the expectation that Patel would surely like to see it before giving his decision. The issue was discussed on the basis of a verbal briefing. Patel gave his decision, showing no interest in seeing the letter. For Iyengar, this was something unusual. Out of sheer curiosity, he asked Patel 'whether he did not want to read for himself' and interestingly, Iyengar records: He turned to me and asked whether I had not told him all that it contained, and whether there was any point which I had forgotten to mention. I said, 'No'. I had given him a gist of all important points in it. He then refused to look at the letter.[18]

On another occasion, Patel asked Iyengar what he thought of a particular political leader who happened to be a senior Congressman. Iyengar felt uncomfortable. He politely told Patel that 'it sounds funny that you should consult me about that particular gentleman' as Patel 'knew a great deal more about him than the official machinery'. Iyengar adds: He turned to me and gravely said that I was making a mistake. 'I may have moved about with him a great deal', he (Patel) told me, 'but how do I know that my impression of the man is not a prejudiced one? It is of the greatest use to me to know what you or the official machinery think. Your appreciation of the person may be based on facts, of which I have no knowledge. Between my own knowledge and what you are able to tell me, I may be able to get a balanced picture.' According to Iyengar, 'he wanted to make the fullest use of the knowledge and experience which the Civil Service had acquired. To him they were the people with whom it was worthwhile discussing a problem before he took a decision.'[19]

Patel had complete mastery over the working of the departments under his control and in addition, displayed an enormous appetite for information on the manifold activities of the government. Despite his ill health, he took pains to formulate the policies of his Ministry and made his own decisions on vital matters. But, he always took the advice of experts and allowed complete freedom to his officers in implementing his policies.

Patel's democratic spirit gave his officers full freedom to express their views without fear or restraint. He expected of them to think and act independently to the best of their knowledge and ability, without shirking their responsibility.

The government faced an extremely difficult administrative problem over the implementation of the Congress Working Committee resolution directing it to take immediate steps towards the formation of a linguistic Andhra State. Iyengar, as Home Secretary, was however, opposed to making a move in the matter. Being in a quandary, he asked Patel: 'Sir, the gentlemen who have passed this resolution include Shri Jawaharlal Nehru, Maulana Azad, Dr Rajendra Prasad and you yourself. All of you are Cabinet Ministers and you have taken this decision. What do you expect of me to do about it?' Without a moment's hesitation, Patel asked me, 'Are you or are you not, the Home Secretary?' Iyengar was little taken aback. 'Of course, I am', he replied. 'Then', Patel said, 'do your duty as Home Secretary. Prepare a note to the Cabinet stating what exactly, in your judgment, are the implications of the proposal and how they should be further examined. It must make no difference to you who are the parties to the Working Committee resolution. You must clearly and frankly analyse the whole problem'. Iyengar did exactly that, 'subjecting to a cold analysis' the decision which Patel and others had taken. As a result, the proposal to create the State of Andhra before the Constitution which came into force was postponed. In fact, such a linguistic State could never materialise so long as Patel was alive. After the Cabinet meeting, Iyengar called on Patel and told him in a rather lighter vein: I have succeeded in getting you as Home Minister to overrule yourself as Sardar Patel of the Congress Working Committee.[20]

Patel openly stated that the formation of linguistic provinces would unmistakably retard the process of consolidation of our gains, dislocate our administrative, economic and financial structure, let loose forces of disruption and disintegration. He did not allow that to take place so long as he was alive. Subsequently, Nehru could not resist pressures and yielded to the creation of the first linguistic State of Andhra in December 1952. That was two years after Patel had passed away.

The nightmare which haunts officers is the fear of being scapegoats if their calculations go wrong. This breeds caution and habit of sitting on-the-fence. But Patel encouraged his officers to act boldly. If events took a wrong turn, he would not shift the blame on them. He put trusted officers in key posts and gave them freedom to act. He had the gift of leadership—the habit of delegating power to men on the spot.

Iyengar gives a classic example of Patel standing by his Home Secretary. He had to take a most crucial decision in the absence of Patel and other senior Ministers from Delhi, including the Prime Minister. The decision brooked no delay. Iyengar acted on his own to the best of his knowledge and ability. Later, when Iyengar reported to him the action he had taken, Patel 'shook his head with evident disapproval and said that, if I had consulted him beforehand, he would have taken a different decision. I pressed my arguments. He then patiently explained to me the reasons'.[21] Iyengar further states: I was very unhappy about this, but he asked me not to worry and said that every human being makes mistakes. When the matter subsequently came up before the Cabinet, he told them that the decision was his, and there the matter ended. The incident made a striking impression on me.[22]

Patel had a quick eye for merit and could gauge the potentiality of each officer and knew what use to make of him. From his officers he demanded fidelity and integrity; and in return he gave them his trust. A striking example of Patel's trust in civil servants is typified by the confidence he reposed in his redoubtable States Secretary, VP Menon, which he enjoyed to a degree as no other civil servant perhaps did, even when he was a non-ICS. Such confidence Patel had expressed as early as July 1946, when he told him: Menon, you and I are working for a common purpose. Let there be no mistake about our determination to achieve Independence. If the British are under the impression that they can hang on because of the difference of opinion between the Congress and the League, they are mistaken. We will not consider any sacrifice too great to achieve our objective.[23]

A year later, in July 1947, after Menon had secured Patel's approval to the basic contents of the draft Instrument of Accession, he did not trouble him with the changes which the draft underwent from time to time without affecting its main features. The *Hindustan Times* managed to get hold of a copy of the draft and published it. That very morning when Menon was with Patel, the latter mischievously put on an innocent and serious face, pretending as if he had been ignored, told his States Secretary: Menon now that the *Hindustan Times* has published the Instrument of Accession, can I see a copy of it? As I (Menon) was reporting to him twice daily on what was happening in the subcommittees appointed to finalise the Instrument of Accession and Standstill Agreement, I was rather puzzled. But Sardar smiled and said he was only joking. Sardar had that saving sense of humour which is so great an attribute, especially in a man of his position and responsibility.[24]

Menon describes Sardar's leadership in these words: Leadership is of two kinds. A leader like Napoleon, who was master of both policy and detail, wanted merely the instrument to carry out his orders. Sardar's leadership was of the second category. Having selected his men, he trusted them entirely to implement his policy. Sardar never assumed that he knew everything and he never adopted a policy without full and frank consultation. Whenever we entered into any discussion, we did so as personal friends rather than as Minister and Secretary.[25]

Patel's Secretaries always got a status which commanded respect. As Secretary, Menon enjoyed a status far more powerful than he had enjoyed as Reforms Commissioner under Wavell and Mountbatten, even when he had played a crucial role in the preparation of the 3 June Plan. Under Patel, Menon could rub shoulders with the tallest among the Princes and get the integration plans executed expeditiously. He used 'the device of countering resistance or recalcitrance with the threat of taking them to the Sardar'.[26]

As Home Secretary, Iyengar also enjoyed a similar status. He was with Patel one day when the Maharaja of Patiala arrived. Since he was the Rajpramukh of PEPSU, Iyengar volunteered to wait in the drawing-room outside till he finished with the Rajpramukh. Patel disagreed, but invited the Maharaja to his bedroom and asked him 'to take another chair till my work is finished'. Next morning, Iyengar asked Patel why he had shown 'such exceptional courtesy' to him. The reply was typical of an administrator: It was nothing personal, but he felt that the position of a Secretary to the Government of India was a very high one and should be maintained at a high level in public estimation.[27]

Though accommodating and generous, Patel could be unsparing in upbraiding erring colleagues and irresponsible politicians. He treated them all with the same yardstick, though his style of reproach or expression of dissent would vary in degree from individual to individual. The administrator in him was conscious of the other's status. Patel's genius lay in changing his mood and style, which was in direct proportion to the individual concerned. His correspondence reflects matter-of-fact directness of the head rather than the impulsiveness of the heart. He strictly adhered to administrative discipline, being governed by the spirit of law. As Home Minister, he considered it his duty to preserve and promote administrative etiquette. He pulled up Dr BC Roy, Chief Minister of West Bengal, for showing discourtesy to the Prime Minister: I was distressed to find you writing to the Prime Minister like this. Had it been a personal letter, or had you been talking to him, perhaps as an elder, you could afford all this liberty. But, in an official communication to him as Prime Minister, I had expected that you would be deferential as is appropriate to the dignity of the high office that he holds, as well as the office which you yourself occupy as serving your own interest.[28]

Similarly, Patel was also critical of Govind Ballabh Pant, Chief Minister of Uttar Pradesh, for declaring open a Congress exhibition at Varanasi showing pictures of atrocities committed by the police during the Quit India movement in 1942. It amounted to undermining the administration. He wrote to Pant: ...The punishment of persons who were concerned with the 1942 atrocities is quite a different matter.... But caricaturing of official activities in the manner reported in the press at a time when we are in office is open to serious objection. This is likely to affect the morale of the police force which in the present emergency, can hardly be considered proper. It is also likely to agitate the public mind against the Services. For obvious reasons, this must be avoided if administrative efficiency is to be maintained in these difficult times.[29]

Patel hadn't spared Wavell or Mountbatten or Churchill either. He told Wavell on 14 February 1947, that 'a corporate body like the Central Government has ceased to exist, and that the sooner the present state of affairs is put an end to, the better'.[30] And in view of the deteriorating law and order situation, Patel did not hesitate to tell Mountbatten: Since you have come out here, things have got much worse. There is a civil war on and you are doing nothing to stop it. You wouldn't govern yourself and you won't let the Central Government govern. You cannot escape responsibility for this bloodshed.[31] His firmness was, on occasions, tinged with 'a delightful sense of humour'. At their first meeting, on 25 March 1947, when Mountbatten expressed pleasure that Patel's first Cabinet meeting went off so smoothly, Patel told him 'with a twinkle in his eye, that this was only because all the members had previously decided not to give me a stormy passage the first time'.[32]

The most telling illustration of the punch and power Patel packed may be cited from the manner in which he silenced Winston Churchill, who, as late as June 1948, while 'bemoaning the disappearance of the title of Emperor of India from the Royal titles', had the audacity to make the derogatory remark that the Government of India had been handed over to 'men of straw'. In reply, Patel called Churchill 'an unashamed imperialist at a time when imperialism is on its last legs', and 'the proverbial last ditcher for whom obstinacy and stupid consistency count more than reason, imagination or wisdom'. Patel gave a grim warning from his sick-bed in Dehradun: I should like to tell His Majesty's Government that if they wish India to maintain friendly relations with Great Britain, they must see that India is in no way subjected to malicious and venomous attacks of this kind and that British statesmen and others speak of this country in terms of friendship and goodwill.[33]

Churchill, great as he was, despite his being a blue-blood, diehard conservative and unabashedly anti-India, however, took Patel's attack in good spirit. He conveyed to Patel through Anthony Eden, who was second to Churchill in the Conservative hierarchy, during his visit to India in 1949, that he (Churchill) had 'thoroughly enjoyed the retort Sardar had made and that he had nothing but admiration for the way the new Dominion had settled down to its tasks and responsibilities, particularly those involving relations with the Indian States'. Eden went on to say that Churchill had specially said that the Sardar should not contain himself within the limits of India but that the world was entitled to see and hear more of him. Patel was taken aback by both the forthrightness and warmth of the massage. He asked Anthony Eden to thank Churchill warmly for the kind words and sentiments he had expressed and said that he would bear his generous and friendly advice in mind.[34]

Patel, as an administrator, was precise, direct, sometimes biting but always strong. He could be soft and soothing, or cut through like a razor. But he was never indiscreet in the use of words. His effectiveness lay in his restraint, in his unerring judgment, fair-mindedness and inflexible determination. Iyengar calls him a 'genius in the art of administration' who had 'a tremendous capacity for listening—and listening patiently and carefully—before he made up his mind. And, thereafter, he was a rock'.[35] And, 'after listening and reflection', when he had made up his mind, then, 'you knew that a giant had got up and moved inflexibility into action'.[36]

Patel did not forget those who executed his plans—the ICS. He never doubted their loyalty, appreciated their work and offered them full protection by acting as their Godfather. He told the Constituent Assembly, 'I need hardly dilate at length on the necessity of maintaining their discipline and morale, and keeping them contented. In no other circumstances can we get out of the Services loyal and efficient service except by trying to appreciate their difficulties and their work ... it is our duty to see that the machine with which we have to work is kept in good humour and good temper'.[37] Later, on 10 October 1949, Patel again told the House: 'I must confess that in point of patriotism, in point of loyalty, in point of sincerity and in point of ability, you cannot have a substitute. They are as good as ourselves.'[38]

Little wonder that the death of Sardar Patel (16 December 1950) was mourned by the civil servants with all the poignancy of personal bereavement. 'His exit from the political stage', says a retired civil servant, 'was the death-knell of the ICS, whose decline now became quite evident'.[39] After his death, a condolence meeting was held in the Central Hall of Parliament in New Delhi when, over fifteen hundred, both senior and junior civil servants paid their tribute of tears to his memory. The meeting, which was presided over by Sir Girija Shankar Bajpai, passed a resolution re-affirming the officers' determination to render devoted service to the nation. The resolution stated that they owed 'a special debt to him (Patel) for his confidence and support, and for his keen and unfailing solicitude for our welfare. In grateful remembrance of his services to India and his trust in us, we pledge our complete loyalty and unremitting zeal in service to the land that he helped to liberate and to strengthen'.[40]

References

1. VB Kulkarni, *British Dominion in India and After*, Bhartiya Vidya Bhavan, Bombay, 1964, p-139.
2. *Hindustan Times*, 11.10.1949.
3. On 10.10.49, Nandurkar (ed), *Sardar Patel: Birth Centenanry vol-I*, pub Sardar Vallabhbhai Patel Smarak Bhavan, Ahmedabad, 1975, p-122-30.
4. See PN Haksar in *Premonitions*, pub:Interpress, Bombay, 1979.
5. HM Patel in Nandurkar, (ed), *Centenary, vol-I*, 1975, p-143.
6. VB Kulkarni, *The Indian Triumvirate*, Bhartiya Vidya Bhavan, Bombay, 1969, p-438.
7. Sir Surendranath Banerjea, *A Nation in Making*, Oxford University Press, 1925, p-27.
8. *The Civil Servant in India*, Ed:KL Punjabi (105), Bhartiya Vidya Bhavan, Bombay, 1965, p-47.
9. Creation of IAS in place of ICS.
10. *The Times of London*, 23 October, 1946.

Administrative Unifier and a Great Administrator | 237

11. Leonard Mosley, *The Last Days of British Raj*, Jaico Publishing House, 1965, p-6.
12. BK Nehru, *Thoughts on our Present Discontents*, Allied Publishers, New Delhi, 1966, p-97-98.
13. *Bombay Chronicle*, 21 April 1947.
14. *The Statesman*, 16 December 1950.
15. Judith M Brown, *Modern India*, Oxford University Press, 1994, p-347.
16. HVR Iengar, The Image of the Police, *The Indian Express*, September-8, 1966.
17. See HM Patel in Nandurkar (ed), *Sardar Patel: Birth Centenary, vol-I*, pub:Sardar Vallabhbhai Patel Smarak Bhavan, Ahmedabad, 1975, p-18-20.
18. HVR Iyengar, *Administration in India: A Historical Review*, p-34-40.
19. Ibid.
20. HVR Iyengar: Making of Decisions by Government, *The Indian Express*, February 4, 1964.
21. HVR Iyengar, Officials and Ministers, *The Indian Express*, July 8, 1964.
22. HVR Iyengar, *Administration in India: A Historical Review*, p-40.
23. *Harijan*, January 26, 1951, p-422.
24. VP Menon, *Integration of the Indian States*, Orient Black Swan, New Delhi, 2014, p-101.
25. Ibid, p-103.
26. V Shankar (ICS) *My Reminiscences of Sardar Patel*, pub:Macmillan company of India, 1975, vol-I, p-185.
27. HVR Iengar, The Image of the Police, *The Indian Express*, September 8, 1966.
28. *Sardar Patel's Correspondence*, ed:Durga Das, Navjivan Publishing House, Ahmedabad, 1971, vol-IX, p-35, letter dated December 6, 1949.
29. Ibid, vol-V, p-325, Letter dated January 31, 1947.
30. Ibid, vol-IV, p-6.
31. Manmath Nath Das, *Partition and Independence of India*, pub:East-West Publications, London, 1982, p-52.
32. Mountbatten, His Final Act of Friendship, *This was Sardar*, commemorative volume, vol-I, p-241.
33. *Sardar Patel, In Tune with Millions*, Sardar Vallabhbhai Patel Smarak Bhavan, Ahmedabad, 1975, vol-II, p-305-307.

34. V Shankar, *My Reminiscences of Sardar Patel*, The Macmillan Company of India, 1974, vol-I, p-126.

35. HVR Iyengar, Making of Decisions of Government, *The Indian Express*, 7 May, 1964.

36. HVR Ingar, Sardar Patel — a Man of Decision, *The Indian Express*, 7 May 1964.

37. Constituent Assembly of India (Legislative) Debates, vol-II, Part-II, February 4 to March 18, 1949, p-1451.

38. *Sardar Patel, In Tune with Millions*, Sardar Vallabhbhai Smarak Bhavan, Ahmedabad, 1975, vol-III, p-123-24.

39. *The Civil Servant in India*, ed:KL Punjabi, ICS (Retired), Bhartiya Vidya Bhavan, Bombay, 1965, p-300.

40. *Bharat Jyoti*, dated 17 December 1950.

Patel: Greater than Bismarck

By far the most important achievement of the present government is the unification of the States into the Dominion of India. Had you failed in this, the results would have been disastrous ... Nothing so added to the prestige of the present government than the brilliant policy you have followed with the States.
—Lord Mountbatten to Patel

THE INTEGRATION of the Princely States by the astonishing process of bloodless revolution will stand out as the most outstanding achievement of Sardar Patel, entitling him to a place among the great statesmen of the world.

At no time during the post-mutiny period of the British rule had the abolition of the Princely States been regarded as either necessary or possible. While Britain undoubtedly needed them to consolidate her position in India, even nationalist opinion had not made any categorical demand for their elimination. Indeed, the Congress party's attitude towards them lacked both consistency and clarity. In any case, the Congress party would have been satisfied if the Princes had agreed to associate their people with the management of their affairs. The ignorance about the gravity of the States' problem was widespread.

While addressing the Royal Empire Society, after his return to England, Lord Mountbatten declared that 'when he came to study the practical details of transfer of power from the British hands in India, he (Patel) found in the Indian States a problem which seemed even more complex and difficult than that of the separation of Pakistan from the Indian Union'.[1] It was not easy for any Prince, however small his State, to abdicate his authority or to renounce his possessions, which he and his ancestors had enjoyed for centuries, in response to what he could understandingly regard as some idealism of no tangible benefit to himself. There were indeed many rulers who, far from agreeing to make any sacrifice for their country, insisted on the enlargement of their own interests even if it meant national disintegration.

Even during the British period, the Nizam of Hyderabad had threatened to go to the League of Nations on the question of the retrocession of Berar to him. The Sardar himself referred to the seriousness of the States' problem when addressing the Constituent Assembly in October 1949. If, after the British withdrawal, the Princes had exercised their technical right to remain independent or if some of them had chosen to join Pakistan, they would have found considerable support from influential elements hostile to the interests of India. The successor government did not possess either the prestige or the instrumentalities of Paramountcy held by the previous regime in order to secure the Princes' submission and yet Patel won the country's cause so magnificently.

From a mere Accession to a total disappearance from the map of the country was not a short step and yet dispossessed Princes accepted the new dispensation, not with sullen resignation, but with commendable appreciation of the requirements of the altered situation. Very few members of the Princely order nursed any hatred or personal grudge against the Sardar for bringing about its dissolution. Being a fair-minded man, Patel was fully conscious of the tremendous sacrifices they had made for their motherland and was liberal when settling their civil list, their property rights and their privileges and immunities. He ensured that his settlement with them was sanctified by constitutional guarantees. In spite of Patel's generosity, what the Princes received was modest compared to what they were accustomed to take as a matter of right before the merger of their States.

The position of the Indian Princes in the Indian polity 'afforded no parallel to or analogy with any institution known in history'. Yet through 'peaceful and cordial negotiations' the Chiefdoms had dissolved themselves, and become 'hardly distinguishable from the other democratic units comprising the Indian Union'. The words are from a booklet issued by the Government of India in 1950. The self-congratulation was merited. Whereas the British-directed partition of India had exacted such a heavy toll, over 500 'centres of feudal autocracy' had, with little loss of life, been 'converted into free and democratic units of the Indian Union'. The 'yellow dots on the maps' that marked these fiefdoms now 'disappeared. Sovereignty and power have been transferred to the people'. 'For the first time', the booklet went on, 'millions of people accustomed to living in narrow, secluded groups in the States, became part of the larger life of India. They could now breathe the air of freedom and democracy pervading the whole nation'.

This being an official booklet, the credit for the job was naturally given to the man in charge. 'What the British proconsuls failed to achieve after two centuries of ceaseless efforts', wrote the publicists, 'Sardar Vallabhbhai Patel accomplished through his persuasive appeal to the nobler feelings of the Princely Order'.[2]

Stafford Cripps thought that it would take at least ten to fifteen years to liquidate the Indian States and to merge them with the rest of India. It was 'a welcome surprise to him—and a great tribute to the ability of Sardar Patel—that the integration of the States with the rest of India has not taken even ten to fifteen months'.[3] KM Panikkar praised it in glowing words, 'How all these grand and grandiose title-holders were swept under the carpet of history in the twinkling of an eye. Many are amazed that Vallabhbhai Patel was able to sweep them away in so short a time. The *Puranas* say that Parasurama fought twentyone battles before he could exterminate the Kshatriya princes, but the new Parasurama needed no battle to make a clean sweep of kingship in India. One by one they queued up to sign their Instrument of Accession, collected their pensions and left with good grace'.[4]

Patel was gentle to them, persuasive, but firm—under no circumstances willing to barter away India's interests. His feat was revolutionary—perhaps unique in world history for its speed and boldness. He was himself the executioner of the revolution he had dreamed of in 1938 when he had publicly stated, 'The Princes should be made to dissociate themselves from their reign. They should be given annual pension, and we should ourselves rule'.[5]

For such a historic achievement, Patel has been compared with Bismarck who had, likewise, consolidated Germany by integrating a handful of Princely States and who was considered the greatest master of diplomacy in Europe. President Zakir Hussain considered Patel 'even greater than Bismarck, because he has unified the country within a short time and without much noise and trumpeting'.[6] President VV Giri stated that Patel possessed 'the organising ability of Bismarck, the astute statesmanship of Chanakya and the single-minded devotion to the cause of national unity of Abraham Lincoln'.[7]

Patel's unification and consolidation of 562 princely States, in a country of continental size and diverse people, was epoch making—of greater importance than Bismarck's role in

Germany: 562 States were reduced to 26 administrative units of the Indian Union, and democracy was extended to 80 million people comprising of 27 per cent of India's population in a matter of months, not years. 'When the British left India', writes Foreign Secretary KPS Menon, 'the unity even of divided India was in danger. Some 560 Princely States had been left in the air. It was open to them to adhere to India, to accede to Pakistan, or to remain independent.... It almost looked as if India was going to be Balkanised. But this danger was averted by firm handling of the Princes by a man of iron, Sardar Vallabhbhai Patel'.[8]

Patel and Bismarck possessed totally dissimilar personalities: differing from each other in physical appearance, mental make-up and the means each employed in achieving the ends. Bismarck struck awe through his fierce moustache, huge jackboots, a spiked helmet and a sword; he was a civilian despite his military tunic. Patel had, in contrast, the looks of a simple, unsophisticated peasant, with whom he had completely identified in his traditional dress of *dhoti*, *jubba*, waistcoat and a pair of country made *chappals*.[xix] Patel's round clean-shaven head made him look like a venerable Buddhist monk. Patel's Gandhian humility was fully mirrored in his statement after his victory in the 'Police Action' in Hyderabad, 'On the chessboard of this world, we are like small or trivial pawns, and are instrumental, at times for small or bigger events.... Let us express our gratitude to God'.[9]

Bismarck was a thorough aristocrat and a crafty dictator, 'always impulsive and always exaggeratedly nervous of the aggressive designs of others',[10] whereas Patel was ever cool and unruffled, possessing the serenity of a volcano covered with snow, and devoid of malice and unscrupulousness. If he did not like someone, he did so openly. Bismarck had 'no friends, only sycophants'.[11] Patel's friendships were deep and lasting, but he did not like either fools or flatterers.

[xix] *dhoti*–a wraparound; *jubba*–a overcoat; *chappal*–slippers

Unlike Bismarck, Patel was a born democrat but a party disciplinarian who remained content throughout his political life with a number two role—first under Gandhi and later under Nehru. Yet, he played a role independent of either. Because of his forceful personality and his hold over the party machine, Patel wielded the weapon of people's support, and ruled through the Princes' willing surrender; whereas Bismarck ruled through a policy of 'blood and iron', court intrigue and ruthlessness. Bismarck 'did not value the Princes nor respect them', as Patel did. Bismarck also 'trusted no one else. Suspicion grew with power'.[12] Patel, in comparison, secured the lasting trust and friendship of the Princes. Patel's approach was Gandhian—nonviolent, high-minded, principled statesmanship, which believed in befriending, rather than in eliminating the Princes.

Like a kind shepherd, Patel brought the Princes under his umbrella and adopted them as his own flock. His winning over the hearts was a great achievement at a personal level. His wisdom and far-sightedness were reflected in his directive to his aides: Do not question the extent of the personal wealth claimed by them, and never ever confront the ladies of the household. I want their States—not their wealth.[13] Such was Patel's judicious benevolence towards the Princes. He had won their goodwill; even earned their gratitude and admiration.

Mountbatten took special pride in telling Patel: By far the most important achievement of the present Government is the unification of the States into the Dominion of India. Had you failed in this, the results would have been disastrous... Nothing has so added to the prestige of the present Government than the brilliant policy you have followed with the States.[14]

During his visit to India in 1956, Soviet leader Khrushchev felt so overwhelmed by Patel's achievement as to observe: You Indians are an amazing people. How on earth did you manage to liquidate the Princely rule without liquidating the Princes?[15]

Patel advised the people to change their outlook towards the rulers. 'They are ours, and we can make them understand and appreciate our point of view... the days of vilifying the Princes, calling them names and maligning them are gone.'[16] He set an example by being gentle and forgiving, generous and gracious, considerate and loyal to those who put their trust in him. He openly acknowledged, 'None is more conscious than myself that all this could not have been achieved but for their willing cooperation and their intense patriotism, which was latent but which had blossomed forth in all its fullness with the acquisition of the country'.[17]

Unlike Patel, Bismarck was 'a political conspirator, not a fighting man, by nature and by experience'.[18] Patel was a fighting man, but as a Gandhian. He could not dream of conspiracy as a means to achieve the ends, whereas Bismarck's 'greatest gift was in packing the cards, not in playing the hand... he had gained power by court-intrigue and never learnt a better trick'. To Bismarck, 'His family was always more important than any political affairs'.[19] Patel had completely detached himself from his family: in his lifetime, he had kept his son at bay; and he did not leave behind any property for his unmarried daughter,[xx] Maniben.

An eloquent tribute to Patel's genius, though not directly paid to him, is to be found from what Lord Curzon wrote about the Princes to Lord Hamilton in August 1900: 'For what are they (the Indian Princes) for the most part, but a set of unruly and ignorant and rather undisciplined schoolboys? What they want more than anything else is to be schooled by a firm, but not unkindly, hand, to be passed through just the sort of discipline that a boy goes through at a public school...'[20] Patel proved the ideal schoolmaster. None could have been more kind and firm than he. Patel's paternalism was unlike the autocracy of the British, or the iron hand of Bismarck. It was humane, benevolent, essentially Gandhian.

[xx] Dahyabhai Patel
Maniben Patel
Later both were Members of Parliament

References

1. *The Round Table: A Quarterly Review of British Commonwealth Affairs*, December, 1948, p-36.
2. *Democracy on the March*, New Delhi, Publication Division, 1950, p-1-9-10.
3. Jagjivan Ram, The Great Administrator, *The Statesman*, 31 October 1950.
4. KM Panikkar, *An Autobiography*, Oxford, 1979, p-190-191.
5. *Sardar Patel's Speeches*, in Hindi, p-363.
6. Dr Zakir Hussain, *The Statesman*, 1 November 1968.
7. VV Giri, *Times of India*, November-I, 1969.
8. KPS Menon (ICS), *Many worlds Revisited: An Autobiography*, Oxford, 1966, p-262.
9. *Sardar's Letters-Mostly Unknown*, ed:Manibehn Vallabhbhai Patel, vol-V, Pub-Sardar Vallabhbhai Smarak Bhavan, Ahmedabad, 1977, p-129.
10. AJP Taylor, *Europe: Grandeur and Decline*, Penguin, 1990, p-101-102.
11. Ibid, p-88.
12. APJ Taylor, *Bismarck: The Man and the Statesman*, pub-Hamish Hamilton, United Kingdom, 1955, p-195-200.
13. CS Venkatachar (ICS), *The Hindu*, 11 July 1999.
14. *Sardar's Letters-Mostly Unknown*, vol-V, ed:Manibehn Vallabhbhai Patel, pub-Sardar Vallabhbhai Patel Smark Bhavan, Ahmedabad, p-152.
15. KPS Menon (ICS), *The Sunday Standard*, 12 September, 1976.
16. *For a United India:Speeches of Sardar Patel*, Compiled by Publication Division, Ministry of Information & Broadcasting, Government of India, p-57-58.
17. *Sardar Patel, In Tune with Millions*, Sardar Vallabhbhai Patel Smarak Bhavan, 1975, vol-II, p-82.
18. APJ Taylor, *Bismarck: The Man and the Statesman*, Hamish Hamilton, United Kingdom, p-108.
19. Ibid, p-258-59.
20. CH Philips, *The Evolution of India and Pakistan : 1858-1947, Select Documents*, Oxford University Press, 1962, p-425.

Appendices

Letter from Vallabhbhai to KM Panikkar regarding Princes' getting out of cordon
417

New Delhi
16 March 1947

My dear Sardar Panikkar,

I have your letter of the 10th instant. I am glad that so many Princes are getting out of the cordon. Let us hope that they will all come in now. You must have seen our resolution of the Working Committee. It has been very well received all throughout.

You have seen what is happening in the Punjab. I hope there will be no sympathy from any quarters for the Muslim League any more, not even amongst any of the Princes.

Yours sincerely,
Vallabhbhai Patel

Sardar KM Panikkar
Prime Minister
Bikaner

Source—Sardar Patel's correspondence, Ed:Durga Das, Navjivan Publishing House, Ahmedabad, 1973, vol-V, p-384

Letter from Patel to Desabandhu M Sankar Lingegowda
432

New Delhi
2 February 1947

Dear Friend,

I have received your letter of 21 January.

I do not understand what is your stand regarding the demand for responsible government in Mysore. This is an old demand which has so often been repeated by the Mysore Congress and its representatives in the Assembly that no exception can be taken by anybody to such a demand. The words 'wherein sovereignty vests in the people' added to the 'demand for responsible government' are superfluous, and its addition in the principal demand makes no change in the meaning.

Your inference that these words would mean ending the Princely Order is only unjustified. Sovereignty in England vests in the people of England and not in His Majesty the King. It is a constitutional phrase and its meaning is clear. No man in his senses in the modern world believes that sovereignty vests in any single individual, whether he be a prince or a monarch, or a Czar or a Hitler.

Responsible administration means nothing. What is wanted is responsible government in the Indian States, and any attempt to draw difference between responsible government and responsible administration is bound to create suspicion. Therefore, I would advise you to join the demand for responsible government with the Mysore Congress; and if you make a unanimous demand of that nature from the Legislature, I am prepared to advise the Mysore Congress to drop the words to which you object about the vesting of sovereignty in the people. Even without your admission in that behalf, sovereignty is not going to vest anywhere else. I do not understand this kind of quibbling. Let us tackle this problem in a more practical manner. If Mysore, which has been one of the most advanced States in India, gibes even at this stage in granting the long overdue demand of the Congress for responsible government, you may take it that the State will have to face serious troubles in the near future. Nothing in the world can prevent the rapidly marching forces of progress, and it is wise to recognise the writing on the wall.

Yours sincerely,
Vallabhbhai Patel

Desabandhu M Sankar Lingegowda
Member of the Assembly
Nagamangala Post (Mysore State)

Source—Sardar Patel's correspondence, Ed: Durga Das, Navjivan Publishing House, Ahmedabad, 1973, vol-V, p-401

Letter from BL Mitter* to Vallabhbhai about the conspiracy of the Regent and Political Agent to declare independence of Kathiawar States
407

Narendra Niwas
Mount Abu
17 June 1947

My dear Sardar Sahib,

Jatashankar Pathak came today from Rajkot to Abu. He gave me the following information which I am conveying to you for what it is worth.

There was a gathering of Rulers in Kathiawar with the Jamsaheb as leader. The Resident and Political Agent are out to Balkanise India and advised the Rulers accordingly. The argument is that if Travancore can declare independence the Kathiawar States, being maritime States, can do likewise. The advantage is that they can rule without any interference from Delhi and develop their ports and they need not depend upon India for anything.

A secret meeting was held under the presidency of the Resident. It was decided that a 'Union of Kathiawar' should be formed covering the whole peninsula and that it would declare sovereign independence, subject to the right of Junagadh to declare separate independence or to join Pakistan. In case Junagadh separated, it would enter into inoffensive and defensive treaty with the Union of Kathiawar and they would resist Baroda's claim to tribute. The Jamsaheb would be the President of the Union and seven States should constitute a council to govern the peninsula. The seven States are Jamnagar, Bhavnagar, Gondal, Porbander, Morvi, Dhrangadhra and Junagadh. Pattani of Bhavnagar was at the meeting. The constitution of the Union is under way. The Resident is helping and the Jamsaheb has promised to put up a crore of rupees in furtherance of the scheme. Baroda was severely criticised for joining the Constituent Assembly and all the States decided to repudiate Baroda's claim to tribute.

Pathak asked Major Hailey, the Political Agent, why Baroda should not get its tribute. Hailey said that the tribute was more than a hundred years old and when Britain was resigning sovereignty, Baroda's sovereignty fell with it. Whatever the logic may be, there it is.

Junagadh's position is that it will either declare separate independence or join Pakistan.

A document was signed, but it is secret at the moment. Major Hailey refused to disclose the contents.

Yours sincerely,
BL Mitter[1]

Sardar Vallabhbhai Patel

---

* Member, Viceroy's Executive Council; Federal Advocate-General; Dewan of Baroda; acting Governor of West Bengal.

Source—Sardar Patel's correspondence, vol-V, p-472

Letter written by Aravamudh (Nizam's Executive Council Member) to Gopalaswami Ayyangar regarding Nizam's plan to utilise respite of two months to arm himself to crush Hindus
51

Hyderabad (Dn)
31 August 1947

My dear Gopalaswami Ayyangar,

Monckton returned yesterday. He seems to have stayed at the Governor-General's House on the 28th until the GG left for Lahore on the 29th inst.

Monckton has written a long letter to HEH complaining about the manner in which the president of the local Muslim League has attacked him, expressing want of confidence in him and that the GG also agreed with him that unless and until the allegations were withdrawn and the statement about want of confidence also withdrawn, it would not be possible for him to continue the negotiations. But in his letter he has adverted to two points which I consider to be unnecessary.

1. He has warned the Nizam that the States Department seems to know everything that is going on here even though it may be extremely confidential. I think there was no need for him to make that statement.

2. He has stated that he would try to prolong the negotiations as long as he can. In the meantime, the Nizam may consider about what he is going to do. He has also promised that he will try to persuade the Union to consider some via media which will neither be a treaty nor an accession but will be in the form of an agreement. The Nizam's reaction is not yet known.

Lord M seems to have sent a very strong letter to Monckton criticising the attitude of the Nizam as regards his attempt to get arms through Pakistan. He has referred to the conversation he has had with the Prime Minister of India while they were going together in the plane. That letter is a strongly-worded one and says that it makes his (GG's) position very difficult. While on the one hand he is requested to persuade the Indian Union to stretch a point or two in favour of Hyderabad, the way in which the Nizam is acting is likely to alienate the sympathies of the Union Govt. He seems to have remarked further that he (GG) has been told that the respite of two months is being utilised by the Nizam to arm himself with a view to crushing the Hindu subjects.

Today in the Council, the President brought to the notice of the Council the fact that the Czechoslovakian Government had informed the Indian Dominion Government that the Hyderabad Government had approached them for the purchase of arms and ammunition to the tune of three crores of rupees and what they had to say. It seems the Indian Government sent a reply to the effect that if they complied with the order they would be regarded as doing an unfriendly act. This Government is going to reply that they were only negotiating but that they had not yet got the arms or ammunition.

The situation in Secunderabad has not yet come to normal. People are still going away and warrants, I understand, are being issued against members of the Andhra Sangham because it is on the strength of their being there that some of the Hindu families are bold enough to stay on.

Mr Brunyate, the solicitor, who has accompanied Monckton, is preparing the standstill agreement. I do not know if an advance copy of the proposed draft which will be submitted by this Govt would be considered useful. If so, I shall send it on.

With kind, regards,

Yours sincerely,
Aravamudh

Source—Sardar Patel's correspondence, Ed:Durga Das, Navjivan Publishing House, Ahmedabad, 1973, vol-VII, p-55-56

Letter from Aravamudh (Nizam's Executive Council Member) to Gopalaswami Ayyangar informing worsened communal situation in Hyderabad

58

25 September 1947*

My dear Gopalaswami Ayyangar,

It is learnt on reliable authority that HEH asked Sir Nizamat Jung and Sir Ameen Jung (Ahmed Hussain who is a Madrasi) to go to Delhi for negotiations. Both of them declined. So HEH seems to be very angry. It is rumoured that nowadays he has become extremely irritable and melancholy.

I learnt that on a requisition by telegram by Pakistan 16,000 ampules of cholera vaccine have been despatched, as it was reported that cholera had broken out in a virulent form in Pakistan. It was not stated where it had broken out, may be in Eastern Pakistan.

The delegation from Hyderabad returned day before yesterday. My information is that they had no talks with Sardar Patel but only with Lord M. Lord M seems to have told these people that he already knew the viewpoint of the Prime Minister and Sir Walter Monckton. What is it that the other two delegates had to say? Ali Nawaz Jung, it seems, was the spokesman and he said that HEH definitely declines to accede. It seems Lord M told him, 'Do you know what grim consequences will follow such a decision?' to which the Nawab replied that they knew it. Hyderabad is quite prepared for it. It may affect it for two years but after that everything would become normal as Hyderabad was big enough to be an independent State. Then, it seems, the Governor-General told them to leave the papers and that he would intimate to them what decision his Government would come to.

The version from the official side is that it is no longer the State that has got to initiate anything but it is now the Indian Union to re-establish contacts and initiate any further negotiations.

Chhatari is expecting to leave for good on Saturday. He is giving a farewell dinner tomorrow night to the Members of the Executive Council.

Nothing is known about who is to succeed. Rumours are to effect that Ali Nawaz Jung is to succeed and some say Laik Ali, who has gone to the UNO, is going to succeed. A third version is the Nizam is going to carry on his own administration without a Prime Minister which he did years ago.

Yesterday, it seems, a telegram was received from VP Menon to Monckton enquiring as to why the Nizam issued the ordinance regarding the Government of Berar, to which a reply has been sent by Monckton saying that he was the author of it and that it was only meant to continue the existing position without a break and that it was not intended to assume powers which were not already existing.

Monckton seems to have written a private letter to Lord M to the effect that if communal strife begins, the Hindus will suffer in Hyderabad city, while in the districts and villages the Muslims are likely to be wiped out.

There is absolutely no doubt that every Englishman is pro-Pakistan and pro-Muslim. Griggson, who was till recently Revenue Member, and Major Maunsell, who was secretary to the Resident, have got employed in Pakistan. Mr Savidge, who is the Director General of Revenue, is going to Pakistan. Mr Anderson, who was the Director General of Police, is in quest of employment in Pakistan.

The Berar legislation was the joint handy work of Monckton and Ali Yavar Jung. As I have already told you, Ali Yavar Jung, though he is considered to be not so very extreme in his views, is sufficiently mischievous and unreliable. I want that the States Department should know this, because there is an impression here that he is considered to be a safe man by them, which is not the case.

I am herewith enclosing two documents, one dated 15 September 1947 being a note submitted by Sir Walter Monckton to the Council, explaining his policy and giving a final opinion and warning on the situation; the other, dated 18 September 1947, is the corrected copy of the letter which HEH has sent to Lord M. I dare say that the latter document must be in the hands of the States Department by now. Perhaps, the former document will be interesting as showing the mentality of the Constitutional Adviser.

You will remember that I wrote to you some time back that HEH has handed over letters prepared presumably by Sir Walter Monckton for being handed over to His Majesty the King, Mr Attlee and other prominent Members of the British Cabinet. That letter was sent through a special messenger and that messenger is no other than Mr Laik Ali who was, I understand, especially appointed as additional representative to the UNO on behalf of Pakistan, although he is not a Pakistani subject, simply to show to the world that he is being sent to the UNO whereas really he was carrying these letters to be delivered to the above-mentioned people. Yesterday, it seems a cablegram has been received to the effect that the letter to His Majesty was handed in Scotland and that the other letters to Mr Attlee and others were duly handed over, that Mr Attlee was very sympathetic and that everything was very hopeful there.

With kind regards,

Yours sincerely,
Aravamudh

---

* (Second batch of Hyderabad letters received by Gopalaswami Ayyangar and passed on to Sardar Patel.)

Source—Sardar Patel's Correspondence, vol-VII p-66-68

Telegram from Nizam to Monckton (Legal Advisor of Nizam) explaining no need of hurry for agreement with India

6 January 1948

Sir Walter Monckton
3 Paper Buildings,
London EC 4

IN CONTINUATION OF MY TELEGRAM TO YOU OF 5 JANUARY I AGREE WITH YOUR OPINION THAT NO GOOD OF OUR HURRYING UP MAKING LONGTERM AGREEMENT WITH INDIAN UNION AT THE BEGINNING OF THE YEAR BUT TO WAIT AND SEE WHAT FURTHER DEVELOPMENTS ARISE BEFORE WE DO IT NAMELY TOWARDS THE END OF THE YEAR. BESIDES WE MUST SEE HOW KASHMIR AND JUNAGADH'S CASE IS GOING TO BE SETTLED BY UNO. AFTER THAT WE CAN THINK ABOUT OUR OWN AFFAIR. IS LORD MOUNTBATTEN GOING TO GET EXTENSION AFTER APRIL NEXT AS WAS RUMOURED BEFORE? IN ANY CASE SINCE HE HAS NOT GOT POWER WHAT HELP CAN HE GIVE TO US IS OBVIOUS. IN THAT CASE HIS BEING IN OFFICE OR NOT DOES NOT AFFECT US MATERIALLY SO WE MUST MANAGE OUR AFFAIRS IN THE BEST WAY WE CAN AFTER TAKING EVERYTHING INTO CONSIDERATION.

NIZAM

Source—Sardar Patel's Correspondence, vol-VII, p-134

Letter from Vallabhbhai to Gadgil regarding need for timely action in Hyderabad
164

Dehra Dun
21 June 1948

My dear Gadgil,

Thank you for your letter of 18 June 1948.

I am rather worried about Hyderabad. This is the time when we should take firm and definite action. There should be no vacillation; and the more public the action is the greater effect it will have on the morale of our people both here and in Hyderabad and will convince our opponents that we mean business. We should, therefore, go ahead with determination and vigour in applying the economic sanctions as well as in dealing effectively with border and other incidents. There should be no lack of definiteness or strength about our actions. If, even now, we relax, we shall not only be doing a disservice to the country, but would be digging our own grave. About this I am quite clear. We should also put our military in a state of preparedness for all eventualities. It is no use taking a complacent attitude on these questions.

Regarding Ajmer-Merwara, the position is not as easy as some imagine. Ajmer-Merwara is the heart of Rajasthan, and Rajasthan itself is in a ferment. We have, therefore, to be careful about what we say and what we do in Ajmer-Merwara. Its repercussions will be felt throughout Rajasthan, and therefore I would advise you to emphasise in your speech loyalty to the country above loyalty to any sectional or regional interests and that the people and politicians of Ajmer-Merwara as also of Rajasthan must take a broader view of their responsibilities and their position. They should not think only of their own individual or parochial interests, but consider their place in the polity of India as a whole. On the constitutional question, you might take the position that the whole case is being actively considered by the Constituent Assembly, which will no doubt decide the issue after bearing in mind all the relevant considerations. In the meantime, the system of Advisory Council is the only suitable and feasible one, and its machinery can always be improved to suit popular demands. The people should, therefore, concentrate not on asking for something which, in the present transitory stage, is impossible, but for something which can easily be conceded by adaptation of the present system.

I am also writing to Dr Pattabhi in the same sense and enclose a copy of my letter to him. You might take it to Ajmer-Merwara and give it to Dr Pattabhi, because I am not certain if my letter will reach him in time.

As regards the question of capital, I have throughout maintained that Delhi is unsuitable as a capital. Any idea of a subsidiary conclave or subsidiary capital does not, therefore, appeal to me. We must have a capital where we can work all the year round with reasonable efficiency and in reasonable comfort. Dispersal of offices sometimes seriously prejudices efficiency, and therefore we have got to avoid it. However, I can only offer comments on your proposal after studying the details.

I have no intention of changing my residence. The present house suits me very well and I like it for sentimental as well as practical reasons.

As regards your occupying 17 York Road, it would of course be nice if you came there, but you have to consider the accommodation. I do not think the accommodation available in 17 York Road will suit you. I should not like you to inconvenience yourself and the children merely on account of being near me.

With kind regards,
Yours sincerely,

Vallabhbhai Patel
The Hon'ble Dr N V Gadgil
Minister for Works, Mines and Power
New Delhi

Source—Sardar Patel's Correspondence, vol-VII, p-217

Telegram from Vallabhbhai to Major General Chaudhuri congratulating him for efficient arrangement for takeover of Hyderabad
237

Camp Nagpur
28 February 1949

Major General Chaudhuri
Military Governor
Hyderabad (Dn)

PLEASE ACCEPT FOR YOURSELF AND CONVEY TO THE PEOPLE OF HYDERABAD AND MEMBERS OF YOUR ADMINISTRATION CIVIL AND MILITARY MY SINCERE GRATITUDE FOR THE WARM AND AFFECTIONATE WELCOME THEY EXTENDED TO ME. HYDERABAD HAS BEEN CONSTANTLY IN MY THOUGHT AND I HAD BEEN LOOKING FORWARD TO A PERSONAL ACQAINTANCE WITH ITS PEOPLE AND THE ADMINISTRATION. I WAS VERY HAPPY TO FIND THAT THE PEOPLE WERE SETTLING DOWN TO THE CHANGE FROM THE RECENT PAST WITH COMMENDABLE DISPLAY OF SPIRTT OF ACCOMMODATION AND THAT THE ADMINISTRATION UNDER THE WISE AND SKILFUL GUIDANCE OF YOURSELF AND YOUR COLLEAGUES WAS MEETING EFFECTIVELY WITH THE MANY DEMANDS WHICH THE CHANGING ORDER AND CHANGED SITUATION WERE MAKING ON IT AND WAS TACKLING WITH ORDERLINESS AND PRUDENCE THE MANY DIFFICULTIES WITH WHICH IT IS FACED. I SHOULD IN PARTICULAR LIKE TO THANK THE POLICE AND ARMED FORCES FOR THE EXCELLENT TRAFFIC AND SECURITY ARRANGEMENTS MADE IN CONNECTION WITH MY VISIT. I AM ALSO

HAPPY THAT MY VISIT WAS UTILISED BY THE STATE CONGRESS TO EVOLVE A SETTLEMENT OF THEIR OUTSTANDING DIFFERENCES WHICH I HOPE WILL ENDURE. I PRAY THAT THE PEOPLE OF HYDERABAD WILL MAINTAIN THE PROGRESS THEY HAVE MADE AND WILL IN COURSE OF TIME DECIDE UPON THEIR FUTURE CONSISTENT WTTH THEIR NEEDS, SUITED TO THEIR GENIUS AND IN ACCORD WITH THE LESSONS OF HISTORY AND FACTS OF GEOGRAPHY.

VALLABHBHAI

Source—Sardar Patel's Correspondence vol-VII, p-308

Letter from Vallabhbhai to Major General Chaudhuri congratulating him and all members for restoration of normalcy in Hyderabad

238

New Delhi
1 March 1949

My dear Chaudhuri,

We landed here safely this morning, and directly after that I have plunged into the usual rounds of interviews, meetings and engagements. But my mind is full of my tour, and I thought I should write to you to thank you both for the generous hospitality extended to us during our stay in Hyderabad. I know how much strain our stay imposed on both of you and on your staff. You will, of course, make light of it, but that would be only out of the regard and consideration you have for us.

I have come back with a full appreciation of the tremendous task in which you and your colleagues are engaged. That has enabled me to recognise all the more the value of their work and the contribution which the Military Administration, under your able and inspiring leadership, has made to the restoration of normal condition in Hyderabad and to the many improvements which have been effected in the affairs of the State.

Please convey to your colleagues and your staff my sincere thanks for all that they have done and, in particular, for the pains they took over my visit to Hyderabad.

With kindest regards to both of you,

Yours sincerely,
Vallabhbhai Patel

Major-General J N Chaudhuri
Military Governor
Hyderabad (Dn.)

Source—Sardar Patel's Correspondence, vol-VII, p-309

Letter from Dy PM Vallabhbhai to Nizam appreciating former's meeting with the latter

239

Hyderabad (Dt.)
3 March 1949

My dear Friend,

I was glad to get an opportunity of making my acquaintance with you when you paid a visit to Hyderabad, and hope that this will prove to be a happy augury for the future of the premier State of Hyderabad which has got a peculiar traditions of its own among the other Indian States.

2. I trust you enjoyed your visit and safely reached Delhi and are quite well.

Yours sincerely,
Mir Osman Ali Nawaz
(Nizam VII)

Sardar Vallabhbhai Patel
Deputy Prime Minister
Dominion of India
New Delhi

Source—Sardar Patel's Correspondence, vol-VII, p-238

Letter from Vallabhbhai to Nizam of Hyderabad expressing his happiness over Nizam's adapting to the changed situation
240

New Delhi
4 March 1949

Dear Exalted Highness,

I should have written to you earlier, but unfortunately I have been plunged in work ever since my return and have hardly had any time to myself.

2. I was very glad to meet you and to make your acquaintance. As I have written to General Chaudhuri, it was very reassuring to find Hyderabad settling down to recent changes so well.

3. I was also happy to learn that Your Exalted Highness had adapted yourself so readily to changed conditions. As I told Your Exalted Highness, while error is a human failing and divine injunctions all points to forgetting and forgiving, it is the duty of human beings to contribute their share to this process by sincere repentance and by employing the period that is left in discharging their duties to their people and to their God. I should once more like to repeat that advice which, I can assure Your Exalted Highness, is in all sincerity intended to be friendly.

With kind regards,

Yours sincerely,
Vallabhbhai Patel

His Exalted Highness
Asaf Jah Nawab Sir Mir Usman
Ali Khan Bahadur
Nizam of Hyderabad
Hyderabad

Source—Sardar Patel's Correspondence, vol-VII, p-310

Congratulatory Telegrams

Vallabhbhai Patel was congratulated from many quarters for his unique victory over Junagadh

327
TELEGRAM

Bombay
10 November 1947

Hon'ble Sardar Vallabhbhai Patel
New Delhi

MY WARMEST FELICITATIONS ON LATEST HAPPY DEVELOPMENTS IN

JUNAGADH. MAY EVERYTHING END WELL BY GRACE OF GOD AND

YOUR NOBLE EFFORTS IS MY EARNEST PRAYER.

MAHARAJA PORBANDAR

328
TELEGRAM

New Delhi
11 November 1947

His Highness Maharaja of Porbandar
Taj
Bombay

MANY THANKS YOUR TELEGRAM OF FELICITATIONS AND GOOD WISHES. CREDIT FOR SUCCESS IS AS MUCH OF FRIENDS LIKE YOU AS OF MINE.

VAllABHBHAI PATEL

329
TELEGRAM

Jetpur
10 November 1947

Hon'ble Sardar Vallabhbhai Patel
Deputy Prime Minister
New Delhi

PLEASE ACCEPT MY VERY SINCERE CONGRATULATIONS ON THE UNIQUE VICTORY OVER JUNAGADH WITHOUT CAUSING LOSS OF LIFE OR PROPERTY. CROWNING SUCCESS IN JUNAGADH HAS AMPLY PROVED THAT TRUTH AND JUSTICE MUST PREVAIL. ALL KATHIAWAR PRINCES AND PEOPLE ARE GRATEFUL FOR PRESERVING INTEGRITY AND UNITY OF KATHIAWAR BY YOUR TIMELY ACTION. KINDEST REGARDS.

JETPUR DARBAR

330
TELEGRAM

New Delhi
11 November 1947

Ruler of Jetpur
Jetpur
MANY THANKS YOUR TELEGRAM OF CONGRATULATIONS. CREDIT FOR SUCCESS BELONGS AS MUCH TO FRIENDS LIKE YOU.
VALLABHBHAI PATEL

Source—Sardar Patel's Correspondence, vol-VII, p-392-393

Vallabhbhai thanking Ramasamy Mudaliar for representing the case of Hyderabad before UNO with skill and ability
559

New Delhi
24 November 1948

My dear Sir Ramasamy Mudaliar,

Thank you for your letter of 20 November 1948.

I shall discuss the matter with Reddy and yourself when you come here.

I should like to say how much I appreciated the skill and ability with which you represented India's stand on Hyderabad before the Security Council. When you come here, we shall discuss more about it.

With kindest regards from us both.

Yours sincerely,
Vallabhbhai Patel

Sir Ramasamy Mudaliar
Dewan
Mysore State
Carlton House
Bangalore

Source—Sardar Patel's Correspondence, vol-VII, p-646-647

Letter written by Vallabhbhai Patel to Maharaja Hari Singh that he himself and his party never harboured any sentiment of disloyality against him
34

New Delhi
3 July 1947

My dear Maharaja Sahib,

Rai Bahadur Gopaldas [a prominent Hindu of Lahore] saw me today and conveyed to me the substance of your conversation with him. I am sorry to find that there is considerable misapprehension in your mind about the Congress. Allow me to assure Your Highness that the Congress is not your enemy, as you happen to believe, but there are in the Congress many strong supporters of your State. As an organisation, the Congress is not opposed to any Prince in India. It has no quarrel with the States. It is true that recent events resulting in the arrest of Pandit Jawaharlal Nehru and the continued detention of Sheikh Abdullah have created a feeling of great dissatisfaction amongst many Congressmen who wish well of your State. Pandit Jawaharlal Nehru belongs to Kashmir, He is proud of it, and rest assured he can never be your enemy.

It is unfortunate that none of the Congress leaders has got any contact with Your Highness. Personal contact would have removed much of the misunderstanding, which probably is based largely on misinformation gathered through sources not quite disinterested.

Having had no personal contact, my correspondence has been with your Prime Minister since the arrest of Sheikh Abdullah and my efforts have been to persuade him to have a different approach to the problem, which in the long run would be in the interest of the State.

Is it necessary to assure you that in your domestic affairs the Congress has no intention whatever of interfering? If it had not been so, the Constituent Assembly would not have been able to attract a vast majority of Princes who have joined it, and I have no doubt that the rest will also join with very few exceptions who have no choice owing to peculiar circumstances, for instance Bhawalpur, Kalat etc. In the Negotiating Committee, your Prime Minister was present, and our decisions were unanimous in the four meetings that he attended. In these meetings, all the Princes got complete satisfaction from us about their special rights, privileges etc. which they enjoyed.

I fully appreciate the difficult and delicate situation in which your State has been placed, but as a sincere friend and well-wisher of the State, I wish to assure you that the interest of Kashmir lies in joining the Indian Union and its Constituent Assembly without any delay. Its past history and traditions demand it, and all India looks up to you and expects you to take that decision. Eighty per cent of India is on this side. The States that have cast their lot with the Constituent Assembly have been convinced that their safety lies in standing together with India.

I was greatly disappointed when His Excellency the Viceroy returned without having a full and frank discussion with you on that fatal [fateful] Sunday, when you had given an appointment which could not be kept because of your sudden attack of cholic pain. He had invited you to be his guest at Delhi, and in that also he was disappointed. I had hopes that we would meet here, but I was greatly disappointed when His Excellency told me that you did not avail of the invitation.

May I take the liberty of suggesting that it would be better if you even now come to Delhi, when you will certainly be his guest? We want an opportunity of having a frank and free discussion with you in an atmosphere of freeborn, and I have no doubt that all your doubts and suspicions, of which I have heard from Gopaldas, will completely disappear. In Free India, you cannot isolate yourself, and you must make friends with the leaders of Free India who want to be friends with you.

Yours sincerely,
Vallabhbhai Patel

Lt Gen. His Highness Rajrajeshwar Maharajadhiraj
Sir Hari Singh
Maharaja of Jammu & Kashmir

Source—Sardar Patel's Correspondence, vol-I Ed-Durga Das, Navjivan Publishing House, Ahmedabad, 1971, p-32-34

Letter written by Jawaharlal Nehru to Vallabhbhai Patel forwarding therewith the letter written by Dwarkanath Kachru.
57

New Delhi
5 October 1947

My dear Vallabhbhai,

I enclose a letter I have received from Dwarkanath Kachru [Secretary, All-India States Peoples' Conference] from Srinagar. A subsequent message says that he is staying on for a few more days.

Yours sincerely,
Jawaharlal

The Hon'ble Sardar Vallabhbhai Patel
New Delhi
Encl. 1

ENCLOSURE

Srinagar
4 October 1947

My dear Panditji,

I am now here for the last four days. Probably I will fly back on Monday. The position here can briefly be summarised thus:

1. Sheikh Sahib and his close associates have decided for the Indian Union.
2. But this decision has not been announced yet and the impression is being given that so far the National Conference have taken no decision.
3. The leaders of the National Conference are mostly in jail and only Sheikh Sahib has been released so far.
4. The stand taken by Sheikh Sahib is that the political prisoners must be released and the Working Committee and the General Council must be allowed to meet to consider the problem and to place their decision before the people.
5. Meanwhile Sheikh Sahib is delivering speeches to educate public opinion and to prepare the people for what seems to be the inevitable decision of the National Conference.
6. Speeches are delivered to show that killings of Hindus and Muslims are un-Hindu and un-Islamic; that the issue of accession cannot be decided by a religious sentiment and that the friends and sympathisers of Kashmiris during these years of struggle or sufferings have been Gandhiji, Jawaharlalji and the Congress and not the Muslims or the League or Mr Jinnah. Attempts are being made to show that Jinnah and the League have done great harm to the popular movement in Kashmir and that the objective of the League and Mr Jinnah is the preservation of the Princely Order and feudal oppression.
7. It is also emphasised that the objective of the Kashmir National Conference is the attainment of people's sovereignty, with the Maharaja enjoying a constitutional position and that this would be the main factor determining the decision of the Conference in the matter of accession. In short, they would join the Dominion

which enables them to achieve these objects or helps them in the achievement of their objective.

8. Another Important fact which must be borne in mind is the utter collapse of the administrative and governmental machinery. An atmosphere of fear and insecurity pervades the place. There is no competent or reliable person to talk or negotiate on behalf of the Government or the Maharaja and so far no step has been taken to begin talks with Sheikh Sahib.

9. The Maharaja is incapable of taking a decision and though Sheikh Sahib has written a nice letter to him and the Maharaja too has expressed a desire to meet sheikh sahib and his wife, there has really been no move from the Government or the Maharaja.

10. All this has made Sheikh Sahib very uneasy and the continued imprisonment of his colleagues adds all the more to the seriousness of the position.

11. Sheikh Sahib feels that unless there is a transfer of power to a substantial degree, the National conference may find itself in a difficult position. To fight the League, to maintain law and order inside the State and to carry the masses with them it is highly essential that a settlement with the National Conference should be brought about simultaneously with the accession to the union.

12. Alternative to the National Conference is undiluted Muslim communalism of the most militant type and the National Conference urges that it be taken into confidence and be closely associated with the governance of the country.

13. This is the demand of the progressive elements amongst the minorities and they also urge that all progressive sections should stand behind Sheikh Sahib and strengthen his hands.

14. The threat to Kashmir is real and unless the Congress takes up a strong stand and forces the Maharaja to come to some agreement with the National Conference, Kashmir is doomed and there will be nothing to prevent the conquest of Kashmir by Muslim League leaders and private armies. The Maharaja is doomed and so are the National Conference and the minorities.

15. Sheikh Sahib has received, your letter today and tomorrow a reply will be prepared for you.

16. I shall most probably fly back on Monday and shall bring it along with me. This letter will be a detailed one and will explain the case of the National Conference.

17. Sheikh Sahib was most anxious to fly to Delhi to meet you but the situation here is such that he cannot leave the place for some days more. He has therefore asked me to go back in order to explain the whole case to you and Sardar Patel.

18. I hope you will realise the urgency of the situation here and bear it in mind while talking with the representatives of the Maharaja.

19. I need hardly repeat that you realise the whole position much better than most of us but I hope your colleagues will also take a similar view of the situation here.

Yours,
Dwarkanath

Source—Sardar Patel's Correspondence vol-I p-53-55

Letter written by Vallabhbhai to Jawaharlal informing that half of NC prisoners had already been released and the other were to be released within next two or three days. Also indicating the misconception of difference between him and Nehru
58

New Delhi
8 October 1947

My dear Jawaharlal,

I am returning herewith Kachru's letter to you, which you so kindly sent to me for perusal. After you received this letter, Batra, the Deputy Prime Minister of Jammu & Kashmir State, was here. He told me that Sheikh and Begum Abdullah were to meet His Highness the Maharaja that day, ie. 6 October. He also told me that about half the political prisoners had already been released and the other half were to be released within the next two or three days.

2. We all realise that the position is full of dangerous potentialities. We are giving the Kashmir Government as much assistance as possible within the limited resources available. There are all sorts of difficulties in our going all out to assist the State. But I am sure things would improve when Justice Mahajan takes over the Prime Ministership. He is at least keenly alive to the dangers which surround Kashmir and knows his own mind. I hope there would be an end to the almost fatal indecisiveness which has so far been the bane of the Kashmir Government. In the meantime, all that we can and should do is to assist the State to the best of our capacity. I have also impressed upon Batra the need for mobilising popular opinion on the side of the Government. I am sure they themselves realise it.

3. Para 19 of Kachru's letter has a fling which is obviously aimed at me. I do not think that anything which could have been done for Kashmir has been left undone by me; nor am I aware of any difference between you and me on matters of

policy relating to Kashmir. Still it is most unfortunate that persons down below should think that there is a gulf between us. It is also distressing to me.

Yours sincerely,
Vallabhbhai Patel

The Hon'ble Pandit Jawaharlal Nehru
New Delhi

Source—Sardar Patel's Correspondence vol-I, p-56.

Letter written by Dalip Singh, Agent to the Government of India in J&K, to Vallabhbhai with copy to Jawaharlal explaining the position of J&K and differences between Maharaja and Sheikh
74

Camp Residency Guest House
Jammu
7 November 1947

My dear States Minister,

I wish to explain the psychology of the people I am now supposed to deal with. His Highness is extremely bitter. I neither praise nor condemn his attitude, which is easily understood. The Prime Minister is a man of ability and straightforwardness. He is however an Arya Samajist with all the mentality and fanaticism of that body. The IG of Police is talkative and intelligent, but he does not impress me as reliable. The Governor [of Jammu Province], Mr CR Chopra, is an intelligent man and I find him the most reasonable and unbiased of officials here. The State's Brigadier Rawat is a good man according to Brig Paranjpe under whose orders he is working. I have not had any occasion to test his mentality.

The refugees from west Punjab and of the local villages are extremely bitter. It is impossible to control their lust for vengeance and retaliation whenever possible. I arranged a scheme with the approval of the Governor for the evacuation of refugees from West Punjab to East Punjab. They have made the scheme unworkable by collecting opposite the Indian Brigade Headquarters, causing confusion and trouble and endeavouring to board the military lorries en masse, with the result that the evacuation has been delayed. They refused to leave the ground occupied even though the Brigadier wanted it for camping the rest of a battalion expected here. The IG of Police telephoned me and I told him that, if necessary, force must be used, however regrettable, because the military must not be hampered. The refugees themselves, whom I tried to address, declared that they had suffered untold grievances at the hands of the State Administration and preferred to lie down and die at the hands of the military. No appeals to them that without the military no evacuation was at all possible and if the military were hampered their lives were in great danger, affected them at all. The officials here fully realise the danger of all this kind of thing or at any rate agree with all the arguments I put forward while in my presence. I have a strong suspicion that they agree only seemingly with a few exceptions. Whether they agree or not, however, it is extremely difficult to cope with the refugees who can neither be made to understand nor will listen and are so blinded by self-interest that they would not have evacuation rather than see some fortunate person get ahead of them in the process of evacuation.

I have formed a high opinion of Brig Paranjpe's abilities and straightforwardness. Even he, however, told me that his experience showed that a Muslim could not be trusted where the cry for religion was raised. He told me of two Muslim officers who worked admirably under him in what is now Pakistan and saved many Hindus and Sikhs, but when they came to Ferozepur and saw what had happened to their co-religionists, they went completely 'haywire' and forgot all duty as officers. I can fully appreciate this Muslim attitude. It is not altogether blameworthy, though again I neither praise nor condemn.

The troops, the Brigadier assures me, are unable to give protection to Muslim citizens in Jammu city. The Muslims were concentrated in two mohallas (localities). Mahajan tells me that he asked them to come out and reopen their shops and he would post pickets to prevent any danger to their persons. But perhaps rightly they realised that they could not be protected and refused to do so. Their concentration in two mohallas was certainly dangerous in the sense that shots used to be exchanged between them and Hindus round about and much alarm and panic caused. It was in these circumstances that it was decided to evacuate them to Pakistan. I went to their camp today and one man came up to me and said that he, a member of the national conference and a loyal subject of His Highness, was being treated the same as a Leaguer. I believe he was telling the truth. But I can think of no method of keeping back selected persons and giving them protection from Hindus and Sikhs in the city. As you know already, the Muslim districts of Jammu near the frontier are really in the hands of raiders and mobs with a few pockets where State troops and non-Muslims are shut up and surrounded. In these circumstances, it is impossible to promote friendly feeling between Muslims and Hindus or to give protection to Muslims in Hindu areas and I am unable to see what more can be done. Severe action involving the death of 150 attackers was taken yesterday. This, I believe, is the largest number of attackers ever shot. It was due to the death of a Rajput trooper that his comrades went mad and opened fire with LMGs and rifles, causing severe casualties. As far as I can ascertain, 300 Muslims were killed due to the connivance of the Sikh lorry drivers who deliberately stopped the lorries. The occupants in alarm jumped out and tried to escape making it impossible for the escort to guard them. The rest were brought back safely. As soon as this becomes known, I fear repercussions in Kashmir State and weakening of Sheikh Sahib's authority there. As I have repeatedly stated, it is impossible, however, to do more. These are the circumstances which make me feel that my mission is hopeless.

HH personally dislikes Sheikh Sahib and Sheikh Sahib's endeavours to try and maintain authority in Jammu without reference to HH are merely causing friction and tension, No result is obtained as he Is not in touch and to appoint a Muslim IG of Police would probably mean that he would be murdered or his authority would be defied with the connivance of his own men.

The Muslim police have largely deserted and hence only Hindu police are functioning. I am glad to say that these police have dealt humanely with the evacuees. I have this from an evacuee, who does not inspire me with any confidence and who privately admitted that he was a Leaguer and a Pakistani.

All this however is probably due to the personal influence of one or two officials and does not disturb the general picture which I have sketched above.

I got the wire informing me of Mr Brijlal Nehru's going to Srinagar. As no reference was made to my going there and as Mr Nehru was to contact me here, I did not go to Srinagar today either. I should be obliged if I am given clear instructions as to the evacuation of the second mohalla of Muslims from Jammu. I should also like clear instructions as to what is meant by the Kashmir Government. I would suggest that where Sheikh Sahib is concerned, he should be mentioned by name; where HH is concerned, he should be mentioned by name; and where the concurrence of both is desired, the phrase 'Kashmir Government' might be used. I have already explained the difficulty arising in carrying out instructions where this phrase is used. It is not always possible to contact Sheikh Sahib on the phone and everyone here says the phone is tapped. Hence I cannot speak very freely over the wire.

I have, etc.,
Your most obedient servant,
Dalip Singh
(Agent to the Government of India in J&K)

The Hon'ble Sardar Vallabhbhaiji Patel
Minister for States
New Delhi
Copy to: The Hon'ble Pandit Jawaharlal Nehru
Prime Minister
New Delhi

Source—Sardar Patel's Correspondence, vol-I p-85-88

Letter written by Mehrchand Mahajan* to Sardar Patel explaining the need for formation of Interim Government
81

Jammu
22 November 1947

My dear Sardar Patelji,

Kindly excuse these few lines amongst your multifarious engagements. As advised I am quietly watching the trend of events without in any way interfering in the administration, but I wish to emphasise two things:

1. There should not be further delay in the formation of an Interim Government. Sheikh Sahib, I suppose, is in no hurry about it having got dictatorial powers which are being exercised in a dictatorial manner regardless of all rules and forms of law. This will not be in the interests of the administration. There is no reason why an Interim Government on the Mysore model should not be formed. I will however act as advised.
2. The Indian Dominion forces in Jammu province should be immediately strengthened and reinforced. At least two more battalions are needed. In spite of repeated signals nothing is coming through.
3. Would you advise me to visit Mysore and see Sir Ramasamy Mudaliar[1] and get a complete picture of the recent Mysore constitution and its working and its future plans?

I entirely depend on your advice.
With kindest regards,

Yours sincerely,
Mehrchand Mahajan

* Dewan of Mysore State, a former Member of Viceroy's Executive Council

Source—Sardar Patel's Correspondence, vol-I, p-96

Letter written by Vallabhbhai to Gopalaswami Ayyangar to persuade Maharaja to agree for Mysore Model of Government.
89

New Delhi
10 December 1947

My dear Gopalaswami Ayyangar,

I have seen your letter dated 9 December 1947 addressed to HH the Maharaja of Kashmir. (See enclosure.)

I am afraid you have probably misunderstood me on these matters. The proposals which you have made may ease matters from the point of view of Sheikh Abdullah, but whether they would ease matters from the point of view of the Maharaja is difficult for me to say. We have to bear in mind that it was we who suggested to the Maharaja to agree to the Mysore model and unless the Maharaja can be persuaded to agree to alter it, I feel that we cannot insist on him to accept any change. We have also to take into account that it is the Maharaja who has entered into a commitment with Mr Mahajan and, therefore, it is for him to decide whether or not he could release himself from that commitment. All we can do is to persuade him to agree to this position.

Yours sincerely,
Vallabhbhai Patel

The Hon'ble Mr N Gopalaswami Ayyangar
Minister without Portfolio
New Delhi

Source—Sardar Patel's Correspondence, vol-I, p-107

Letter from Jawaharlal to Vallabhbhai informing him that Kashmir issue would be dealt with the PM and not by the States Ministry

98

New Delhi
23 December 1947

My dear Vallabhbhai,

Gopalaswami Ayyangar has sent me copies of correspondence which has, passed between him and you last night regarding 150 motor vehicles being sent from East Punjab to Kashmir.

I must confess that I am greatly surprised to read this. I do not appreciate the principle which presumably the states Ministry has in view in regard to its work. That Ministry, or any other Ministry, is not an imperium in imperio, jealous of its sovereignty in certain domains and working in isolation from the rest. If that was so then the government would not be a close-knit organism working together with a common purpose, and the PM would have no function to perform. But I do not wish to consider the wider question of principle at this stage though it may have to be discussed later.

The present issue relates to Kashmir. This raises all manner of connected issues—international, military and others—which are beyond the competence of the States Ministry as such. That is why it has to be considered by the Cabinet as a whole frequently and by various Ministers separately or together. And that is why I have to take personal interest in this matter as PM to bring about co-ordination in our various activities.

Gopalaswami Ayyangar has been especially asked to help in Kashmir matters and at our request has visited the state twice. He has to deal with East Punjab also and the MEO organisation there. Both for this reason and because of his intimate knowledge and experience of Kashmir he has to be given full latitude. Accordingly, after repeated talks with representatives of the Defence Ministry, all manner of arrangements have been made about supply of arms and equipment etc. In this connection the urgent need of motor vehicles has been repeatedly raised. Ultimately it was decided to ask the East Punjab Government to relieve a number of these for Kashmir and steps were taken accordingly.

I really do not understand where the States Ministry comes into the picture, except that it should be kept informed of steps taken. In any event I do not understand why the States Ministry should intervene and come in the way of arrangements being made. All this was done at my instance and I do not propose to abdicate my functions in regard to matters for which I consider myself responsible.

May I say that the manner of approach to Gopalaswami was hardly in keeping with the courtesy due to a colleague?

Yours,
Jawaharlal

Sardar Vallabhbhai Patel

Source—Sardar Patel, Correspondence, vol-I, p-121-122.

Vallabhbhai Ready to Resign over J&K

In reaction to Nehru's letter, Vallabhbhai submitted his resignation. However, after Gandhi's intervention, the letter did not reach Nehru

Draft*

99

23 December 1947

My dear Jawaharlal,

Your letter of today has been received just now at 7 pm and I am writing immediately to tell you this. It has caused me considerable pain.

Before I received your letter I had already written to Gopalaswami a letter of which a copy is enclosed herewith. If I had known [that] he had sent you copies of our correspondence I would have sent to you a copy of my letter to him straightaway.

In any case, your letter makes it clear to me that I must not or at least cannot continue as a Member of Government and hence I am hereby tendering my resignation. I am grateful to you for the courtesy and kindness shown to me during the period of office which was a period of considerable strain.

Yours sincerely,
Vallabhbhai Patel

Pandit Jawaharlal Nehru

---

* The letter is marked 'draft'. It was not sent presumably because Sardar was persuaded to, drop the controversy.

Source—Sardar Patel's Correspondence, vol-I p-122

Letter written by Sheikh Abdullah expressing loyalty to Maharaja

26 September 1947

It May Please Your Highness,

It is after about one and a half years' incarceration as long wished—I had opportunity of having derailed talks with Thakur Nichantchandji [brother of the Maharani]. What unfortunate things happened during this period in the State I need not mention. But this is now realised by every wellwisher of the State that many of the regrettable happenings of the past have mainly been due to the misunderstandings which appear now to have deliberately been created by interested people in order to achieve their own ends. R B Ramchandra Kak, the ex-Prime Minister, through his mischievous methods and masterly manoeuvrings, brought these misunderstandings to a climax and succeeded in his attempt, though temporarily, to a certain extent. He painted me and my organisation in the darkest colours and in everything that we did or attempted to do to bring Your Highness and your people closer, base and selfish motives were attributed to me. But God be thanked that all these enemies of Your Highness and State stand exposed today.

In spite of what has happened in the past, I assure Your Highness that myself and my party have never harboured any sentiment of disloyalty towards Your Highness' person, throne or dynasty. The development of this beautiful country and the betterment of its people is our common aim and interest and I assure Your Highness the fullest and loyal support of myself and my organisation. Not only this but I assure Your Highness that any party, within or without the State which may attempt to create any impediments in our efforts to gain our goal will be treated as our enemy and will be treated as such.

In order to achieve the common aim set forth above, mutual trust and confidence must be the mainstay. Without this it would not be possible to face successfully the great difficulties that beset our State on all sides at present.

Before I close this letter I beg to assure Your Highness once again of my steadfast loyalty and pray that God may grant me opportunity enough to let this country attain under Your Highness' aegis such an era of peace, prosperity and good government that it may be second to none and be an ideal for others to copy.

Yours Highness' most obedient subject,
SM Abdullah

Source—Sardar Patel's Correspondence, vol-I p-130

Letter from Gopalaswami to Vallabhbhai Patel reporting about extraordinary behavior of the Security Council in dealing with Kashmir question
158

New Delhi
5 June 1948

My dear Sardar Sahib,

I am so grateful to you for your letter of the 4th.

2. Nothing has caused me greater disappointment than my inability to proceed to where you are, spend a little time with you and talk over many matters. I programmed a visit to Mussoorie more than twice since my return from New York, but at the last moment something or other stood in the way and I was obliged to postpone it. I cannot find time to get away tomorrow and go over and see you at Dehra Dun, but I trust I shall be able to do so the following week-end.

3. The ways of the Security Council have been extraordinary and in dealing with the Kashmir question it has behaved in a manner which has surprised even a person like me with three months' day-to-day contact and experience with its members. Its last resolution giving the Commission the discretion to make enquiries about Junagadh, genocide and implementation of inter-Dominion agreements is a dishonest surrender to Pakistan intrigue.

4. As you say, we have entangled ourselves with a set of persons who will not see things straight and we have to do our best under the circumstances in which we find ourselves today. We are today informing the Security Council that in view of our previous clear indications to it, its Commission cannot, on arrival here, proceed to take steps to implement the tasks cast upon it by a resolution which we have declined to accept in essentials. But we have only intimated our willingness to confer with it if it comes over in spite of our objection. We are asking it further to let us know in advance the point or points

on which it proposes to confer with us. The Council apparently wants to push its Commission out, to plant it in India and slowly to hustle us into agreeing to all things recommended in its resolution. I am not sure even the telegram we are sending today will have the intended effect of making it hesitate to carry out the programme of the Commission coming out to this country.

5. Since returning from New York and especially after my visit to Srinagar during the freedom celebrations, I have not been feeling too happy about the internal affairs of the State. I have had more than one talk with VP[Menon] about Kashmir. There are a number of matters to be straightened out and I shall be only too glad to carry out your wishes. I am arranging to proceed to Jammu and Srinagar on the 8th and am asking V P to accompany me. I hope his Hyderabad pre-occupations will permit of his doing so. We shall jointly try to do our best and hope that at the end of our visit things there would look more satisfactory than they do now.

6. I am daily getting myself posted with the state of your health and am glad to learn that it has much improved. I trust this improvement will be even more rapid in the future than in the past and that you will be able to resume your normal activities here to the full at the earliest possible date.

With kindest regards,

Yours very sincerely,
Gopalaswamy

The Hon'ble Sardar Vallabhbhai Patel
Dehra Dun (UP)

Source—Sardar Patel's Correspondence, vol-I p-201-202

EXTRACTS
From Nehru to Sardar Patel
159

New Delhi
6 June 1948

My dear Vallabhbhai,

Our experience in Kashmir has shown us that it is easier to begin military operations than to end them. I think on the whole our army in Kashmir, officers and men, have not done badly. I have gone fairly deeply into this question and balanced the enormous difficulties they have had to face. They have erred and made mistakes, they have also shown sometimes an unnecessary caution. Nevertheless on the whole they have done well. I do not think most people realise the tremendous difficulties of the undertaking. At the present moment there is little doubt that the Pakistan army, or a. part of it, is functioning against us in Kashmir territory. They have a tremendous geographical advantage over, us. Kashmir is a very big area and possesses most difficult terrain from the point of view of military operations. Also the climate in winter is a very hard one and large areas like the Ladakh Valley are completely unapproachable in winter. The first lesson that a military commander is taught is that of concentration. Nothing is more dangerous in war than a dispersal of forces. This concentration leads to large areas being left unguarded, unless the forces we use are tremendous in numbers. Even so it is practically impossible to guard every mountain valley or cave. We fight to win and to break the enemy. They fight to harass and annoy and cause us injury. The latter method does not need concentration. In any event we have to think of our army as it is and not as it might be. We have, in technical matters, to take advantage of our military experts. Our policy, specially when it involves military operations or the possibility of them, cannot ignore the hard facts of the situation, as judged by the military experts. I have, little doubt that our officers are exceedingly anxious to produce results in Kashmir. Their own reputation depends upon that. We cannot bring them about by expressing our dissatisfaction of the army, which can only do what it is capable of doing and no more. The fight that is going on near Domel-Muzaffarabad is of great significance and that is the reason why Pakistan has thrown its forces and some armour into it. our victory there will no doubt make a great difference to our campaign. Because of this Pakistan will try its utmost to prevent that victory.

I have written to you about Kashmir already. I found there that quite a good effort in the shape of propaganda has been made by the Kashmir Government. They have published attractive pamphlets and have very effective popular plays about the struggle which are performed in large numbers of urban and rural areas. Their difficulty is lack of paper and lack of broadcasting equipment. Pakistan radio repeats the most infernal lies by leaflets etc. The only way to check it is to have our own broadcasting. Therefore, the urgency of this.

Propaganda in Kashmir must obviously take into consideration the psychology of the Kashmir people, both Muslim and non-Muslim. It must be largely addressed to large masses of people who can make a difference this way or that way. I am told that Kashmiri broadcasting from AIR[*] is rather colourless and does not appeal to the listeners in Kashmir. It seems necessary to associate a competent Kashmiri to give the background to our broadcasts.

My study of the Kashmir situation has led me to believe that the Maharaja cannot play. He just does not know how to. When there is an obvious, possibility of his losing everything he still wants to hold on to relatively simple things, not realising that this has a bad effect both internally among the people as well as on external observers. His mere absence

---

[*] Sardar Patel was I&B Minister

from Srinagar is bitterly resented because everybody of any consequence functions from Srinagar now. Even the military situation requires this.

This leads me to the State Forces which have become not only not helpful but a tremendous nuisance. By their passivity and sheer funk, they have done injury to our cause. The only way to pull them up is for the Indian Army to take complete control over these forces. This, of course, will not mean that the State army will lose its identity or will become absorbed in the Indian Army. The State army will be kept distinct and will certainly stay on in Kashmir even when our troops decide to withdraw. Our own officers feel this strongly and they cannot make full use of existing State troops in present circumstances. It has thus become an urgent necessity, from the point of view of military operations as well as the possibility of a plebiscite, that quick action be taken in such matters. It is equally important that the Maharaja should live in Srinagar for the greater part of the summer months, as Srinagar is the place now where important decisions have to be taken both by civil authorities and our military commanders. Unless he lives in Srinagar he cannot keep in touch. From some other points of view too it is not desirable for him to live long in Jammu during summer. This would be entirely opposed to the old policy when the Maharaja spent the whole summer in Srinagar.

Yours,
Jawaharlal

The Hon'ble Sardar Vallabhbhal Patel
Dehra Dun

Source—Sardar Patel's Correspondence, vol-I, p-203-205

Letter from Jawaharlal to Vallabhbhai with enclosure of Mountbatten's letter, who urged compliance with the ceasefire order of the UNO
177

New Delhi
30 August 1948

My dear Vallabhbhai,

Some days ago I received a personal and confidential letter from Lord Mountbatten. I showed it to the Governor-General* today. He was of opinion that as this letter dealt with important and grave matters, all the Members of the Cabinet should see it.

I am therefore sending a copy of it to you....

Jawaharlal

* GS Bajpai, Secretary-General, External Affairs Ministry

ENCLOSURE

Copy of a Letter from Lord Mountbatten to Pandit Nehru, dated London 15 August 1948

We have just come back from a great meeting at the Albert Hall where over 4,000 people joined together to celebrate the first anniversary of India's independence. No doubt you will see the full report in the press, but I thought you would like to know that every time your name was mentioned it brought all proceedings to a standstill; so long and so genuine was the applause.

Edwina and I are off tomorrow morning to Ireland and after that to Canada, and will not be back until the end of the month, and I know that you will have in the meanwhile to take some very vital decisions. How I wish I could still be with you in Delhi and help you to make them by giving you a chance to discuss all the points with me as you used to in the old days.

Although I have no right whatever to make any comments, let alone give you any advice now, I feel in a way a continuing responsibility for the situation you are now faced with, for it was I who encouraged you to take the Kashmir case to UNO.

Since I have been over here, I have had an opportunity of discussing this problem with every sort of person and all shades of opinion. I have been struck by the unanimity of thought over here that India was absolutely right to go to UNO. I know that you (and I) have been criticised in India for having gone to UNO because UNO handled the matter in a way that caused disappointment in India. But in the comparatively detached atmosphere of London, it is more than ever clear that the alternatives before India were and still are open war or a decision by UNO. There are really no other alternatives except perhaps a continuation of undeclared war with all the risks that entail of eventually turning into a declared war.

I think you will agree with [me that] Pakistan is in no position even to declare war, since I happen to know that their military commanders have put it to them in writing that a declaration of war with India can only end in the inevitable and ultimate defeat of Pakistan.

Therefore a declared war can only come about by India making the declaration.

I know that you will instinctively shrink from taking such a course, but I also know that there are some of your colleagues in the Cabinet and the more noisy and unthinking elements in the country who will press you to declare war. I therefore feel it may be of some use if I enumerate again the disastrous consequences of such an act on the part of India.

After all that the leaders of free India have said and stand for, after having won your long battle against Imperial rule, can we honestly contemplate that India's first major international act should be a declaration of war, and the final and open abandonment of all other methods of settling an international dispute? This will inevitably be of the gravest possible prejudice to Indians future international position; indeed UNO might well outlaw her, in my opinion, naming her as the aggressor. What a paradoxical tragedy that would be!

I am certain I do not need to reassure you as to the sincere friendship which HMG feel towards India. The decisive voices in the British Cabinet are extremely sympathetic and well disposed towards India. If there was any doubt, surely Attlee's remarks in the recent debate in the House on Hyderabad and Stafford's remarks at the Albert Hall today would reassure you. But whatever their feelings would be, they would have no option, in my opinion, but to conform with UNO's decision if they were to name India as the aggressor.

The converse seems equally true to me; if the United Kingdom were named an aggressor by UNO, the Government of India would be bound to conform to UNO unless indeed they were to abandon UNO.

I need not remind you that you have 4 crores of Muslims spread all over India to whom communal peace was given by Gandhiji's teaching and finally by his death. Can anyone doubt that all Gandhiji's teaching would be thrown by the board, and that communal massacres which would make the Punjab look mild by comparison would follow open warfare with a Muslim State. A declaration of war would be signing the death warrant of a great number of innocent women and children within India and not merely within the war zone. In this respect I submit that India is in an almost unique position.

This would be a most inglorious end to the whole conception of the secular State for which you and Gandhiji and your followers have devoted your whole life's work.

Have you asked your Chiefs of Staff Committee to give you the advantages and disadvantages of declaring war? If you had a thousand heavy bombers, or a hundred, or even fifty, which could completely flatten out the Pakistan bases, then I could understand the military temptation to declare war. But what have you got? A few old Dakotas with a somewhat doubtful Harry Tate contraption to drop bombs which I have seen for myself at the Hindustan Aircraft Factory. To hit the target with this arrangement would entail flying at so low a height that the Pakistan anti-aircraft gunners could not miss. And we know from our own experience in England how ineffective even a first-class bombing force can be until after years of training and war experience.

If therefore you will agree that no sane man could subscribe to a declaration of war, what is the alternative? Apart from going on with an undeclared war, which is so likely to lead to ultimate disaster, the alternative must be UNO.

I think that India should show some patience with UNO, for after all it is the first time humanity has got together to try and find an alternative to war. All my discussions here have convinced me that it was not malice, power politics or any sinister motive which brought about the unsatisfactory treatment of our case. I admit that they took a long while to send the Delegation; that they failed to deal with India's complaint against Pakistan as you would have wished them to, and that things have dragged on interminably; but now you have the Delegation with you, and now is your opportunity to bring all possible legitimate pressure to bear to make them understand your position. I know that you, unfortunately, did not share my view that the last resolution of UNO was not unfavourable for India, but if you will look at it again, I think you will find that if UNO were to implement it, it can provide a reasonable solution for India. Certainly an infinitely better solution than plunging all the rest of India into the consequences of war.

If UNO, as Krishna [Menon] seems to think likely, order a cease-fire, with all the forces in their present positions, you might feel that this was giving an unfair advantage to Pakistan. But is it? If there are enough competent and honest observers, they can prevent the forward movement of troops and ammunition, and they can prevent any form of consolidation by Pakistan, or at least report any infringement which would finally put Pakistan out of court before UNO und the world.

The only satisfactory conclusion that I can see would be for UNO to condemn Pakistan publicly for sending their army into Kashmir on the ground that this is Indian territory. I do not myself see how such a condemnation could precede the acceptance of the order to cease fire. As I said just now, the act of complying with the cease-fire order could in no way prejudice India's military position, as your military advisers will tell you, but the condemnation of Pakistan by UNO which can then follow would be the justification of the policy which you have pursued from January and the beginning of peace in Kashmir. In effect this would enormously strengthen your position with your followers, and public opinion would certainly establish India's rightful position in the world.

For God's sake don't get yourself plunged in 'war' however great the internal pressure, for once in you cannot get out of the consequences.

Source—Sardar Patel's Correspondence, vol-I, p-219-222

Letter from Vallabhbhai to Jawaharlal expressing his displeasure over Sheikh Abdullah who critised Maharaja at a press conference.
183

New Delhi
30 September 1948

My dear Jawaharlal,

I was surprised to read this morning an account of the Press Conference which Sheikh Mohammed Abdullah is reported to have held here yesterday. He said he would be seeing me today and I was waiting for him, but since he did not turn up, I am writing to you as well as to him about it.

It is rather odd that he should have found the venue of a Press Conference to ventilate his alleged grievance against the Maharaja. No one should know better than he that the Maharaja is not in a position to resist the demands of the popular Ministry. We, the Maharaja and Sheikh Mohammed Abdullah himself came to a settlement last March. That settlement has not only been faithfully adhered to by the Maharaja but, in certain respects, he has acquiesced in departures from that settlement to the advantage of Sheikh Mohammed Abdullah and his Ministry. [I] refer in particular to the position regarding the reserved subjects of which the jagirdars form one. I am not aware of any single instance—at least Sheikh Sahib has not brought it to my notice—in which the Maharaja has obstructed or resisted any of the popular reforms. As a constitutional head, he may have asked for reconsideration in one or two matters, but this could hardly be treated as the subject of a grievance. It is undignified and constitutionally improper for a Prime Minister to attack the constitutional head of his administration, knowing full well that the latter is not in a position to defend himself or to retaliate. On top of it, to insinuate that he is trying to retain power, or that he has strong friends in India or that he could buy friends is, in my opinion, to say the least, most unfortunate.

Sheikh Sahib has also referred to certain people in India who believe in surrendering Kashmir to Pakistan, I should like to be enlightened who they are. As far as my information goes, there are many more of such people in Jammu and Kashmir State than in the whole of India put together.

Sheikh Sahib also refers to the Hindu fanaticism of the East Punjab. This again is a generalisation which, I hope, Sheikh Sahib in calmer moments will regret. It certainly is a most unfortunate attack on a neighbouring province of the Dominion to which his State has acceded.

I hope Sheikh Sahib realises that nobody has been more accommodating to him than the Government of India and none has extended to him greater understanding and sympathy in his struggle than the people of India. In spite of the fact that he has departed from an accepted position from time to time, we have tried our best to put pressure on the Maharaja and make him concede the position which he has taken up. I thought that, having made the Maharaja accept the position regarding the Army, he would now accommodate himself to the Maharaja and would not at least carry controversy in public. He has, however, thought it fit to do so, without having any regard for the fact that he is, after all, constitutionally the Maharaja's Prime Minister, I think it would be difficult to find a parallel in constitutional history to the sort of attack which he has made on the Maharaja. I hope you will succeed in impressing upon him the mistake he has made. We shall have gained something if at least it is not repeated. I thought I would let you have my reactions so that if an opportunity arises you might speak to him some time. I am sending herewith a copy of my letter to Sheikh Sahib.

Yours sincerely,
Vallabhbhai Patel

The Hon'ble Pandit Jawaharlal Nehru
New Delhi

ENCLOSURE

New Delhi
30 September 1948

My dear Sheikh Sahib,

I have seen a report of your yesterday's Press Conference which has appeared in today's Statesman. You made no reference to it when you saw me yesterday nor did you give me any indication that you were going to deal with certain controversial matters with which we, in the States Ministry, are undoubtedly concerned. Indeed, in respect of some matters we are seized already. I thought, as you told me yesterday, you would be coming to see me, but since you did not come, I am writing this to you.

I had hoped that with the Army question now out of the way and with practically no resistance or obstruction from the Maharaja in regard to the many schemes of reforms which you have introduced and are introducing, you would now accommodate yourself to your new constitutional relationship with him. I had never imagined that you would ventilate your grievance in public and I had thought that at least in fairness to ourselves and, having regard to the agreed arrangements between ourselves, if you had any grievance, you would first come to the States Ministry and seek a satisfactory solution through our medium. In fact, so far whenever you have had any difficulty we have not hesitated to put pressure on the Maharaja to accept a position, even though in certain matters it went against the arrangements agreed to last March.

No one knows better than you that today the Maharaja is powerless to resist your wishes. Even if he feels inclined differently, on merits he has to endorse your wishes if you pressed them. It is within my knowledge that he has deferred to your wishes in matters which concerned him intimately such as allowances to the family of the Raja of Poonch or to the handing over of guest houses or in regard to tenancy reforms. I am, therefore, unable to comprehend your reference to his trying to retain power.

I am also rather mystified at your reference to his having strong friends in India, or his being in a position to buy friends. During the three or four weeks that he was in Delhi he was quite inaccessible to interviewers and to the Press because he felt that, constitutionally, it was improper for him to deal in public with any matters affecting his State. If you have any particular information about these strong friends, I would be glad if you could communicate it to me. You have also referred to certain people who believe in surrendering Kashmir to Pakistan. I should like to be enlightened on this point as well. You will agree that we should know who these traitors are. You have also referred to the Muslim fanaticism of Pakistan and the Hindu fanaticism of East Punjab. As far as I know none of the Hindus or even Sikhs of East Punjab would like Kashmir to go to Pakistan. There has undoubtedly been some dissatisfaction in India with certain measures which have been put into force, but such dissatisfaction is by no means so general as to justify your dubbing a whole province as having succumbed to any kind of fanaticism, particularly when that province happens to be your neighbour and one whose goodwill and assistance would be of some help to you. You have also referred to the view that 'we deserted the Frontier'. This is probably a criticism of our attitude to the referendum in the Frontier. Jawaharlal would know this best how to deal with criticism of yours which, I can only say, is based on complete ignorance of facts. I don't blame you for it because you were in jail at the time.

I hope you will not mind my speaking to you frankly about your inter-view because I do feel that row when we are engaged in a common struggle against a foreign foe this sort of interview or thinking aloud does no one any good. On the other hand, it merely gives a loophole to our enemies to harp on dissensions and dissatisfactions and to pick out phrases here and there which could be magnified into more serious proportions on which a great deal of hostile propaganda can be built. It is much better our trying to solve our difficulties round a table in an atmosphere of friendliness and cordiality than to try to discuss them in public in an attempt to collect popular support for it. You know very well that our relations are such that any propaganda or publicity for your views in India is unnecessary. You also know that whenever you have had any difficulties we have tried our best to help you to overcome them and have mostly succeeded. Either the difficulties which you experience in India are formidable or they are not. If they are formidable, we have the right to be told what they are before you take the public into confidence. If they are not, they are hardly worthy of public notice.

With kindest regards,

Yours sincerely,
Vallabhbhai Patel

Hon'ble Sheikh Mohammed Abdullah
C/o The Prime Minister of India
New Delhi

Source—Sardar Patel's Correspondence, vol-I, p-227-230

Letter from Jawaharlal to Vallabhbhai Patel expressing his faith on Sheikh Abdullah
187

New Delhi
4 October 1948

My dear Vallabhbhai,

Thank you for your letter of 3 October about Sheikh Abdullah's press conference. I did not reply to your previous letter as I was leaving for Kashmir. I entirely agree with you that some of the statements that Sheikh Abdullah made in regard to the Maharaja were very indiscreet and should not have been made.

In Srinagar I had a long talk with Sheikh Abdullah and Bakshi Ghulam Mohammad about a large number of matters, more specially the whole background of our approach to these problems. I hope this did some good. Sheikh Abdullah is, I am convinced, a very straight and frank man. He is not a very clear thinker and he goes astray in his speech as many of our politicians do. He is of course obsessed with the idea of meeting the challenge of Pakistan and keeping his own people from being influenced by Pakistan's propaganda. I made it clear to him that while I entirely agree with this, the approach should be different.

Yours,
Jawaharlal

The Hon'ble Sardar Vallabhbhai Patel

Source—Sardar Patel's Correspondence, vol-I, p-232-233

EXTRACT

Extract from letter of Jawaharlal Nehru to Sardar Patel explaining his point of view on Kashmir 194

Paris
27 October 1948

Both Hyderabad and Kashmir have troubled people a lot here and in London, It is recognised, of course, that the Hyderabad affair is over from the international point of view. It was very fortunate that we could dispose of it rapidly. Otherwise reactions would have been very much adverse to us as it is difficult to explain everything and the simple fact of a large country attacking a small one impressed people unfavourably. So far as Kashmir is concerned, I think it is generally recognised that our case is a good one; nevertheless this business of a plebiscite and the conditions governing it fills people's minds. Of course people cannot get rid of the idea that Kashmir is predominantly Muslim and therefore likely to side with Muslim Pakistan. They say that if it is agreed that there should be a plebiscite, why is there any difficulty in having a ceasefire and truce? Liaquat Ali has laid stress on one fact only, ie. that the conditions of the plebiscite should be fixed now and then he will gladly agree to the ceasefire etc. in accordance with the UN Commission's resolution. He says those conditions should be according to the Security Council's resolution. I have made it clear that we cannot accept this for obvious reasons. The next suggestion is to come to some other agreement about the conditions. I do not think all this will lead to anything at present, at least. We cannot possibly agree to any outside intervention in the Government of Kashmir.

I am mentioning all this to you just to keep you in touch with the developments here. I might mention also that the position I have taken up about Kashmir is either a full acceptance of the UN commission's resolution on ceasefire, or a partition on the lines we have previously talked about, ie. Western Poonch etc., Gilgit, Chitral, most of Baltistan etc. to go to Pakistan. Neither of these is acceptable to Liaquat Ali.

The whole point I should like to impress upon you and my colleagues is that the Kashmir affair as well as Hyderabad developments are being very closely followed in other countries, though they may not say much about them. They follow them in order to judge what India stands for and is going to be. We have therefore to keep this fact in mind in regard to any steps that we take in both these places.

Source—Sardar Patel's Correspondence, vol-I, p-249

Letter from Vallabhbhai to Gopalaswami about Sheikh's interview to Michael Davidson whereat he advocated for independent Kashmir
213

New Delhi
1 May 1949

My dear Gopalaswami,

You have probably seen the interview by Sheikh Sahib to Michael Davidson which was published in *The Scotsman* of 14 April 1949. A vehement exponent of accession to India seems to have been converted to an 'independent Kashmir'. He wants absentee landlords, most of whom have gone to Pakistan, to be expropriated. At the same time, he has got, according to the information brought here by Sethi of the Agriculture Ministry, large tracts of valuable irrigated lands vacant lest non-Muslims should settle down on them, and this is at a time when elsewhere we are asking for every inch of land to be cultivated. [See enclosure]

Yours sincerely,
Vallabhbhai Patel

The Hon'ble Mr N Gopalaswami Ayyangar
New Delhi

ENCLOSURE

Extract from a report of an Interview with Sheikh Abdullah by Michael Devidson published in *The Scotsman*

'Accession to either side cannot bring peace', he [Sheikh Abdullah] declared. 'We want to live in friendship with both Dominions. Perhaps a middle path between them, with economic co-operation with each, will be the only way of doing it. But an independent Kashmir must be guaranteed not only by India and Pakistan but also by Britain, the United States and other members of the United Nations.....'

'Yes, independence—guaranteed by the United Nations—may be the only solution. But why do you talk of partition?...'

During the communal riots in the Punjab after partition, we tried in our humble way to stem the wave of fanaticism. That is why I urged we should wait before deciding our affiliation. I pleaded with both Dominions to help us first to win internal emancipation before asking us to choose! India replied by refusing to make a standstill agreement with the Maharaja; Pakistan did so. When, during the crisis India accepted the Maharaja's accession, Pandit Nehru insisted that it was only provisional and that the people must decide later....'

Source—Sardar Patel, Correspondence, vol-I, p-266-267

Letter from N Gopalaswami, condemning Sheikh's interview to Michael Davidson
215

New Delhi
1 May 1949

My dear Sardarji,

I have just received your letter about the interview given by Sheikh Abdullah to Michael Davidson of *The Scotsman*. My attention was drawn to the contents of this interview earlier in the day. It is a most astonishing performance. Kachru, who is going to Kashmir tomorrow, has just been to see me, and I am sending a message through him to Sheikh Abdullah. I have asked him to tell the latter that I condemn the Sheikh's action and that I feel that what he has told Michael Davidson and what the latter has published will have the most serious and mischievous consequences both in India and abroad. I have asked him to inform the Sheikh that, reading between the lines, I suspect a plan, the first step of which is this blessing by the Premier of Kashmir of the idea of an independent Kashmir and this public expression of his conviction that accession to India will not bring peace, and the final step of which may well be perhaps one of the greatest betrayals in history. He will also be told that India will expect him publicly to repudiate some of the things attributed to him by Michael Davidson.

It is all so distressing.

Yours sincerely,
N gopalaswami

The Hon'ble Sardar Vallabhbhai Patel
New Delhi

Source—Sardar Patel's Correspondence, vol-I, p-267

Letter from Vallabhbhai to Jawaharlal regarding former's talk to Maharaja, J&K, suggesting he be absent from the State

216

New Delhi
11 May 1949

My dear Jawaharlal,

You will recall that, just before you left for the UK, you wrote to me regarding His Highness the Maharaja of Kashmir. I sent for His Highness who has been here since 28 April. I had a talk with him on 29 April and 1 May, when I explained to him the whole position and commended to him my view that, in the circumstances of his relations with the Ministry and the situation created by the reference to UNO and the plebiscite issue, it would be best for him to absent himself from the State for some time and to make the Yuvraj Regent. Both of them [Her Highness was also present] were visibly taken aback by this proposal, and I could notice that there was a sense of shock and bewilderment at the end of my discussion with them on 29 April. However, I asked him to reflect over the matter. I asked Shankar also to have a talk with him, and he had two or three long discussions both with His Highness the Maharaja and Her Highness separately. They now seem to be reconciled to the proposal, and I send herewith a, copy of the letter which I have received from His Highness and which would require our very careful and urgent consideration. I suggest that we meet some time tomorrow to discuss our final attitude in this matter. I am, therefore, sending copies of His Highness' letter and of my letter to you and to Gopalaswami.

Yours sincerely,
Vallabhbhai Patel

The Hon'ble Pandit Jawaharlal Nehru
New Delhi

ENCLOSURE

Imperial Hotel
New Delhi
6 May 1949

My dear Sardar Patelji,

With reference to the discussions I had with you on 29 April and 1 May 1949, I have been revolving the matter in my mind and am now in a position to let you have my settled reactions to the proposal in regard to my temporary absence from the State which you put to me.

I should like to say at the outset that I was completely taken aback by this proposal, but coming as it did from you, in whom I have since the very beginning placed implicit trust and confidence and whose advice I have throughout followed on the many questions affecting me personally and my State both in the present and in future, I have been able somehow to adjust myself to it. I would not, however, be human if I did not express my sense of keen disappointment and bewilderment at having been called upon to make such a sacrifice of personal prestige, honour and position when all along I have been content to follow, sometimes even against my own judgment and conscience, the advice in regard to the constitutional position in the State which I have been receiving from the Prime Minister of India or yourself, sometimes even against arrangements which were agreed to only a few months before. Nor would it be fair on my part to conceal from you my own feeling that while Sheikh Abdullah has been allowed to depart, from time to time as suited his inclinations, from the pledged and written word, to act consistently in breach of the loyalty which he professed to me prior to his release from jail and the oath of allegiance which he took when he assumed office, and to indulge openly along with his colleagues in a campaign of vilification and foul calumny against me, both inside the State and outside, I should have had to be driven from position to position—each of which I thought I held on the advice of the States Ministry.

The contrast naturally fills me with poignant feelings. However, once again putting my complete trust in your judgement and benevolent intentions towards us, I might be prepared to fall in with your wishes and to absent myself from the State for a period of three or four months in consideration of the fact as emphasised by you, namely, complications created by the reference to UNO and the plebiscite issue.

There are, however, certain questions arising out of this proposal on which I would venture to make my position clear to you and on which I would be grateful to have your assurance. I hope you will kindly appreciate the necessity of my seeking these assurances. I have to think of the immediate future in the light of my bitter experiences of the last several months and I owe it to myself, my family and dynasty to procure a clear declaration in respect of these matters:

1. I should like to be assured that this step is not a prelude to any idea of abdication. I should like to make it clear now that I cannot entertain the latter idea even for a moment and am fully prepared to take the consequences. I regard such a demand from my Prime Minister and his colleagues as a clear breach of the many understandings on which constitutional arrangements have been based from time to time and a positive act of his disloyalty treachery and deception.
2. Sheikh Abdullah should be clearly told to stop the campaign of vilification against me and to abandon all activities, both on his part and that of his followers, aimed at securing my abdication. I feel that the sacrifice which I am being called upon to make would be in vain if I continued to be the target of their public and private attacks.
3. There should be a clear assurance of protection of myself and my adherents against any victimisation. In this connection I should like especially to draw your attention to the facts that have been reported to me about persons having been detained in jail for their failure to sign for my abdication.

4. The question that I should remain out of the State for three or four months for reasons of health, will, I am afraid, not be believed by anybody and is likely to give rise to many misgivings and speculations within and outside the State as
   (i) everybody knows that I am not in such a state of health as would necessitate a long rest outside the State. I have, on your advice, been recently touring parts of Jammu province in the heat of April;
   (ii) for everybody in bad health Kashmir is considered to be the best health resort and it will certainly look strange if I went outside the State giving out that I am doing so for reasons of health;
   (iii) wherever I take [up] my temporary residence, I cannot confine myself to the four walls of the house. I am bound to meet people, who, when they meet me, will never believe that I am staying there for reasons of health;
   (iv) some other reason which may be plausible and may also at the same time not compromise my dignity and position should be given out. The best thing would be that the Government of India should find a suitable position for me in Delhi where my services may be utilised in a fitting manner during the above period of 3 to 4 months.
5. It is a matter of paramount necessity that Her Highness should remain with the Yuvraj in the State during the period of my absence. He is young and impressionable and requires paternal guidance and personal supervision of at least one of his parents. I can see no reason either of political expediency or justice in insisting on the separation of a mother from her only child, whom she is seeing after thirteen months of absence abroad. Considerations of humanity alone should suffice to rule out this altogether.
6. My private estates, houses and other property should be protected against the aggressive acts of Sheikh Abdullah's

party. They will attempt to take possession of my houses, gardens, lands and other property. The Indian Dominion should guarantee against that act of aggression. While I am there they dare not do these things, but in my absence they will attempt this. I have received information that even during the last few days, after I left Jammu for Delhi, encroachments have been made on my lands at Srinagar.

7. No change should be made without my consent in the present arrangements regarding the State forces or the constitutional position, prerogatives, etc. of the Ruler as now subsisting. Arrangements will continue for me to draw my staff (both State and Private Deptts.) from amongst officers of my forces, guards mounted by my forces at my palaces will also continue as at present as per agreement reached, *vide* my letter of 30 August and Mr [VP] Menon's reply of 3 September, thereto. I shall also take whatever staff etc. I require with me outside.

8. I should be entitled during my stay in India to suitable strength of military guards wherever I stay.

9. Yuvraj's safety and protection should be the concern of the Indian Dominion. State and Indian military should guard his person.

10. Outstanding matters with the State Ministry, Civil Lists, Hazur Departments* etc. should be decided with me immediately.

In conclusion I wish to say that I shall take the final decision on getting assurances from you on the points above mentioned.

With kindest regards,

Yours very sincerely,
Hari Singh

* Departments under personal control of Maharaja.

Source—Sardar Patel's Correspondence, vol-I, p-268-271

Letter from Jawaharlal to Vallabhbhai regarding proposed visit of US Ambassador to meet him

235

New Delhi
30 August 1949

My dear Vallabhbhai,

I am sorry, I have not written to you for some days. I went to Kanpur and then I had to go to Allahabad for a brief visit owing to Indira's* illness.

There are a host of matters of importance on which I should like to have a talk with you. But it becomes difficult to write lengthy letters on each subject. HVR Iyengar came to me today and gave me your message about my visiting Bombay. I shall certainly try to do so. I am going to Allahabad on Saturday and Sunday next, 3 and 4 September. I shall try to come to Bombay early on the morning of the 5th from Allahabad, returning the next day. I do not want any engagement in Bombay except to meet you.

The UN Kashmir Commission people came to see Bajpai today and put forward their proposal for arbitration regarding the truce, [Admiral] Nimitz as arbitrator. The US Ambassador is coming to see me tomorrow with a special message from President Truman about this matter. The UK High Commissioner is also seeing me tomorrow, probably with the same object in view. All this barrage is, I suppose, meant to sweep us away. But I am quite clear in my mind that we should not accept this proposal. I am sure you must be of the same opinion. I shall meet the Commission myself day after tomorrow.

* Indira Gandhi, daughter of Nehru.

Source—Sardar Patel's Correspondence, vol-I, p-294

Sardar Patel in his teens.

In the late 1920s, Patel with his brother, Vithalbhai Patel.

Sardar Patel during the Nagpur Flag Satyagraha, 1923.

Sardar's Mother with her five sons in 1927 (Sardar-extreme right).

Maulana Azad, Sardar Patel, Abdul Ghaffar Khan and Kanayalal Munshi during a visit to Bardoli in 1928. The women here first addressed him as 'Sardar'.

Sardar, Bapu and Maniben during the Shimla Conference, 1945.

Maniben Patel with her father Vallabhbhai in 1946.

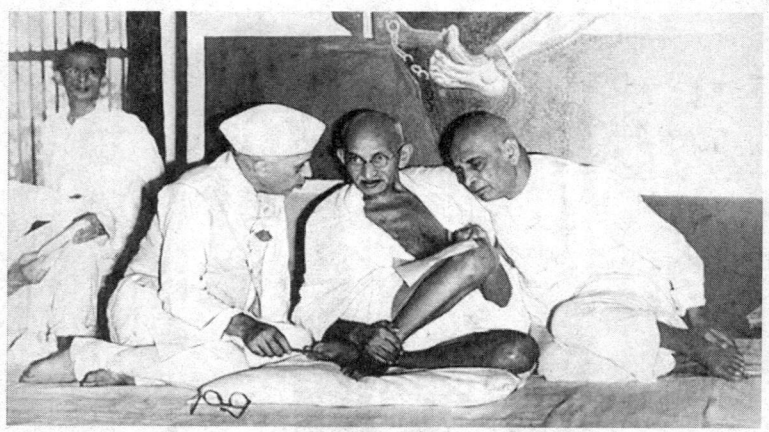

The Troika: Nehru-Gandhi-Patel, who led the last phase of India's freedom struggle from 1921 to 1947.

Gandhi's 'muscle man': Congress success lay in Patel lending his 'muscle' power as a great organiser to Gandhi's 'soul' force. The *Manchester Guardian* wrote: Without Patel, Gandhi's ideas would have had less practical influence, and Nehru's idealism less scope.

At a conference on the partition of India in June 1947, are (from left) President of the Indian National Congress Acharya JB Kripalani, Sardar Vallabhbhai Patel, Advisor to the Viceroy Sir Eric Melville, Pandit Jawaharlal Nehru and Lord Mountbatten.

A photograph taken during the Independence Day Session of the Constituent Assembly held on 15 August 1947. Standing in the first row can be seen Sardar Vallabhbhai Patel, KM Munshi, NV Gadgil and Amu Swaminathan.

Photograph taken on the occasion of Vallabhbhai Patel's visit to the Broadcasting House, New Delhi on 14 October 1947.

Sardar Patel was India's first Information and Broadcasting Minister.

C Rajagopalachari with Sardar Patel and Maniben Patel on arrival at aerodrome, New Delhi on 9 November 1947. Rajagopalachari was to act as Governor-General during the leave period of Lord Mountbatten.

Sardar Patel visited Calcutta in 8 January 1948. Photo shows Patel speaking at the Calcutta Club Lunch.

Photo taken on the occasion of Sardar Patel's visit to Calcutta in January 1948.

Sardar Vallabhbhai Patel's tour of Bombay and Ahmedabad (January 1948). Patel addressing a rally organised by the All-Mahajan Associations and Societies of Ahmedabad on 22 January 1948.

Nehru with Sardar Patel during Sardar's convalescence at Dehradun (1948).

Photo taken on the occasion of the Conference of Industrialists held under the agies of Sardar Patel in Mussoorie in May 1948, in connection with the Gandhi Memorial Fund.

Chandulal Trivedi, Governor of East Punjab and Chancellor of the East Punjab University presenting the degree of Doctor of Laws (Honoris Cause) to Sardar Patel at the first convocation of the University held at Ambala on 5 March 1949.

Lord Mountbatten greeting Sardar Vallabhbhai Patel at the Government House, New Delhi at reception held by Mountbatten in honour of the members of the Constituent Assembly, May 1949. At right is Lady Mountbatten.

Sardar Vallabhbhai Patel watching the Police tattoo at Phillaur Fort which he visited in March 1949. On his right appear Chandulal Trivedi, Governor of East Punjab, Maniben Patel is on the extreme right.

Sardar Patel, Deputy Prime Minister of India and the Minister-in-charge of States, administers an oath of office of the Rajpramukh to the Maharaja of Jaipur, at the inauguration ceremony of the Greater Rajasthan Union held at Jaipur on 31 March 1949. The new Union is the Biggest union of Indian States comprising 15 ancient Rajput States with an area of 120,000 square miles, population of 13,000,000 and an approximate annual revenue of Rs 10 crore.

XIV Indian Athletic Championships, August 1949 in Delhi. A view of the distinguished visitors' gallery in the Irwin Stadium. Sardar Patel, the Deputy Prime Minister, Shankar Lal, President of the organising committee and the Maharaja of Patiala are seen in the picture.

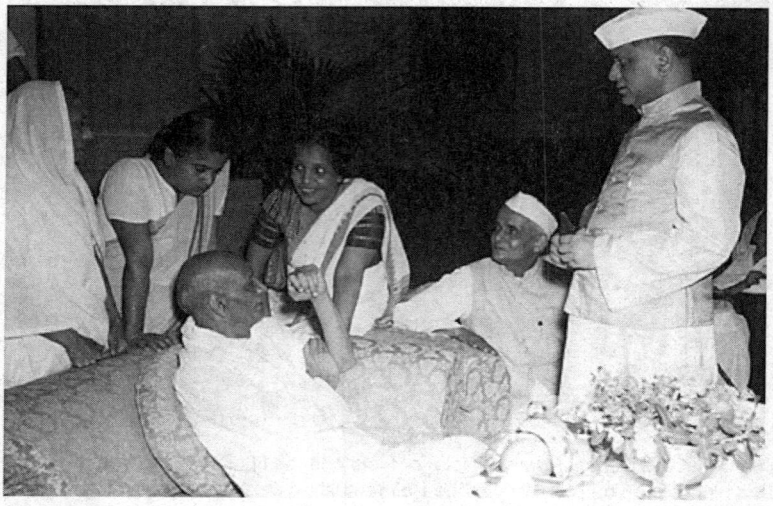

Sardar Patel, RR Diwakar and Satyanarian Sinha photographed at the party held by Patel for the Members of the Constituent Assembly (MCAs) at New Delhi on 17 October 1949. Standing at extreme left is Maniben Patel.

Satyanarian Sinha, Rajendra Prasad, Sardar Patel and Acharya Kripalani photographed at the party which the Deputy Prime Minister held at New Delhi on 17 October 1949, to meet the MCAs. Maniben Patel stands behind.

Sardar Patel glances through a collection of telegrams that felicitate him on his 74th birthday on 31 October 1949.

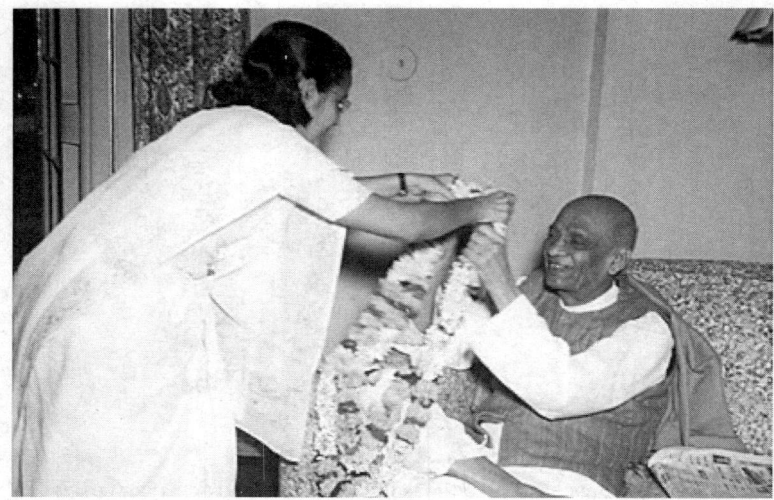

Sardar Vallabhbhai Patel receives felicitations on 31 October 1949, his 74th birthday.

Air Chief Marshal Sir John Slessor, Chief of Air Staff-designate, RAF who was in Delhi on a three-day visit, called on Sardar Patel, Acting Prime Minister of India on 5 November 1949. He was accompanied by Air Marshal Sir Thomas Elmhirst, C-in-C, RIAF.

Sardar Patel in 1950, on the day the first President of Free India, Rajendra Prasad, took the oath at the Darbar Hall of the Government House.

The Cabinet of India on 31 January 1950, along with the newly appointed President Rajendra Prasad. (L to R sitting) BR Ambedkar, Rafi Ahmed Kidwai, Sardar Baldev Singh, Maulana Abul Kalam Azad, Jawaharlal Nehru, Rajendra Prasad, Sardar Patel, John Mathai, Jagjivan Ram, Rajkumari Amrit Kaur and SP Mukherjee. (L to R standing) Khurshed Lal, RR Diwakar, Mohanlal Saksena, N Gopalaswami Ayyangar, NV Gadgil, KC Neogy, Jairamdas Daulatram, K Santhanam, Satya Narayan Sinha and BV Keskar.

JB Kripalani, Sardar Vallabhbhai Patel and Maniben Patel.

Rajendra Prasad, Sardar Patel, Maulana Azad and Khan Abdul Ghaffar Khan eating together.

Sardar Vallabhbhai Patel with TK Narayana Pillai, premier of the United State of Travancore-Cochin, V Shankar and others when he visited the Kanyakumari temple at Cape Comorin in May 1950.

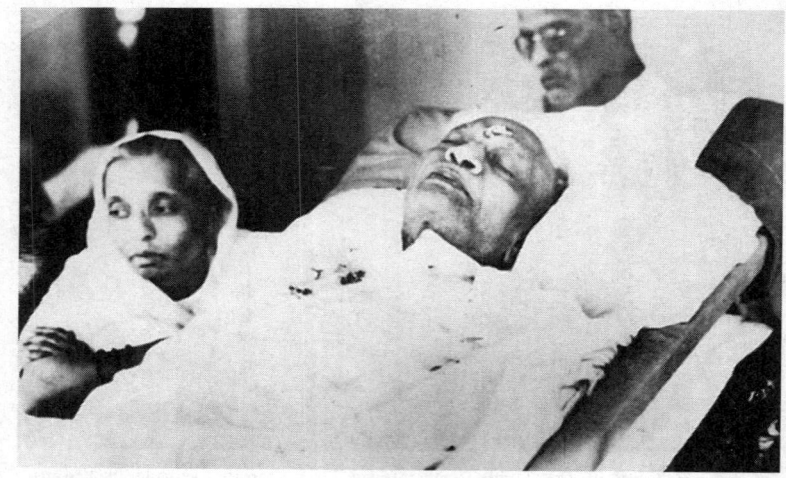

Sardar Patel took his last breath on 15 December 1950. Seated beside is Maniben, the Sardar's daughter.

Index I

The indexing in this book is based on alphabetical order of initials for persons and places, also includes words of political importance keeping in mind the context of the book. This is just to facilitate referencing for interested readers and scholars.—Ed.

A

Abdicate   94, 182, 185, 190, 225, 240, 287, 314

Accede, accession, accession to the Union   X, 1, 7, 8, 28, 29, 33-42, 47, 57, 62, 67, 70, 74, 75, 81, 83, 84, 89, 90, 99, 100, 102-106, 108-119, 130, 132, 135-139, 141-144, 164, 166, 167, 170, 171, 173, 174, 176-179, 183, 185-187, 190, 191, 195, 197, 198, 231, 240, 242, 243, 253, 255, 275, 276, 302, 309, 311

Accession Plan   74

Accession Satyagrah   139

Administration   viii, ix, xv, 2, 3, 22, 41, 48, 49, 52, 53, 55, 88, 89, 92, 118, 126, 152, 164, 184, 220-227, 233, 235, 237, 249, 256, 261, 263, 281, 284, 301

Advisors   8, 34, 39, 118, 123, 141, 144

Agent-General, Agents   6, 100, 130, 136, 140, 148, 226, 227

Agreement of Association   132

Airfields   141

All India Radio   198

All India States People's Conference   20, 165

Allies   12, 210

Ambassadors, American Ambassador   27, 200

Ammunition   127, 135, 145, 169, 209, 218, 254, 300

Anglo-American machinations   208

Annule   188

Anti-Indian   39, 63, 137

Appeasement   131, 174

Arabs   135

Armed forces   xv, 26, 41, 72, 90, 210, 261

Arms airdrops   145

Army Headquarters   41

Articles 35A, 314, 356, 357, 369, 370, 370 (I), 392   187, 190-195, 222

Artificial barriers   5

Arzi Hukumat   38, 39

Asafia flag   135

Assembly of Jammu & Kashmir   193, 195

Attachment Scheme   89

Autocracy   3, 47, 57, 241, 245

Automatic   7, 22, 94, 114, 197

Autonomy, Autonomous   7, 50, 110, 111, 190, 192, 204, 214

B

Balkanisation, Balkanised   x, 42, 73, 100, 156, 243

Banks   128

Bhavan's Journal   203, 204, 207, 211

Black market operations   89

Boycott   22, 188

Brahmins   145

British Assistant Political Agent   164

British Commonwealth of Nations, Commonwealth   11, 14, 32, 129, 130, 246

British crown   6, 14, 16, 98, 124, 221,

British government   5, 9-12, 18, 21, 25, 35, 48, 50, 73, 92, 98, 128, 129, 166, 168

British High Commissioner   200

British India   6, 7, 10, 11, 14-20, 24-26, 30, 33, 61, 98, 103, 127, 128, 175, 210, 221

British Parliament   73

British power   5, 125

British Residents   6

British-Maratha war   125

Buildings   4, 138, 139, 258

C

Cabinet Mission Plan of 1946   7

Cash balances   4, 117

Ceasefire   176, 197, 198, 199, 296, 307

Census, census of 1961   109, 192

Central Excise   192

Central government, Centre   vii, 2, 3, 25, 34, 49, 52, 64, 65, 71, 73, 74, 138, 223, 234, 241

Central Hall of Parliament   236

Central India   60, 66, 81, 90

Central Reserve Police   20, 116

Chamber of Princes   13, 16, 17, 21, 22, 23, 27, 35, 50, 83, 99, 102, 103

Chancellor   13, 23, 25, 26, 83, 99, 102,

Charter Accounts Law   192

Chief Commissioner's Province   3

Chief ministers   xv, 146, 153, 157, 159, 225

Chief of Combined Operations   172

Chiefs of Staff Committee   199, 299

Chinese forces   208, 214

Circars   124, 135

Citizens   111, 152, 194, 196, 281

Civil and Military Gazette   105

Civil Aviation   192

Civil liberties   9

Civil Service   xv, 128, 221, 222, 223, 224, 226, 227, 229

Clause 7 of the Indian Independence Bill   129

Co-architects   3

Coercion   3

Coinage Act   192

Commission   viii, 3, 104, 117, 137, 183, 191, 192, 200, 232, 291, 292, 307, 317

Commissioner for the States of Western India and Gujarat   117

Communal riots   134, 165, 310

Communications   33, 35, 50, 89,

127, 134, 174, 190, 216, 218

Communist imperialism   209, 215

Communists, Communist Party of India   49, 75, 139, 209, 215, 217

Compensation   4, 5

Complacent   150, 217, 259

Comptroller and Auditor General   191, 192,

Compulsion of circumstances   3

Compulsory levy   139

Confederation of States   14

Congress, Congressman   xiv, xv, xvi, 9-12, 15, 19-22, 24, 27, 30, 37, 51, 63, 69, 74-76, 102, 138, 139, 152, 159, 165, 176, 189, 198, 224, 227-231, 233, 240, 249, 250, 262, 271, 275, 276, 322, 323,

Congress Parliamentary Party   189

Congress Working Committee   12, 229, 230

Conservation of Foreign Exchange and Prevention of Smuggler Activities Law   192

Conservative, Conservative Party   12, 133, 226, 234

Constituents   6

Constitution, Constitution of India   3, 8, 11, 12, 13, 15, 21, 23, 25, 26, 28, 49, 56, 74, 101, 187, 188, 189, 190, 191, 192, 193, 194, 195, 196, 203, 230, 251, 284

Constitutional development   10

Constitutional doctrines   6

Constitutional head   184, 301

Constitutional history   7, 207, 302

Constitutional validity   188

Constitution-making body   11

Contempt of Courts Law   192

Conversion   137

Cooperation   14, 23, 24, 25, 30, 31, 34, 105, 110, 132, 136, 165, 168, 172, 245

Coordination   50

Copy Right Act   192

Cordon   24, 248

Corps   136, 138

Correspondence   39, 43, 44, 96, 121, 156-159, 180, 202-204, 212-214, 233, 237 248, 250, 252, 254, 257, 258, 260, 262-265, 269-271, 273, 277, 279, 283-290, 292, 295, 300, 305, 306, 308, 310, 311, 316, 317

Cripps Proposal of 1942   7

Crown Representative   7, 8, 15, 20, 35, 103, 128, 155

Currency   4, 128, 140

Customs, custom's buildings, customs law   70, 74, 117, 192 139, 192

D

Daily Telegraph   119

Deccan States formula   51

Defence   12, 14, 29, 33, 35, 50, 127, 149, 150, 169, 170, 171, 190, 191, 206, 209, 215, 217, 218, 222, 224, 286

Defence Committee   149, 150, 169, 170, 171

Delhi Agreement (1952)   191

Delimitation   192

Demi-official   206

Demobilised   225

Democracy   92, 220, 211, 241, 243, 246

Democrat   244

Dengerous Drugs Act   192

Dewan   3, 22, 33, 36, 38, 67, 70, 71, 72, 73, 89, 108, 110, 111, 113, 115, 118, 152, 172, 252, 270, 284

Dewanship 190
Dictatorial 179, 186, 284
Dispossessed 240
Division 6, 7, 44, 45, 67, 73, 156, 157, 164, 167, 246
Domestic issue 148
Dominion 11, 19, 26, 32, 35, 39, 71, 75, 81, 104, 105, 108, 111, 113, 129, 130, 132, 139, 142, 155, 164, 166, 174, 235, 236, 239, 244, 254, 264, 275, 284, 291, 302, 316

E

Eastern States Union 49, 50
East India Company 6, 88, 124, 125, 162
Economic 5, 6, 9, 19, 66, 95, 108, 109, 116, 127, 132, 147, 149, 195, 196, 230, 259, 310
Elected members 190
Election Commission 191, 192
Electoral college 11, 94
Emergency 10, 127, 170, 192, 233
Emissaries 8, 9, 37
Emperor of India 234
Empire 5, 6, 10, 42, 61, 62, 81, 87, 134, 162, 211, 224, 240
Ex-army 142
Exile 183, 188, 190
Expansion 210, 214, 215
Expiry of the Agreement 141
Export 71, 74, 89, 140
External Affairs 35, 114, 115, 146, 205, 213, 296
External Affairs Minister 115

F

Faithful Ally of the British Government 128

Famine 81
Federal 7, 8, 10, 16, 98, 179, 252
Feudal 6, 55, 66, 241, 275
Feudal autocracy 241
Fighting man 245
Firman 129, 135, 139
First Sikh war 162
Fissiparous tendencies 63, 224
Fixed rate of exchange 128
Foodgrains 117, 128
Forcibly occupied 205
Foreign affairs 14, 33, 190
Foreign policy 206
Foreign Secretary 243
Formula 50, 51, 134
Franchise 119, 220
Freedom 9, 24, 28, 29, 30, 43, 47, 58, 62, 73, 85, 98, 106, 121, 146, 159, 172, 188, 211, 222, 229, 230, 241, 292, 322
Free port 81
Frontiers 115, 127, 206, 209, 214, 217, 218
Frontier tribesmen 42, 168
Ist battalion of the Sikh Regiment 172

G

Gaddi 51, 106, 164
Gandhian principles 210
General election 12, 115
Gilgit Scouts 164, 168, 169
Government of India Act 1935 7
Government of Junagadh 110, 111
Governor, Governor-General 7, 11, 39, 40, 41, 52, 105, 109, 112, 113, 125, 128, 132, 142, 144, 146, 150, 152, 162, 163, 168, 169, 170, 175,

190, 191, 199, 252, 253, 255, 261, 263, 280, 296, 325, 328, 329

Governor-General of Pakistan 105

Governor-General's Executive Council 11

Great Revolt 126

Guru 83

H

Harijans 137, 141

Heir 6, 52

Hindu 45, 64, 71, 83, 102, 109, 111, 114, 115, 119, 128, 129, 134, 135, 138, 153, 161, 165, 168, 176, 182, 190, 196, 246, 254, 271, 275, 282, 302, 304

Hindu fanaticism of East Punjab 182, 304

Hindustan Times 121, 231, 236

His Majesty 7, 10, 11, 13-15, 17, 18, 21, 22, 26, 29, 102, 129, 135, 139, 224, 234, 249, 257

His Majesty's Government, HMG 10, 11, 13, 14, 16, 18, 21, 26, 102, 129, 224, 234, 298

Historical 161, 215

Home 10, 15, 17, 27, 71, 81, 125, 150, 151, 199, 201, 226, 227, 229, 230, 232, 233

Home Minister 150, 227, 230, 233

Home Rule Movement 71

Home Secretary 81, 151, 227, 229, 230, 232

Home Secretary, Government of India 151

House 11, 18, 43, 44, 52, 57, 58, 65, 83, 84, 96, 121, 129, 152, 158, 159, 168, 188, 201, 202, 203, 204, 222, 225, 235, 237, 248, 250, 253, 254, 260, 270, 273, 280, 298, 315, 324, 328, 333

House of Commons 11, 18

Houses of the Central Legislative 10

Hyderabad Independence Act 135

I

IAS, Indian Administrative Service 192, 222, 224, 225, 226, 236

ICS, Indian Civil Service 85, 119, 156, 221-227, 231, 235, 236, 237, 238, 246

Ideological 6, 215

Immunities 224, 241

Imperial 6, 14, 16, 66, 83, 122, 298, 313

Imperialist 211, 215, 234

Imperial Strategy 14, 16

Independent treaty 214

Indian army, Indian forces, Indian troops 3, 41, 65, 113, 115, 119, 127, 137, 141, 147, 150, 151, 152, 170, 171, 173, 198, 209

Indian Constitution 191, 194, 203

Indian Dominion 19, 81, 104, 108, 139, 142, 254, 284, 316

Indian federation 7

Indian government 9, 148, 183, 196, 206, 207

Indian independence 5

Indian National Congress 165, 323

Indian peninsula 69, 127

Indian Police Service, Police 20, 49, 116, 136, 137, 146, 150, 152, 156, 216, 222-225, 237, 243, 256, 280, 282, 329

Indian representatives 11

Indian States Forces Scheme of 1939 127

Indo-Pakistan Question 175

Infiltration 216, 217

Instrument of Accession   7, 8, 28, 35, 36, 37, 67, 75, 84, 103, 104, 110, 116, 130, 132, 142, 171, 178, 179, 197, 231, 242

Integration   1, 3, 4, 5, 19, 39, 43, 44, 45, 47, 57, 58, 61, 64, 67, 76, 77, 85, 96, 106, 120, 121, 155, 156, 157, 158, 201, 202, 224, 232, 237, 239, 242

Integration of 554 Princely States   3, 5, 155

Intelligence bureau   183

Interests   2, 4, 6, 17, 18, 25, 26, 29, 30, 31, 33, 36, 42, 66, 75, 76, 94, 101, 103, 105, 134, 176, 206, 209, 240, 242, 259, 284

Interim Government   15

Internal security   127, 149, 150, 172, 210, 217, 218

International law   118, 148

Invaders   30, 60, 114, 174, 199

Invasion of Kashmir   42, 168, 197, 199

Investments   4

Islamic State   128, 156

Islands   39

Ittehad-ul-Mussalmeen   129, 130, 135, 141

J

Jagirdars   83, 301

Jammu and Kashmir Question   175

Jurisdiction of Parliament   191

Jurisdiction of the Supreme Court   91

K

Kathiawar Rajakeeya Parishad   91

Killed in action   173

Korean War   218

L

Labour, Labour government, Labour Party   12, 133, 192

Lapse   14, 26, 28, 71, 72, 98, 99

Law and order   2, 54, 89, 91, 145, 149, 151, 170, 171, 172, 177, 226, 234, 276

Leadership   27, 32, 57, 81, 138, 230, 232, 263

League of Nations   240

Legal advisor   190

Legislations   193

Liberty of thought   195

Lok Sabha   192, 222

M

Machinations   18, 35, 177, 208

Madhya Bharat Union   3

Mahavir Chakra   173

Mahura Power House   168

Manoeuvres   35, 62

Map of India   3, 57, 96

Maritime tradition   71

Mauryan bureaucracy   220

Membership of the United Nations Organisation   208

Memorandum   16, 26, 98, 111, 127

Merger   2, 3, 47, 49, 50, 52, 53, 55, 56, 57, 80, 93, 95, 132, 241

Metcalfe House   225

Middle path   186, 310

Military Governor   41, 152, 261, 263

Ministry of External Affairs   114

Ministry of States   4, 130

Minority   25, 39, 48, 123, 131, 144, 155, 165

Missionaries   209, 216

Motherland   30, 34, 62, 221, 224, 241
Mughal Empire   61
Museums   4
Muslim Conference   165, 176
Muslim League   11, 12, 15, 21, 24, 80, 111, 135, 167, 175, 248, 253, 276
Mysore model   179, 180, 284, 285

N

National Coalition Government   10
National Conference   165, 166, 168, 171, 173, 174, 176, 177, 191, 192, 196, 275, 276, 277
National Flag   138
Nationalism   6, 73
Nationalist   5, 62, 66, 176, 198, 240
Nationalist storm   5
National Revolt   5
Negotiating Committees   18, 22, 23
Nizam's Executive Council   131, 144, 156, 253, 255
Non-salute States   61, 88
Non-violent   40, 56, 244
Northern Circars   124

O

Occupation   111, 118, 152, 162, 174, 208, 211
Officer on Special Duty   163, 164
One India   47, 100
Open-door policy   147
Operation Polo   41, 151, 153
Oysters   103

P

Pakistani-dominated Secretariat   101
Pakistan Radio   137

Pakistan territory   112, 118
Palaces   4, 51, 316
Paramountcy   6, 12, 14, 15, 16, 18, 19, 20, 23, 24, 26, 27, 28, 30, 32, 65, 70, 71-73, 89, 98, 99, 102, 119, 125, 202, 240
Paramount Government   126
Part III of Constitution of India   194
Part XXI of the Constitution of India   194
Partition   5, 16, 18, 84, 108, 112, 154, 167, 195, 201, 221, 224, 226, 237, 241, 308, 310, 323
Patriots   76
Pension   242
PEPSU   3, 40, 66, 96, 232
Plan of 3rd June 1947   26
Plebiscite   113, 115, 116, 118, 119, 170, 171, 174, 175, 176, 179, 183, 187, 189, 197, 198, 200, 295, 307, 312, 314
Police Action   146, 150, 152, 156, 243
Policy of abstention   9
Political   5, 6, 7, 9, 10, 11, 13, 16, 26, 39, 51, 61, 63, 66, 71, 73, 89, 91, 95, 99, 100, 116, 123, 127, 132, 133, 142, 152, 155, 163, 164, 165, 176, 191, 195, 210, 216, 217, 218, 226, 228, 236, 244, 245, 275, 278, 315
Political Officers   20
Political Service   8, 164
Popular ministries   2
Population   5, 6, 48, 53, 62, 88, 89, 99, 102, 109, 114, 128, 130, 165, 166, 167, 170, 179, 183, 196, 198, 209, 215, 216, 220, 243, 329
Postal, telegraphic   127, 192
Post-mutiny   239
Prajamandal   49, 54, 92

President 15, 21, 99, 120, 132, 138, 175, 188, 191, 192, 194, 203, 242, 251, 254, 317, 323, 330, 333

Presidential Order 194

President's Rule 192

Princes 1, 2, 3, 4, 6, 7, 9, 10, 12, 13, 14, 15, 16, 17, 19, 20, 21, 22, 23, 24, 25, 26, 27, 28, 29, 30, 31, 32, 33, 34, 35, 36, 37, 38, 50, 53, 54, 55, 57, 60, 62, 63, 64, 65, 66, 71, 76, 83, 89, 90, 93, 98, 99, 100, 101, 102, 103, 112, 119, 120, 127, 156, 165, 232, 240, 241, 242, 243, 244, 245, 248, 272

Privy purses 2, 4, 50, 51, 53

Pro-Chancellor 103

Pro-consuls 241

Propaganda 64, 136, 174, 182, 294, 304, 305, 306

Provinces 2, 3, 6, 7, 9, 11, 13, 41, 46, 50, 57, 95, 128, 129, 139, 223, 226, 230

Provincial governments 2, 48, 225

Provincial legislatures 9, 11

Public Relations Officer 141

Puranas 60, 67, 242

Q

Quisling 81

Quit India Movement 233

R

Racial 12, 209, 215

Railways 5, 109, 117, 127

Rajasthan Union 3, 61, 62, 64, 329

Rajatrangini 161

Rajpramukh 94, 329

Razakar 136, 135, 137, 151

Rebellion 5, 153

Recommendations 14, 25

Referendum 115, 119, 304

Reforms 9, 10, 126, 184, 301, 303

Reforms Commissioner 232

Refugees 91, 280, 281

Regional loyalties 5

Religious minorities 12

Reserve Bank 128

Resident 63, 88, 90, 124, 126, 127, 155, 164, 251, 256

Resignation 99, 102, 103, 139, 144, 181, 241, 288

Responsible government 1, 9, 39, 52, 91, 92, 95, 136, 138, 144, 165, 249, 250

Revolution 239, 242

RIAF planes 171

Rights of the rulers 3

Round Table Conference 99

Royal Empire Society 240

Royal titles 234

Rule of Law 225

Ruler 2, 4, 7, 18, 49, 52, 53, 54, 56, 57, 70, 81, 83, 90, 91, 94, 99, 106, 112, 115, 118, 131, 162, 163, 164, 165

S

Sadar-e-Riyasat 190

Safeguard 2, 4, 8, 25, 66, 111, 112, 208

Salute States 61, 88, 92

Seaboard 71, 114, 217

Secede 11, 189

Second World War 10, 26

Secretary 10, 11, 12, 15, 17, 49, 71, 81, 100, 146, 150, 151, 169, 222, 224, 225, 226, 227, 229, 230, 231, 232, 243, 274, 296

Secretary of State 225

Secretary of the External Affairs of Hyderabad 146
Secretary of the Political Department 15, 17
Secularist 198
Security Council 148, 153, 175, 176, 200, 201, 270, 291, 307
Senapatis 87
Separatism 223
Settlement 146
Smuggling 89
Social 6, 9, 128, 195
Social Insurance 192
Social Security 192
Southern Command 41
Sovereign 15, 16, 28, 33, 72, 129, 135, 138, 139, 251
Sovereignty 6, 8, 19, 48, 74, 95, 180, 207, 249, 252, 275, 286
Speaker 222
Standing Committee of the Chamber of Princes 21
Standstill Agreement 35, 36, 40, 65, 75, 100, 103, 140, 141, 144, 147, 167, 179, 231
States 1-58, 61-85, 88, 89, 90-120, 121, 127, 129, 130, 140, 142, 146, 155-158, 161, 164, 165, 169, 175, 176, 180, 181, 185, 186, 191, 193, 197, 200, 201, 202, 221, 224, 226, 231, 235, 237, 239, 240, 241-244, 249, 250, 251, 253, 256, 257, 264, 271, 272, 274, 280, 283, 286, 287, 303, 310, 313, 329
States Department 29, 32, 34, 38, 44, 253, 256, 257
States Ministry 32, 55, 118, 140, 161, 169, 180, 181, 185, 286, 287, 303, 313

States' Negotiating Committee 17, 71, 101
States' Treaties and Paramountcy 98
Subedar 124
Subjects 9, 13, 14, 17, 33, 34, 35, 38, 50, 52, 64, 74, 75, 92, 110, 111, 112, 113, 129, 130, 191, 254, 301
Subservience 5, 6, 127
Subsidiary 79, 124, 125, 163, 260
Successor 6, 14, 16, 28, 70, 98, 103, 222, 240
Sunday Times 119
Superstructure of the modern system 5
Supreme Allied Commander 172
Suzerainty 48, 61, 214

T

Takeover 49, 54, 116, 261
Talukdars 88
Taxes 4, 51
Technical correctness 185
Telephonic 127
The Scotsman 186, 310, 311
Third Force 71, 100
Third Maratha War 61
Toddy trees 139
Trade Agent 33, 72, 140
Trade Unions 192
Transfer of power 2, 15, 18, 20, 22, 23, 24, 25, 26, 28, 36, 37, 71, 88, 89, 91, 102, 119, 164, 166, 168, 177, 224, 225, 226, 240, 276
Transitional provision 194
Travancore State Congress 74, 75
Treaties 6, 12, 13, 18, 34, 70, 127
Treaty of 1766 124
Treaty of 1853 125

Treaty of Association   132
Treaty of Deogaon   125
Treaty of Masulipatam   124
Tribals   196
Tungbhadra Project   5
Twentieth century   6

U

UNCIP   183

Unification   5, 18, 40, 47, 81, 89, 91, 92, 93, 156, 239, 242, 244

Union   2, 3, 4, 11, 12, 14, 20, 21, 28, 31, 33, 37, 40, 47, 49, 50, 51, 61, 62, 64, 66, 70, 72, 74, 80, 90, 91, 94, 95, 96, 98, 100, 102, 130, 132, 135, 136, 137, 138, 139, 141, 142, 143, 146, 167, 168, 177, 178, 179, 181, 190, 191, 192, 195, 196, 207, 210, 222, 225, 240, 241, 243, 251, 253, 254, 255, 272, 275, 329

Union and Concurrent Lists   190, 191

Union Consultative Committee   74

Union of the States   2

Union Parliament   190, 191

United State of Saurashtra   95

United States of Kathiawad   2

UNO, United Nations Organisation   104, 113, 132, 141, 147, 148, 152, 187, 197, 198, 200, 209, 213, 214, 218, 256, 257, 258, 270, 296, 297, 298, 299, 300, 312, 314

Uranium   71

US Kashmir Commission   200

Usurper   105

V

Vacillating   101, 217

Valley   173, 183, 189, 190, 196, 293

Viceroy, Viceroyalty   8, 9, 13, 14, 15, 18, 21, 32, 43, 70, 71, 72, 77, 83, 84, 103, 127, 133, 210, 252, 272, 284, 323

Voluntary   7

W

War   10, 11, 12, 112, 113, 124, 125, 130, 137, 162, 163, 166, 172, 173, 199, 200, 224, 234, 293, 297, 298, 299, 300

War Advisory Council   11

War Cabinet   11

Walrus   103

Weapons of precision   127

Z

Zamindars   48

Index II

A

Abdul Kadir Mohammad 110
Abraham Lincoln 242
AD Gorwala 221
Ahmad Shah Abdali 162
Ajmer Merwara 61
Akbar 60, 61, 62, 88, 109, 162
Ali Yavar Jung 71, 76, 256
Ananthasayanam Ayyangar 222
Annie Besant 71
Anthony Eden 234, 235
Aravamudh Aiyangar 134, 156
Arthur Lothian 8, 126, 155, 156
Asaf Jah 124, 265
Ashoka 57
Attlee 12, 13, 18, 19, 22, 23, 42, 133
Aurangzeb 61, 118, 123

B

Bachan Lal Kalgotra 196
Bakshi Ghulam Mahomed 173
Baldev Singh 143, 333
Balwantrai Mehta 92, 94
Beharilal Gupta 223
Bismarck 47, 239, 242-246
BK Nehru 225, 237
BL Mitter 22, 89, 102, 251

BN Mullik 183, 190, 196, 203, 204
Brigadier Gurdial Singh 118

C

Campbell-Johnson 24, 114
Carpenter 103
CB Nagarkar 119
Chamberlin 135
Chanakya 242
Chandulal Trivedi 52, 328, 329
Charles Bussey 124
Chudasama dynasty 109
Col Cuthbert Davidson 126
Colonel Alexander Walker 88
Colonel Tod 61
Col Thakur Kesri Singh 82
CP Ramaswami Iyer 13, 22, 70, 71, 72, 73, 74
C Rajagopalachari 39, 142, 144, 206, 325
CS Venkatachar 81, 246

D

Dalai Lama 213
Dalip Singh 179, 280, 283
Dewan of Junagadh 3
Dhyan Singh 162
Dogra 162, 179
Douglas Brown 119

D Pattabhi Sitarammayya 51
Dr BC Roy 233
Dwarkanath Kachru 177, 274

F

Farrukhsiyar 124
Field-Marshal Auchinleck 169

G

Gaekwar 88
Gandhi 38, 55, 57, 58, 64, 65, 71, 73, 91, 92, 98, 100, 106, 116, 120, 134, 158, 175, 181, 182, 203, 244, 275, 288, 298, 299, 317, 322, 327
General JN Chaudhuri 41, 148, 152
General SSP Thorat 199
Ghaziuddin Khan Feroz Jang 123
Gondal 88, 89, 90, 109, 116, 251
Gopalaswami Ayyanger 143
Govind Ballabh Pant 233
Gulab Singh 162, 163
Gupta Empire 87

H

Harekrushna Mahtab 43, 50
Harvey Jones 117, 119
Himatsinhji 44, 91
Hitler 12, 19, 135, 249
Hodson 32, 43, 44, 77, 80, 85, 96, 105, 106, 120, 121, 158
Holkar 61
HV Kamath 201, 204
HVR Iyengar 81, 85, 151, 156, 158, 227, 237, 238
Hyder Ali 124

J

Jaichand 79
Jain 109
Jam Saheb of Nawanagar 38
Jawaharlal Nehru 15, 120, 157, 159, 165, 181, 183, 193, 202, 207, 211, 229, 271, 274, 279, 283, 288, 302, 307, 312, 323, 333
Jayaprakash Naryan 200
Jinnah 22, 24, 28, 29, 34, 36, 37, 42, 62, 73, 79, 80, 81, 82, 83, 84, 89, 90, 91, 100, 101, 102, 105, 112, 113, 114, 115, 116, 132, 147, 165, 166, 168, 173, 174, 175, 178, 198, 201, 275
Joseph-François Dupleix 124
Jossleyn Hennessy 119
Judith Brown 227
JV Joshi 144

K

Khiljis 88
Khrushchev 244
KM Munshi 17, 43, 44, 58, 71, 76, 85, 106, 121, 136, 140, 143, 146, 152, 156, 157, 158, 159, 181, 189, 203, 206, 207, 211, 323
KM Panikkar 24, 60, 67, 102, 106, 158, 206, 242, 246, 248
KPS Menon 223, 243, 246

L

Laik Ali 142, 143, 144, 147, 152, 256, 257
Leonard Mosley 225, 237
Liaquat Ali 21, 29, 106, 115, 118, 175, 307, 308
Lieutenant-General BM Kaul 199
Lord Curzon 69, 210, 211, 245
Lord Hamilton 245
Lord Hardinge 162
Lord Hastings 61

Lord Ismay   133, 166, 174, 175

Lord Mountbatten   21, 26, 35, 36, 37, 38, 39, 40, 41, 71, 74, 75, 83, 84, 102, 129, 131, 133, 134, 139, 141, 144, 146, 164, 166, 169, 170, 172, 173, 175, 199, 239, 240, 296, 297, 323, 325, 328

Lord Pethic-Lawrence   12

Lord Reading   127

Lord Wavell   12, 18

Lord Willington   8

LS Amery   10

Lt Colonel Dewan Ranjit Rai   172

Lt General Maharaj Shri Rajendrasingji   41, 152

M

Machiavelli   83

Maharajakumar of Jaisalmer   82

Maharaja Morvi   94

Maharaja of Patiala   23, 25, 101, 103, 232, 330

Maharaja Ranjit Singh   162

Maharaja Umed Singh   80

Maharana Pratapt   62

Mahatma   55, 93, 106, 116, 175, 181, 203

Mahavir Tyagi   188, 203

Mahmud Ghazni   88, 109

Major Brown   169

Major General HL Scott   168

Major-General Janak Singh   168

Maniben   245, 321, 325, 329, 330, 331, 334, 336

Maratha Bhonsles   48

Marathas   61, 88, 124, 125

Marquess of Linlithgow   8

Maulana Azad   165, 189, 229, 320, 334

Maurya   87

Mehrchand Mahajan   168, 170

Michael Davidson   186, 187, 309, 311

Mir Qamruddin Chin Qilich Khan   123

Mir Usman Ali Khan Bahadur   128

Mirza Ismail   13, 102, 139

MN Roy   200, 201, 204

Moghulas   135

Mohammad Zafrullah   38, 80, 103

Moin Nawaz Jung   148

Monckton   129, 131, 132, 133, 139, 141, 143, 144, 253, 254, 255, 256, 257, 258

Montague-Chelmsford   6

Morvi Dharangadhra   88, 90, 94, 251

Mountbatten   18, 20, 21, 25, 26, 32, 35-44, 65, 71-76, 83, 84, 102,-106, 112-118, 121, 129, 130,-135, 139, 140-150, 155, 164, 166, 169, 170, 172-175, 183, 197, 198, 199, 201, 232-234, 237, 239, 240, 244, 296, 297, 323, 325, 328

Mughals   48, 60, 62, 81, 88, 109, 124, 125, 126, 135, 162

Muhammad Shah   124

N

Nagas   209, 216

Napoleon   232

Nasir-Ud-Daula   125

Nawab Deen Yarjung   137

Nawab of Bhopal   26, 37, 80, 98-105

Nawab of Chhatari   139

NB Khare   64

Nehru 20, 21, 23, 114, 115, 131, 133, 147, 150, 181, 182, 185, 187, 188, 189, 190, 196, 198, 208, 283, 288, 322

Neville Chamberlain 10

N Gopalaswami Ayyangar 180, 285, 309

Nizam 4, 22, 33, 36, 39, 40, 41, 72, 73, 76, 100, 102, 113, 115, 123-157, 240, 253-258, 264, 265

Nizam Ali Khan 124, 125

Nizam Radio 137

NM Buch 117, 118

NV Gadgil 120, 147, 206, 207, 211, 323, 333, 259, 260, 323, 333

P

Parasuram 242

Pathans 49, 61, 134, 145, 162

Pindaris 61

Pir Maqbool Gilani 197

President VV Giri 242

President Zakir Hussain 242

Pyarelal 106, 181, 203

Q

Qasim Razvi 39, 135, 142, 145, 152

R

Raja Marthanda Varma 70

Rajdidi 82

Rajendra Prasad 15, 51, 120, 143, 188, 229, 331, 333, 334

Rajputs 60, 61, 62, 63, 64, 66, 79

Ramasamy Mudaliar 152, 270

Rana Partap 63

Ranjit Deo 162

Reginald Coupland 42, 45

RK Shanmukham Chetty 73

Rohillas 134

Romesh Chandra Dutt 223

S

Salbat Jah 124

Samaldas 38, 116, 117, 120

Sardar Vallabhbhai Patel 32, 44, 57, 58, 67, 85, 96, 106, 121, 157, 158, 159, 204, 237, 241, 243, 246, 252, 264, 266, 268, 274, 287, 292, 306, 311, 323, 326, 328, 329, 332, 334, 335

Satyendranath Tagore 223

Saurashtra 38, 39, 81, 95, 114

Scindia 61, 64

Shakespeare 224

Shankarrao Deo 51

Sheikh Abdullah 165, 168, 170, 171, 174, 176, 178-191, 196, 197, 198, 271, 285, 289, 301, 306, 310, 311, 313, 314, 315

Sheikh of Mangrol 116

Shephard 244

Sherkhan Babi 109

Shri Padamnabha 70

Shripad Babaji Thakur 223

Siahji 79

Sikandar Jah 125

Sikhs 162, 163, 168, 281, 282, 304

Sir Arthur Lothian 8, 126, 156

Sir Conrad Corfield 17, 19, 99, 100, 155

Sir Courtenay Latimer 8

Sir Francis Wylie 8

Sir Girija Shankar Bajpai 223, 236

Sir Hanwant Singhji 80

Sir Mirza Ismail 13

Sir Mohammad Zafrullah Khan   38, 103
Sir Shah Nawaz Bhutto   38, 110, 111, 116
Sir Stafford Cripps   7, 11, 12, 13, 242
Suchet Singh   162
Sultan Ahmad   133, 139
Sultan-e-Kashmir   190
Surendranath Banerjea   223, 236
Swami Ramanand Tirtha   138
Sydney Cotton   134
Syed Abdul Latif   22

T

Tipu Sultan   125
Tughlaks   88

U

UN Dheber   94

V

Vallabhi dynasty   87
VP Menon   1, 26, 28, 38, 43, 44, 45, 50, 57, 58, 74, 75, 76, 77, 79, 83, 84, 85, 96, 106, 120, 121, 131, 133, 156, 157, 158, 167, 169, 170, 201, 202, 231, 237, 256
VT Krishnamachari   102

W

Warren Hastings   125
Wellesley   125
Winston Churchill   10, 133, 134, 234

Y

Yasin   164
Yuvraj Karan Singh   182, 190
Yuvraj Regent   187, 312

Z

Zaheer's   146
Zulfikar Ali Bhutto   111

Index III

A

Abotabad 168

Afghanistan 162

Ahmedabad 43, 44, 57, 58, 67, 77, 88, 96, 106, 109, 120, 121, 151, 157, 158, 159, 202, 203, 212, 236, 237, 238, 246, 248, 250, 254, 273, 326

Alwar 61, 64, 65

America 148, 175, 176, 214, 219

Amritsar 163

Andhra State 229

Anhilwad 88

Assam 9, 209, 210, 215, 216, 218

Aurangabad 145

Azad Kashmir 176

B

Babariawad 116, 119

Balasore 49

Banswara 61, 64

Bantwa 119

Baramula 169, 173

Baroda 3, 4, 22, 27, 29, 81, 82, 88, 89, 99, 101, 102, 109, 251, 252

Bastar 17, 48, 49

Baudh 54

Bay of Bengal 135

Beas River 162

Bedi Bandar 81

Beijing 207

Berar 125, 126, 240, 256

Bharatpur 37, 61, 64, 65

Bhavnagar 87, 88, 90-94, 109, 251

Bhimber 162

Bhopal 4, 17, 20, 22-29, 33, 36, 37, 80, 81, 82, 83, 85, 90, 98, 99, 100-106

Bhutan 210, 216, 218

Bidar 150

Bikaner 4, 13, 24, 25, 27, 31, 62, 64, 67, 79, 82, 99, 101, 102, 248

Bilaspur 13, 37

Bombay 2, 3, 21, 22, 42, 43, 44, 76, 77, 79, 85, 89, 93, 95, 106, 116, 121, 127, 138, 150, 151, 157, 158, 159, 204, 211, 236, 237, 238, 266, 267, 317, 326

Bombay-Madras Express 138

Britain 11, 12, 18, 23, 32, 42, 43, 44, 77, 85, 96, 102, 106, 120, 121, 143, 158, 175, 176, 186, 210, 214, 219, 225, 234, 239, 252, 310

Bundelkhand States 67

Bundi 61, 64

Burma 208, 215, 219

C

Carnatic 124

Chamba 163

Chera Kings 70

Chhatari 13, 139, 256

Chhattisgarh 47, 48, 49, 52, 54, 55, 56, 93

Chibal 162

Chilas 164

China 176, 205-219

Cochin 3, 22, 27, 69, 73, 75, 76, 101, 126, 335

Cuttack 52, 54, 55, 56, 93

D

Darjeeling 210, 216, 218

Deccan 2, 51, 95, 124, 135, 136

Deccan States 51, 95

Dehradun 142, 143, 148, 234, 327

Dharangadhra 88, 90, 94

Dhenkanal 54

Dholpur 36, 37, 61, 64

Dhrol 88

Diu 117

Domel 199, 294

Dryden 223

Dungarpur 13, 61, 64

E

England 5, 12, 19, 102, 146, 175, 176, 240, 249, 299

F

Faridkot 66

Formosa 213

G

Germany 210, 242, 243

Gilgit 163, 164, 168-170, 174, 308

Gilgit Agency 168

Gilgit Wazarat 164

Gondal 88, 90

Greater Rajasthan 3, 60, 61, 62, 329

Gujarat 2, 88, 91, 95, 117

Gulmarg 197

Gwalior 4, 64

Gyangtse 218

H

Himachal Pradesh 3, 96

Himalayas 205-208, 211, 214, 215

Hindustan 14, 16, 29, 73, 103, 121, 132, 231, 236, 299

Hunza 164

Hyderabad 4, 9, 13, 17, 22, 29, 33, 36-42, 49, 71, 72, 73, 76, 80-82, 100, 102, 104, 113, 114, 115, 119, 122-156, 159, 188, 199, 201, 240, 243, 253, 254, 255, 256, 257, 259, 261, 263, 264, 265, 270, 292, 298, 307, 308

I

Indore 4, 29, 36, 37, 64, 81, 82

Indus 162, 163

Ishkoman 164

J

Jafrabad 88

Jaipur 4, 9, 13, 27, 62-64, 101, 329

Jaisalmer 62, 81, 82

Jalna 145

Jammu and Kashmir 9, 29, 36, 37, 39, 42, 104, 113, 114, 115, 131, 137, 141, 144, 149, 161-202, 271, 272, 273, 275-287, 291-297, 300, 302, 304, 306, 307, 308, 309-317

Jamnagar 28, 29, 89, 90, 94, 251

Japan 12, 210

Jhabua 79

Jhalawar 61

Jind 66

Jodhpur 4, 28, 29, 36, 37, 42, 62, 63, 64, 79-84, 89, 90, 101, 112

Junagadha 29

K

Kalahandi 54, 55

Kalimpong 216

Kalinga 57

Kannauj 79, 207

Kapurthala 66

Karachi 81, 89, 105, 109, 111, 114-118, 133, 134, 141, 144, 145, 148

Karachi-Jodhpur-Bhopal axis 81

Karauli 61, 64

Kargil 199

Kathiawar 29, 38, 40, 42, 62, 63, 80, 86-95, 108-117, 120, 251

Khalsia 66

Kisengarh 61

Kishangarh 79

Kohala bridge 165

Kolhapur 2

Korea 48, 49, 56

Kota 61, 64

Kuh-Ghizr 164

Kulu 163

Kutch 87

L

Ladakh 163, 206, 293

Lahore 105, 163, 173, 174, 175, 198, 253, 271

Lahoul 163

Lancaster 135

Lat Desha 87

Lhasa 218

Limbdi 88

Loha 145

M

Madhya Bharat 3, 64, 79, 96

Madras 68, 95, 126, 127, 135, 138

Malabar 70

Malerkotla 66

Mallani 79

Malwa 64, 66

Manavadar 38, 116, 119

Mangrol 38, 116, 119

Matsya Union 3, 61, 62, 66

Mayurbhanj 48, 49, 53, 56

McMahon Line 215, 218

Mewar 60

Mount Abu 90, 251

Muzaffarabad 172, 199, 294

Myanmar 208

Mysore 3, 4, 9, 102, 124, 126, 152, 179, 180, 249, 250, 270, 284, 285

N

Nabha 36, 37, 66

Nagir 164

Nagpur 46, 48, 52, 54, 56, 198, 261, 319

Nalagarh 66

Nanded 145

Navsari 82

Nawagadh 117

Nawanagar 13, 38, 81, 88, 89, 91, 94, 95, 109, 120

Nepal 210, 211, 216, 218

New Delhi 43-45, 57, 58, 67, 74, 76, 77, 80, 83, 85, 91, 96, 105, 106, 115, 117, 118, 120, 121, 132, 148, 154,

156, 157, 158, 189, 201-206, 223, 225, 236, 237, 246, 248, 249, 260, 263-271, 274, 278, 279, 283, 285, 286, 291, 293, 296, 301, 302, 303, 305, 306, 309, 311, 312, 313, 317, 324, 325, 328, 330, 331

Nilagiri   49

North-eastern regions   209

North-west   42, 209

North-West Frontier Province, NWFP   9, 167, 172

O

Orissa   9, 47-50, 52-56, 93

P

Pakistan   14, 15, 16, 19, 24-29, 33, 34, 36, 38, 39, 42, 43, 44, 72, 73, 77, 80-85, 90, 96, 99,-121, 129-137, 148, 150, 154, 156, 158, 165-170, 173-176, 178, 182, 183, 186, 195, 197, 199, 200, 201, 204, 209, 215, 217, 240, 243, 246, 251-255, 256, 257, 281, 291, 293, 294, 298-310

Pakistan-Hindustan-Princestan   14

Palitana   88

Parbhani   145

Partapgarh   61

Patiala   4, 13, 23, 24, 25, 27, 40, 66, 96, 99, 101, 103, 146, 232, 330

Patna   53, 54

Pattan   161, 173

Peking   206

Poonch   162, 303, 308

Porbandar   88, 114, 267

Prabhas Patnan   120

Princestan   14, 16, 20

Province of Bombay   2

Punial Jagir   164

Punjab   3, 24, 40, 95, 96, 146, 149, 162, 163, 167, 179, 182, 248, 280, 286, 287, 299, 302, 304, 310, 328, 329

Punjab Hill States   3

R

Radcliff Award   167

Radcliffe Boundary   103

Raichur Doab   126

Rajkot   9, 88, 93, 116, 117, 251

Rajputana   61, 79, 88

Ratlam   79

Red Fort   135, 211

Rewa   27, 66, 67, 101

Russia   164, 210, 211, 216, 219

S

Sailana   79

Sakti   48

Sardargarh   119

Sarguja   48

Secunderabad   126, 134, 139, 152, 254

Shahpura   62, 64

Sikkim   210, 216, 218

Sind   81, 91, 110

Sinkiang   164

Sitamau   79

Skardu   169

Somnath   88, 109, 120

Somnath temple   120

Soviet Russia   164, 216

Srinagar   164, 166, 168-173, 198, 274, 275, 283, 292- 295, 306, 316

Stalingrad   12

Surat   82

T

Talchar 48
Tanmarg 197
Telangana 209
The Central Province 49
Tibet 205-218
Tigira 48
Tithwal 199
Tonk 62, 64
Travancore 3, 4, 9, 13, 22, 28, 29, 33, 36, 37, 43, 68,-76, 80, 90, 126, 251, 335
Turkestan 164

U

Udaipur 60, 62, 64, 81, 82, 102
Union of Greater Rajasthan 61, 62
Union of Kathiawar 90, 251
United States of Matsya 64
Uri 199

V

Vala 87
Vallabhinagar 87
Varanasi 233
Veraval 89, 109, 114
Vindhya Pradesh 3, 66, 96

W

Wadhwan 88
Wankaner 88
Wanthali 87
Warangal 150
Wardha 125
Warrangal 209
Western Ghats 70

Y

Yasin 164
Yatung 218

Vivekananda International Foundation is a non-partisan institute for dialogue and conflict resolution with a nationalist perspective. Some of India's leading experts in the fields of security, military, diplomacy, governance, etc have got together under the institute's aegis to generate ideas and stimulate action for greater national security and prosperity. Independently funded, VIF is not aligned with any political party or business house.

RNP Singh is a Senior Fellow at the Vivekananda International Foundation, a Delhi-based think tank. A former officer of the Government of India's Intelligence Bureau, his distinguished service credentials earned him a coveted President's Police Medal, Indian Police Medal, the Sukriti and Kautilya Awards.

A former Trustee and Director of India First Foundation, New Delhi and Managing Editor of two widely acclaimed Journals, Eternal India and Chirantan Bharat (Hindi), RNP Singh has written a number of books including Riots & Wrongs, Bangladesh Decoded, ISI ka Atank, Pakistan ki Haquiqat (both in Hindi) and Nehru: A Troubled Legacy (2015). His works have won wide recognition for their uniform excellence.